Cover design: Marget Larsen
Book design, editing: Anne Kent Rush
Proofreading: Trish Beall
Typeset: Archetype, Berkeley, California
Text Type: Baskerville, Theme
Photographs: Jerry Mander
Printed and bound under the direction of Michele Koury, Random House.
First Printing September 1976: 5,000 in cloth.

This book is co-published by:

| | |
|---|---|
| Moon Books | Random House, Inc. |
| P.O. Box 9223 | 201 East 50th Street |
| Berkeley, California 94709 | New York, New York 10022 |

Distributed in the United States by Random House, and simultaneously in Canada by Random House of Canada Ltd, Toronto.

Moon Books is an independent women's publishing company operating out of San Francisco, California, with distribution through Random House, Inc. in New York. We are committed to making a wide variety of feminist material available in the general market.

*Library of Congress Cataloging in Publication Data:*

Mander, Anica Vesel.
    Blood Ties.

1. Women—Psychology.    2. Mander, Anica Vesel.

I. Title
HQ1206.M325       301.41'2'0924      76-15954
ISBN 0-394-40766-0
Manufactured in the U.S.A.

98765432


First Edition

# CONTENTS

DEDICATION

TO:

KENT, MICHELE, NINA, ERIKA, ELFI,
JANET, BOBI, ANN, SU, CAROL, PAT,
LISBY, ELZA, ROSA, SIDA, FLORA,
FREUDE, IDA, ANNA, PETE, MARGOT,
ELENA, DEBBIE, SARA, ANN, CAROL, TONI,
ADDIE, SHANNA, LIADAIN, HALLIE, MARI,
VEVA, VERONICA, CAROL, SHIRLEY, SHESSA,
PO, ELEANOR, IRIS, MOLLY, DEE, LAUREE,
DORIS, ELIZABETH, KITTY, CHRISTINE,
RINA, LYNNE, SUSAN, KEJA, EVE, ANITA,
OTA, BONNIE, NINA, LINDA, SUZANNE,
JOAN, SALLY, BARBARA, TRISH, RHODA,
LANNIE, VERNA, JOYCE, HELEN, ANDREA,
KATHLEEN, MAGGY . . .


AND TO: JERRY, KAI, YARI, MAX, KEN,
STEVE, BOB, JACK.

# Prologue

In the middle of my life i look back and i seek my roots. In the middle of my life i look back and i seek my female lineage.

Our stories, whatever they are, contain the secret to our womanhood. I turn to Baki, my maternal grandmother. Her name is Sarika Finci Hofbauer. She is eighty-five years old, i ask her to tell me her story. "Do you want to tell me, Baki?" i ask her. "YES, YES, i want to tell it!" she answers. We sit in my house with a tape recorder and she talks to me in our native tongue, Serbo-Croation. Afterwards, she takes my children, one by one, on her lap and laughs at their jokes.

Her story is my story and so i integrate it with mine. I translate it into English but i don't change her words, her syntax, hers is an oral history. I write mine from memory, it is my version, i don't intend to be objective, i don't mean to represent people as they are, just as i see them, and so i change their names.

Our herstory is about movement: a family migrating, nations at war, cultures transformed by events, people transformed by cultures. Yugoslavia is my childhood, a 'young' country, it has only existed since 1918. Its people, however, come from old cultures; they have been invaded but not colonialized. They maintained their identities by singing their songs, telling their tales from generation to generation. Italy is my adolescence, an 'enemy' nation that saves my life. America is my womanhood, a land of oppression and freedom.

In the middle of my life i looked to my childhood, to my girlhood, to my womanhood for clues. I found some, but i need to find more, i need to hear, read many other women's stories, the untold secrets that will amend history. As we peel the onion we find our true identities, our woman-identity.

San Francisco<br>1 May 1976

# YUGOSLAVIA

# 1

My memory begins on July 29, 1941. I was six years old. My mother walked into my room.

—Wake up, Anili, come, you must wake up. We are leaving.

I remember her face over mine, a young beautiful face, lined with fear.

—We are going on the train, to Dalmatia, to the sea.

—Where we go on summer vacations?

—Yes, yes. Now get up! And hurry! We must leave right away. You may wear your pleated skirt, if you like.

As she walked away, she added:

—Oh, and take your doll with you, just one, we don't have room for any of your other toys. One suitcase each, that is all we are allowed to take.

I lay there in my bed, half asleep, perplexed and excited at the prospect of this new adventure. I knew all this had something to do with the Germans who had arrived in Sarajevo suddenly and occupied the city. They were loud; they wore uniforms and bayonets; they didn't like Jews.

Three months earlier we had gone to the mountains for several days, the women and children in our family. We had slept in tents on the ground, picked berries and my godmother, who was fourteen and studying English, had taught me a song:

My Bonnie lies over the ocean,

My Bonnie lies over the sea,
My Bonnie lies over the ocean,
Oh, bring back my Bonnie to me,
Bring back, bring back,
Bring back my Bonnie to me!

I didn't know what the words meant, but i knew they were sad, by the melody, and so i knew that it was something about love.

When we came back to Sarajevo the Germans were there. As we walked through the city there was broken glass all over the streets; my mother held my hand tight and from time to time she covered my eyes and said:

—Take a large step, don't look . . .

Once i didn't take a wide enough step and i felt something like a body under my foot. The city had been bombed for weeks, there were houses in ruin everywhere and on the streets the only live people one could see were German soldiers. I asked my mother:

—What about *our* house, did it get bombed?

—No, no, it's all right, be quiet, don't talk!

My father was home; he looked tired. He hugged me and told me to go to my room because he and my mother needed to talk. The servants were huddled around the wood-burning stove in the kitchen, whispering. They stopped talking when i walked in. The cook took me on her lap and pinched my cheek. She told one of the younger women to get me a piece of bread and prune butter.

These events changed the course of my life. The preceding years i reconstructed from old photographs and tales told to me by members of my family.

* * *

On October 21st, 1934, in Sarajevo, Yugoslavia, at six-thirty-five in the evening, i was born in a private clinic offering 'the most modern medical services.' There were those who considered it an unnecessary luxury to go to the hospital to have a baby. Hadn't they been having babies at home since the beginning of time?

But my mother was a modern woman with modern ideas and her mother agreed with her: why not take advantage of progress? We must go with the times. Don't listen to those peasants; what do they know about modern medicine? The Austrians know, they all have babies in the hospital—those who can afford to, of course . . .

My father wasn't opposed to the idea either; after all, he was a prominent young lawyer who could well afford to give his wife the best care. His thoughts drifted to the baby: it was going to be a boy. No question about that. He already had one son and now he would have a second, so the family name could be well insured. Like the Pregers; they had just had a second son three weeks earlier and they named him Alexander, like the King.

My father, age 34, would ponder the subject of sons and leave childbirth up to the women; or better yet, up to the doctors. Yes, having two sons would be nice. They could be companions to each other, and then, in case one of them didn't have sons, the other could always carry on the family name. The family name was only one generation old in its present form, but my father had already formed strong attachments to it . . .

Legend has it that, when the nurse announced to the young father that he had been blessed with a healthy 4½ kg. daughter, he accepted the fact with good grace. He went in and kissed my mother and if there was any disappointment in his soul, he hid it successfully from her. My mother was rather pleased to have a daughter: they are easier to take care of and they remain closer to the mother when they grow up. She had never had a sister and now she could make up for that wish. Her mother was overjoyed: one son is enough, it is time to have daughters. Besides, now she could keep her beloved mother's name alive. She had just died the year before. The baby would be named after her: her Hebrew name had been Hannah and that would be the baby's Hebrew name as well. The Yugoslav name would be Anica—pronounced 'Anitsa,' accent on the A. And so i was born and named.

* * *

There was another person in the family who was not completely overjoyed by this event. He was two years, eight months and three days old on the day of my birth. My brother Braco.

*His* memory begins shortly before my birth, or so he tells me, on October 12, 1934, the day of King Alexander's funeral. The King had been assassinated in Marseille and his body had been brought back to Belgrade for burial. On the day of his funeral, national mourning was proclaimed throughout the nation. In Sarajevo, a city well acquainted with assassinations, the street lights were draped in black cloth and there were red, white and blue flags at half mast on all the buildings. The little boy remembers walking with his hand in his mother's toward the back of the garden, and being lifted over the fence to watch the cortège.

He remembers looking up at his mother and noticing, for the first time, her belly protruding from her black dress. He asked her about it and she explained something about a baby being inside. He would soon have a baby brother or sister. Then there was funeral music, people in uniforms walking down the street, banners, murmuring and tears on his mother's cheeks.

—Majmi, Majmi, why are you crying?— he asked her.

—Our King is dead; he has been shot.

He was still thinking about her belly but he said:

—Who will be king now?— And his mother answered:

—Petar. He will be our king now. He is only eleven but he will be King of Yugoslavia, with a regent.

* * *

When his father came home, kissed him, took him on his knees and told him: "You have a little sister now," he was not surprised.

—Where is my Mama, i want my Mama! He started crying.

His father hugged him and said:

—Go have your supper now and tomorrow we will go visit them.

And he was taken by Olga, his governess, to the children's room and that night supper was easy; he wasn't forced to eat spinach or any of the other things that are good for you, and she told him stories and left the light on when she walked out of the room.

The next day he was dressed in his special velvet suit and Omama, the grandmother who spoke German, came over. She was wearing pearl earrings; she was smiling and her cheeks were rosy. They handed him a bouquet of flowers and they got into a horse-drawn carriage so he knew they were going on a very special visit. His father sat next to him and Omama gripped his hand very tightly. In the waiting room nurses asked him questions he didn't want to answer. Then they went into a room where his mother was lying under a big down cover and he went to her timidly. She held out her hand and his father lifted him. He kissed her and she smiled.

—Do you want to see your little sister?

He walked over to the cradle, looked in and saw a shrivelled-up face. He reached out to touch her closed eyes and suddenly everybody was shrieking and pulling him away:

—Don't poke her eyes out, be careful! She is just a tiny baby!

The adults all solemnly proclaimed that he was jealous. Until his mother came home, two weeks later, he referred to the clinic as 'home.'


When everyone left, Maja reclined on her pillows and looked out through the small window in her room, at the mountains. She felt quite good, much better than after her first childbirth. There was discomfort in her crotch of course

and her back still ached but these were like pleasant reminders of the event. She smiled. She picked up her engraved
oval silver mirror from the bed-table and ran her fingers
through her brown hair. She had hoped that the baby would
be a girl and her wish had come true. She was very pleased.
Her husband seemed a little upset, but he would get over it.
"And anyway," she thought to herself, "i already gave him a
son. Poor little Braco, he looked pale when he came today,
i'll have to take special care of him when i go home. A boy
and a girl, that is just right. The boy will be tall and
handsome and he will be very intelligent and very successful.
He will travel all over the world and have grand manners and
play tennis and croquet." The baby, ah the baby, she
fantasied dreamily, would be her daughter-companion, her
daughter-grand-lady. She looked at her face in the mirror and
noticed that her skin was smooth, very pale, almost transparent. Her eyes seemed darker than usual, she thought she
was looking rather dramatic with her cheekbones and her
perfect lips. She lay back on the embroidered pillow and
closed her eyes.

The naming ceremony was a rather simple affair with tea
and cakes, a few tears and some Hebrew words, as compared
to the rather brutal celebrations bestowed upon the male heir
a couple of years beforehand.

## 2

That July night, six years later, when my memory begins, i got up and dressed myself very carefully with the clothes my mother had laid out: a white blouse, a beige and brown plaid pleated skirt, white knee socks, brown leather shoes laced to the ankle and a light brown sweater my mother had just finished knitting for me. Then i picked up my doll and dressed her with equal care. I didn't much care for dolls, but it seemed important to everyone that i take an interest in them so i had pretended to make this one my 'special doll.' She had light brown hair over which i put a knit hat, rosy cheeks, blue eyes that shut when she lay down, with very long eyelashes and a round face with a tiny red mouth.

As i walked out of my room, i saw my brother fully clothed, with his new overcoat, sitting on his suitcase in the hallway.

—What is happening?

—We have to flee from the Germans.

—But why? i insisted.

—Because they want to kill us. You never understand anything!!!

He looked tense and nervous and very grown-up all of a sudden in his short pants and falling knee-socks.

My parents were rushing around the house, packing, talking to the servants, giving them last-minute instructions. There were many 'ifs.' "If such and such should happen, then go tell so and so; if, on the other hand, such and such should happen, then do this and that!" Omama was there also, adding to the confusion. She lived in an apartment on the same floor as ours with an access door through our bathroom. She was busily giving my father advice in German. She wasn't coming with us because of course being German she was safe and anyway they wouldn't touch the older people ... My other grandparents weren't going either, in spite of my parents' admonitions. My mother was sewing dukats (gold pieces) into the lining of her coat. The cook was sewing some into my father's winter coat. There was a basket of food ready for us to take: hard-boiled eggs, goat cheese, goose-liver, a freshly baked loaf of dark bread, dried fruit and nuts. And a piece of Omama's honeycake ...

Then we were sitting in a carriage with a man i had never seen before: he was our guide. He was going to take us 'across' on false papers, from the German-occupied zone to the Italian-occupied zone. My mother was whispering to my brother and me:

—Don't say anything, be very quiet. If they ask you anything just say you don't know.

My father said: —If they ask them their name they have to answer, they can't say they don't know! Braco, you tell them your name is Ivan, and Ani you better not say anything.

—I'll remember. Tell me my name.

—All right. Your name is Mara.

I held my doll on my lap and stroked her leg.

I don't remember much about the voyage. We went by train and we got across, to Dalmatia, on the coast of Yugoslavia. We were apparently questioned by the Germans, they examined our papers, they talked to the guide who in turn talked to some 'Ustaši' (Croatian soldiers working with the Germans as members of the quisling government) and somehow they let us through. In Dalmatia there were soldiers too, but they wore green uniforms and they seemed shorter and sloppier and a few of them smiled at me. They spoke a language i couldn't understand but i liked the sound of it. The main thing i remember about this journey is that i left my doll on the train and when i realized it, i suddenly burst into tears and was very sad. Everyone comforted me profusely thinking that losing my *special* doll had caused me great sorrow. My sorrow was of a different nature but i couldn't explain it. The doll was my last vestige of home. My father promised to get me another doll just like mine, which he did a few months later, no easy matter in time of war. I never played with it.

When we arrived in Split, a port city in Dalmatia, we went to the Pregers' house. They were my parents' best friends who had fled a few months earlier and settled in Split. They had tried to talk my parents into leaving also, but at that time, they wouldn't listen. Now there was rejoicing and much to talk about: how did we finally get out, and what about so and so and so and so and so . . . I was very happy to see Sergei and Alex and we all went to their room after a tour of the apartment. Theirs was a nice square room with a window overlooking the schoolyard, across the street. They told us they were studying Italian. Alex said:

—*Buon giorno, signorina. Buon giorno, signore.*

Sergei said: —There is no comparison between the Italians and the Germans. The Italians are much worse soldiers, but they are more civilized.

We were to be interned by the Italians which was the Italian solution to the 'Jewish question.' This meant that we were assigned to a town on the Dalmatian coast which we were not allowed to leave without official permission from the fascist government. By luck they sent us to Korčula, the main town on a beautiful island of the same name on the Adriatic, between Split and Dubrovnik. We were told that about three hundred other refugee families were assigned to Korčula. As we said goodbye to the Pregers and boarded the 'trabaccola' (fishing vessel) we exchanged promises to visit one another whenever we could obtain permission. In the two and a half years we spent at our assigned location we visited each other often gathering happy memories.

Korčula is small, with a population of about 10,000, mostly fishermen, grape growers and olive growers. The town of Korčula, the old part, is perched on the western tip of the island and is, like Dubrovnik, a walled city, a remnant of the war against the invading Venetians in the Middle Ages. It is a lovely little town, with stone buildings and narrow gabled streets climbing in and around the hill, up to the fortress which sits on top, overlooking blue expanse in all directions. I spent there two of the freest, happiest years of my life.

We were greeted, upon our arrival, by some of the other refugees who had preceded us; friends of my parents, a husband-and-wife bon-vivant team who told us about life on Korčula. They pointed out the one and only car on the island, a black 'Topolino':

—That belongs to Colonello Coronconi: he barks like his name but melts with 'rakija' [distilled prune alcohol], and there is good 'rakija' on this island. And plenty of fish. And the people are not anti-Semitic, they are glad to have us. Be welcome. You can put your worries aside for a while. The war will not last to the end of the year. Mark my word.

That was a phrase which was repeated often with ever-diminishing conviction, year after year . . .

We rented a small house with a large kitchen where we huddled through the winter months around a wood-burning stove. The rest of the house was unheated and the winter winds tore through it. We stayed many waking hours in bed for warmth. Across the street from the house was the sea, the beautiful clear blue Adriatic. We children spent six months of the year on the rocks, climbing, searching and learning about life. The local children were friendly and they soon taught us what we needed to know about the sea:

—Watch out for the sea-urchins. Don't step on them, they hurt! Hee, Hee, Hee. Eat one, they are delicious.

One of the little boys dove off and brought back a lovely

purple sea-urchin which he split open with his pocket knife. He presented it to me with a bow:

—You can't eat the grey ones, those are male. The purple ones, the females, have the eggs and that is what is good to eat. Next time bring a lemon— he admonished.

I started school with the nuns. *'Pasticciona!'* (messy girl) one of them used to call me. But that only lasted three weeks; i was told i couldn't go anymore: Jewish children were not allowed to attend Italian schools. Instead, all the mothers and fathers of this newly formed community undertook the children's education. They split up the subjects and divided the children into age groups. My father taught Latin to the older children and math to the younger ones. My mother taught reading and writing. She also taught geography:

—Sophia is the capital of Romania, no, of Bulgaria. Athens is the capital of Greece— we would recite.

The rest of the time we climbed rocks and played hide and seek or cops and robbers around the fortress in the old city. It was during one of these games that i learned the 'facts of life.'

My brother and some older boys played cops and robbers almost every day, but it was rare that they allowed any girls to participate. One day i was hanging around, waiting for a chance to be included, when a boy, slightly older than i, a handsome open-faced boy who later died at the hands of the Germans, called me over and said:

—Come, you can be with me.

We were huddling behind a rock, when a woman walked by with a large protruding belly.

—What's the matter with her?— i asked. He called over to my brother, the leader of the game, and said:

—She wants to know about that— and he pointed to the woman who kept walking, heavily, her eyes on the stone path.

—Do you want to tell her?— he asked my brother.

—No! You tell her. C'mon, let's go!— and off he went seeking other robbers.

The boy took my hand and led me to a deserted dungeon in the fortress. It was damp and there was little light. He sat on one stone and i sat on another. Then he said in a very serious tone of voice:

—That woman is carrying a baby inside her stomach, she is going to have a baby. She is preg-nant.

—How did that happen to her?— i asked.

—A man implants a seed inside a woman, the seed grows and grows and nine months later the baby comes out. Like a flower. You put a seed in the ground in the fall and in the spring you have a flower.

I had many questions: where does he put it, with what, where did he get the seed? But that was all the information the boy was willing to share with me, all that he had at his disposal, most likely. It sounded rather nice, this planting ritual. My curiosity was thus awakened. I have always associated that information with my brother.

News from the outside filtered in and the adults filtered the news: detecting facts from propaganda became their main occupation. Every evening at six o'clock sharp we would all go to the main piazza to hear the official fascist news, broadcast over a microphone from the Workers' Hall. The voice of 'il Duce' would resound almost every night with soothing familiarity. They repeated his speeches over and over again, some old some new:

> The legend that Italians are not fighters must be dispelled, for yesterday, as today, the prestige of nations is determined almost absolutely by their military glories and their armed power.

He spoke with assurance; he seemed to love his country and his people. When he said *'I-ta-liani e I-ta-liane'* i felt included and good, except that there was this funny expression on my father's face: he looked like he was approving, but i knew that he wasn't. When we went home he launched into invectives against the lies and oratory, so i knew that he was against il Duce and that made me uncomfortable. Uncomfortable and proud at the same time. It made me feel special, like not going to school, like not speaking the local dialect, like knowing that one day we would go 'home,' to the life that my mother referred to as 'before the war.'

Then there was 'Zi Teresa's' place where we used to go to later in the evening, at nine o'clock. This was a little restaurant where they sold Aunt Teresa's 'pita' (spinach strudel), local 'rakija,' contraband, and whatever else was available that day. The old couple who kept the establishment had a short-wave radio, the big attraction for the refugees and for some of the local people who congregated there to listen to the BBC. All the windows were draped with black sheets and a kerosene lamp shed a faint light on the wooden console, with a small cloth circle in the middle, through which the voice of Winston Churchill faded in and out:

> Let me, however, make this clear . . . we mean to hold our own . . . I have not become the King's First Minister in order to preside over the liquidation of the British Empire . . . I am proud to be a member of that vast commonwealth and society of nations gathered in and around the ancient British monarchy, without which the good cause might well have perished from the face of the earth . . .

Another way we gathered information was from people coming 'across.' They were no longer coming with their families or their belongings, now they were mostly coming one by one: a child who had been smuggled out, a man or a woman who had found some residue of courage they didn't know they had and had taken a chance. They bore expressions of disbelief and from their mouths came such tales as had never been heard before.

The arrival of a boat at the port was a major event in the

lives of the islanders and their visitors. Word that a 'trabaccola' was coming in spread so that by the time the ship had anchored there was always a crowd awaiting. The adults would go, in the hope of seeing a relative or a friend disembark or of hearing news from a dear one on the other side. For us children these were always exciting events: we would watch the mooring of the vessel, the unloading, the embracing, the questioning. One day, a few months after our arrival, we saw my two grandmothers and my grandfather coming down the plank of a boat bearing the name 'Dalmacija' in black letters on its side.

Omama, dressed in black as always, came first. She embraced my father and cried. She then kissed my mother, my brother and me. I noticed that she was speaking Serbo-Croation instead of German.

—I never thought we would see each other again, but with God's help . . .— she kept repeating.

Then came Bakica. She was barely taller than i and she hugged me and kissed me and sighed and sighed. My grandfather whom we called Dida, was the tall member of the threesome. He was carrying some bundles. He put them down, embraced us all in turn and said:

—Ya, so we are here, we are here, ya, that is all that matters now.

His face suddenly seemed old, his eyes were enormous and his hat was too big for his head.

We all went to our house and for the next few months lived together. The old people were at first reluctant to talk about their experiences, their capture, their imprisonment, the betrayal of the Yugoslavs. But slowly, in the evenings, around the wood-burning stove in the kitchen, it all came out, their humiliation, their fear, their bafflement, their resourcefulness, their courage. There was much speculation about what had happened to the others, to Baki's sisters and brothers and their families, as well as friends and acquaintances who had all been swept up together in the avalanche.

My brother used to sit with them around the table, ask
questions, listen, give opinions:

—Braco has a good head for politics— somebody would
invariably say —if we can call this politics . . .

I would go upstairs and listen from the top of the stairs:

—The children should not hear all this— my mother would
say —go to bed, both of you.

It was in the course of one of these evenings, at the top of
the wooden stairs leading to the unheated bedrooms, that i
heard for the first time the word 'concentration camp.'

3

We weren't allowed to walk on the streets after six o'clock at night and we had to wear that yellow armband that said 'Jew.' When they started to take people away at night—and in the daytime too!—i started to look for a guide to take us across the border. I did that without asking 'Dida' [grandpa]. I hired a guide, i paid him 25 'dukats' [goldpieces]—that was a lot of money!—and i told him where i had hidden my jewelry so that he can bring it to us later, to Split. This 'Ustaša' [German collaborator] was a great thief. He gave people exit permits and then told the police about it. He didn't take us across, he just took us to the first station.

He came to get us. We left. We sat down in the carriage. My brother and his wife and their children came with us. When we arrived at the first station, the police had already sent the detectives after us and the train stopped. The 'Ustaši' came in: "DOWN! DOWN! DOWN!" they shouted. "Let us at least take our suitcases, who will carry our suitcases?" we asked. "WHAT! What do you think? You have to carry everything! DOWN!!!" We took the suitcases and we brought them into the station. "LEAVE THEM THERE!" they ordered.

Then all of us who had been caught were taken to a large hall and they searched us. They took our earrings, our dukats, they took everything. See, i don't have my wedding band . . . They took the rings, they emptied our pockets. They started shouting: "WHAT! WHAT DO YOU THINK? SO MUCH MONEY!" Then they locked us up. One man had a cane over his arm and inside the handle he had dukats. He put it down. They shouted: "Whose is this? WHOSE IS THIS?" He didn't dare say it was his for fear of being punished even more. When we entered the prison they searched us again, they took everything away. I was left with just a watch, which i still have today, because i had long sleeves . . . In the prison they took away all our hairpins so that nobody could commit suicide.

After ten or twelve days the 'Ustaši' swindled us, Omama [grandma] and me. They came at midnight. We were lying down in a very small room, on the floor, one next to the other. Our overcoats were our blankets and our shoes were our pillows. There was no room to straighten out our legs, we couldn't turn around. This 'Ustaša' came at twelve o'clock at night and said: "We want to help you. We will give you your freedom, you will receive good conduct." All the others were very envious of us. Then this officer saluted very politely and said goodbye.

The next day, again at twelve o'clock at night, they came for Omama, they took her away and nobody knew what was with her, where they had taken her. But they took her to question her about some things she had hidden with a German woman. How they knew about this i don't know. So they asked her: "Where are the things? Where did you hide your things?" And she had to tell them. Then the 'Ustaši' went to this German woman's house at five o'clock in the morning and the police locked her up because she had helped a Jew.

They kept Omama downstairs so she wouldn't tell us what had happened and then they came for me. A policeman took me downstairs. He said: "You still have earrings." I had told that to my guide, but he betrayed me, he handed me over to the police. He repeated: "You still have some earrings. You still have some dukats. Where do you keep them?" I needed a moment to think so i took the opportunity to cry and to tell them that until sixty years of age i had never had any dealings with the police and that this was the first time that i had been arrested. The chief of police said: "Confess. Your husband has confessed." My husband was in the men's prison. I said: "I have told you everything, and that's all." They repeated: "Your husband admitted." I said: "I have nothing else to admit." I thought to myself: "I am in prison, but i didn't admit." I had hidden my jewelry with a very fine Serbian family, real diamond earrings, real pearls, a watch, a necklace, many things, but i didn't tell them.

We sat in prison for about three weeks. We were always locked in a cell and up high there was a small window through which the policeman looked day and night at what we were doing. One day, just before our big holiday, Yom Kippur, a policeman opened the door; "OUT! OUT! OUT!" We didn't know what was happening. We got out, we see the men. I hadn't seen Dida in three weeks. He said to me: "Did you confess?" "I didn't." "They said you confessed." "That's not true." We came out, we were walking, we see each other, my brothers, other people, we don't know what's up.

But before that, what they did to us! When we first came to the prison, after about twelve hours, they marched us outside and they searched us with their fingers. After an hour a woman came to search us. One lady had a diamond hidden between her breasts . . . While she was searching one person the others helped each other hide their things . . . We slept on boards and every eight days they took us to the basement, to a bath-hall where the windows were broken, the water cold. We were supposed to bathe according to regulations and go to the doctor for an examination. After we bathed we had nothing to wipe ourselves with. One woman wiped herself with her shirt, another with her slip . . .

I still had some dukats sewn into the hem of my coat, but while i slept in it, it all came undone and as i left a dukat fell on the stairs . . . I turned to the president of the Sephardic Association who was there and whispered to her: "Please be careful, i have dukats, make sure they don't fall and if they fall, pick them up. And ask your daughter to watch also. If they see this there will be another big search." When we came back from the baths, i didn't have anything to sew my hem up. One lady drew some threads out of her stockings and that is how we mended; she gave me a needle and thread and, at night, i sewed when the policeman wasn't looking. I sat by the door, under the window, so the guard couldn't see me. And this is how i saved two or three dukats.

They day they let us out, they opened the doors for us at twelve o'clock and when we got out we saw the men. We didn't know what was happening. We look at each other, we talk to each other, but we don't know what's up. They started signing us in. But they always cheated. What they said wasn't true! One man says: "You will be freed, you will see the sunshine, you will see the air, you will be treated fairly. Just sign here." And everyone started signing without looking at what they were signing . . . A pharmacist, a man who had also been in jail with Dida, read what he was signing. He signed, but he read. He says to us: "Do you know what you signed?" Dida says: "No." "You signed that you are giving your entire property to the government of Croatia."

They let us out, then, on Yom Kippur eve. We go home. Our house is sealed off. We have given everything away. This house is not ours. We cannot get in. The maid we had left behind is in the house. The kitchen is open and her room, where my son Vito used to sleep, that is all, the rest is sealed off. The maid says to me: "You aren't supposed to be in the house, this is not yours anymore . . ." I say to her: "Let me take a bath. I am very tired." She says: "No!" I plead: "Please, be so kind, i'll leave again. I won't take long, just allow me . . ." She allowed me to take a bath. My bathrobe was still hanging there. I dried myself off. I came out barefoot; she noticed that i was barefoot and so she threw down the slippers that she was wearing which were mine . . .

After that i went to see my sister who was paralyzed from the waist down. I go to her house to stay there. But i am not allowed to be there either because at twelve o'clock at night the 'Ustaši' come and take the Jews to concentration camps. My niece found out from the police that we had been released and where we were. She was a doctor and because she was married to an Italian she was allowed to move around freely. She sent a carriage for us, at night, and we went to her house to sleep. But we couldn't stay there very long either. All around her neighborhood Slovenians had moved into the apartments that had been vacated by the Jews who had been taken away. My niece told us: "Don't walk around much because you wear the 'traka' [armband] and you will be caught again . . . Dida went out somehow . . . He went to see his 'hamal' [Moslem errand boy] who used to work for us; he lived across the street from our store. So he went to him and said: "Come, take my suitcases to the station."

A very good friend of ours took us to her house. She was a doctor and doctors were not taken to the camps because they needed doctors. They were able to save themselves and their families. But some 'Ustaši' were without pity, they worked even beyond the law, they took some doctors also and they made them shave the women before sending them to the camps. They made Jewish doctors examine them to see if they were healthy and to shave them . . . This doctor took us to her house. She knew that we had been imprisoned because her cousin was the 'komisar' at the police station. So she said to this commissioner to give us passes so that we can flee again with the 'traka.' But they always put 'Ustaši' on trains to check for armbands. Whoever had them was sent back again. Some men were clever and got dressed like Moslem women so they couldn't see that they were Jews. Some women also got dressed like Moslems and they got through like that. That day the commissioner told the 'Ustaši' not to search the train and that is how we were able to cross over to Split, in the Italian zone.

But one must believe in fate. When we crossed over by boat to Split, the boat was supposed to stop on the 'Ustaši' side and if it had we would have had to get down because of our 'trake.' We got across because a big wind made it impossible for the boat to dock and we had to go to Split. We didn't know that the 'Ustaši' wouldn't have had the right to take us since we were on an Italian ship. When we arrived in Split the 'Ustaši' came on board and they picked up all the Jews. Dida lay down on a bench and i was watching what the 'Ustaši' were doing. I didn't understand the situation. They took one woman and another woman, a man . . . One man said to my husband: "I left the money over there. Pick it up." We didn't dare touch it. And then we got off, nicely, normally. Your father came to pick us up. We were now under the Italians. They were not like the 'Ustaši,' like the Germans. One could live with the Italians. It was nice with them.

4

We stayed on Korčula from August 1941 until October 1943, a month after the Italian armistice. In these two years my education, albeit unconventional, was well rounded. I learned to read and to write, i learned a little about the geography of Europe, smatterings of Judaism and Catholicism, quite a bit about the sea and its creatures. I was introduced to the mysteries of human reproduction. But most of all i learned a great deal about Hitler.

His face and voice had already become familiar in Sarajevo. As soon as the Germans arrived they ordered a photograph of the 'Führer' to be hung prominently in all public places and they recommended that each household have one as well. We, of course, didn't get one, but in the Hall of Justice, the building across the street from our house where my father used to plead his cases, King Petar's portrait (which had just replaced King Alexander's) was now superseded by a large photograph in faint pastels of a man with a small, stingy mustache and side bangs . . .

> German men and women . . . Posterity will one day be able to weigh up which was more important in the past, the speeches of Churchill or my actions . . . I did not want this struggle. . . . Since January 1933, when Providence entrusted me with the leadership of the German Reich I had an aim before my eyes which was essentially

incorporated in the program of our National Socialist Party. I have never been disloyal to this aim and have never abandoned my program ... Only posterity will clearly see its dimension and depth and will realize that it marked a new era.

While on Korčula the photographs in the public buildings represented 'il Duce' and the voice over the loudspeakers on the public square was that of Mussolini, it was Hitler my parents and their friends talked about. He loomed like an evil spirit over our lives. He was the one who was after us. Ever present. He wanted to catch us and kill us. Kill us in the ovens. In concentration camps.

One evening, in my usual spot at the top of the stairs, i heard my grandfather, Dida, saying:

—They take entire families, women, children, old people, young people and load them on trains like animals.

My German grandmother, Omama, said:

—Say it in German, i can't understand so well ...

My mother interjected sharply:

—You know that you must speak Serbo-Croatian now. You must practice. It is dangerous to speak German when we are running away, in these parts. Here only Jews know German. That's how they can spot us. We must all speak Serbo-Croation.

She sat back victorious. She was gaining in her own private battle with my grandmother. She had always resented having to speak German to her mother-in-law. She identified as a Yugoslav and the language she spoke represented her. She maintained this language in our household through the various countries we subsequently inhabited.

My grandfather resumed his story:

—We were almost sent to Germany, if it hadn't been for ... Ah, but you know about that, we have already told you— and he would gesture the memories away. —The man who traveled with us to Split was put on such a train and he said that people died of starvation, of dysentery, of asphyxiation, before they even reached their destinations. They had to relieve themselves, right there on the floor, and there wasn't even room to stretch out. They just closed the doors to the train cars and never reopened them until they were in the camp. He said that in the camps they separated men and women, they took the babies away from their mothers . . . They shaved everyone, they had to take all their clothes off and they paraded them to the 'showers' . . .

—If it's so terrible, how did this man who told you the story, how did he get out alive? He is exaggerating. We mustn't give in to panic— my father admonished.

—Nobody would invent such things, Hitler is capable of anything. He is a maniac— my mother replied.

The discussion went on. I fell asleep several times at the top of the stairs, listening. My parents would find me there when they went to bed and then they became more cautious and came up to make sure i wasn't listening. My images of these horrors were vague, mixed with my own imaginings, but they were strong, lasting throughout the war and thereafter as well.

Several months after my grandparents' arrival word came from Split that Baki's niece, Sonja, age seventeen, had been smuggled out and was all alone in Split in need of shelter. She was the daughter of my grandmother's youngest sister, my mother's favorite aunt. Of course it was decided that she should come live with us. By then the cramped quarters and various family tensions had led to the decision that Baki and Dida would take a small apartment. Sonja would go live with them, while we would move to another house and live there with Omama.

An air of mystery surrounded Sonja when she arrived. She seemed very grown up and mature to me. She had traveled by herself and knew 'the situation.' Yet everyone treated her like a child, with a tinge of disapproval. Years later i learned that the disapproval came from her student activities—'she was a leftist'—and to make matters worse, she had fallen in love with a communist: a young Jewish intellectual who had been taken by the Germans. She had already made trouble for her mother before the war: she was always demanding that the maid be paid more, that she be given the same rights as the other members of the family. And now her mother and brother had been taken and sent to the camps. Her father, it was said, had escaped, but nobody knew where he was so she was all alone, a young girl with progressive ideas.

—Oy, oy, oy, what shall we do with her? We must make sure she behaves herself!— Baki said sternly.

One day, about a year after our arrival in Korčula, my father came home and said to my mother:

—I have obtained permission for you and the children to go to Split for a visit. The Pregers have been writing for us to come and now you can go.

There was some discussion as to whether he or she should go, but it was soon settled: she needed a break from my grandmother.

All throughout my childhood i remember fights between my mother and my grandmother. It would start over food and spread into other areas. Omama's great concern was whether the food we were eating—or she was eating, to be more precise—was kosher. She was an orthodox Jew and, war or no war, she wouldn't go against her practice. The food was rationed and meat very scarce. When we did obtain some meat, on the black market, it certainly wasn't kosher. My mother, then, had to lie to my grandmother to get her to eat it. My grandmother, in turn, would question my mother's assertions and my mother would lose her patience. It invariably ended up with their screaming at each other. My father would look at one, then the other and shake his head disconsolately. I would watch these scenes and think: "Why doesn't he do *something*?" It was after one of these fights that my father had obtained a pass for us to go to Split.

It turned out to be a very happy journey. We boarded the 'trabaccola' with our suitcases and a case of provisions, our presents for the Pregers: a bottle of olive oil from the Korčula hinterland, some smoked fish, dried figs, raisins, pine nuts and two very special gifts, a dozen eggs and a kilo of sugar. Eggs were so difficult to obtain that when occasionally a peasant woman would come and sell one or two from her basket, my mother would call us children, pierce it and have us drink it right then and there, through the hole, the way the islanders did.

At the Split port the entire Preger family was there to greet us, the two parents, the aunt who lived with them and of course Sergei and Alex. They all looked thinner than the last time we had seen them, but they were smiling and said they were well. When we arrived at their apartment they offered us some 'coffee' (finely ground chicory), served Turkish style in small round porcelain cups edged with gold, brought with them from Sarajevo. The children were each given a cube of sugar dunked in the 'coffee,' the way we used to get it in my grandfather's store in Sarajevo, before the war. It didn't taste as good.

The adults started talking and we went to the boys' room where we were all to sleep. There were two beds and two mattresses on the floor. We agreed that the fair way to arrange it would be to rotate, one night on the bed, one night on the floor. They started asking us about school and when they heard that we didn't go to regular school they said we weren't missing much.

—In Italian schools we mostly learn propaganda— said Sergei.

But they spoke Italian pretty well and they knew all the 'balilla' (fascist youth) songs. They even had some 'balilla' shirts they wore on special fascist holidays. The Pregers had converted and were treated by the fascists the same as all the other Yugoslav nationals.

That night, when we went to sleep, Sergei introduced his newest favorite game. We would all lie very still on the two beds, two by two, in opposite directions and tickle each other's soles. The point of the game was to see how long one could go without laughing. Sergei and Alex were very good at this game, having been practicing every night for months, and Braco caught up with them quickly. As for me, i never became very good at it. I would laugh and say:

—Stop! Stop! That's enough, it tickles too much!

I never quite saw the point of it all. They said it had something to do with building one's character . . .

Another tradition in the Preger family was for Mrs. Preger, whom i called 'aunt,' to bring us a treat while we were asleep for us to find when we woke up in the morning. We soon caught on to this and stayed awake, pretending to be asleep, until she brought the plate of goodies. Then we would quietly get up and divide them. One night she brought a bowl of cherries, our favorite treat of all. Sergei, as the eldest, divided them one by one and when he discovered there were two left over he solemnly opened the window facing the schoolyard across the street and tossed them out.

—This is the only fair way to handle the situation— he proclaimed.

The other two boys agreed. It seemed a stupid waste to me.

We spent about two weeks with the Pregers, mostly in the apartment: it was safer there. Occasionally we would walk around the city, to buy provisions or to hear news by hearsay, an important informational source in time of war. The Pregers had a radio and we listened to the official news there. We heard the interminable Mussolini speeches:

To begin with, history tells us that war is the phenomenon which accompanies the development of man . . . War is for man what motherhood is for woman . . . not only do I not believe in everlasting peace, but I would also hold it as depressing and destructive of the basic virtues of man, which only in bloody effort can shine in the full light of the sun . . .

At night they listened to the BBC, on the short wave, but that was very dangerous and they didn't allow children to be present for fear that we might tell someone about it. People who had been caught listening clandestinely to 'enemy' broadcasts had been known to disappear.

It was at the Pregers' that i first heard of the 'resistance.' It was Sergei's great interest. He was constantly debating whether he would join the Partisans—the communists—or the 'Četniks'—the royalists—if he were old enough to join either . . . According to him both groups fought the Germans, both groups were in the mountains. The Partisans were led by a man called 'Comrade Tito' and the 'Četniks' were led by Draža Mihajlović. It was all a question of leadership: even though Sergei's sympathies tended toward the 'Četniks' (being a patriot, he wanted to remain loyal to the official representatives of the Yugoslav government and not to a foreign nation like Russia) he had to admit that the Partisans seemed to be more effective in their fight against the Germans. Simultaneously, both groups also fought each other, thus weakening their troops and supplies and *that* was clearly idiotic.

The two oldest boys played a game they called 'war.' It consisted of laying their lead soldiers out on the dining room table. Then they would pick lots to see who would represent the English and who would have to play the Germans. Sometimes it was Italians vs. Russians, or Japanese vs. Americans; in that case the table would be the Pacific Ocean and, in the middle, would be something called Pearl Harbor; then they would fly paper airplanes all over the room. But mostly they played soldiers, shooting, ambushing, attacking by surprise, on the ground. That seemed most realistic.

One day when they were playing 'war,' as usual, Alex said to me:

—Come, let's do something else.

As we left the room we heard mocking voices saying:

—Ahhh, the little ones are offended . . . Poor little ones . . .

We went into the kitchen. All the adults were napping. The

house was very quiet. The kitchen was dark and smelled faintly of lard.

Alex brought out some pencils and paper. We sat at the kitchen table which was covered with a cracked grey oilcloth. He said:

—Do you want to see what boys look like?

—Sure— i answered nonchalantly —but i already know what they look like. I have seen Braco, and others as well . . .

—How do you know they all look alike?— he questioned.

—All right, all right . . . What do you have in mind?

—You draw a picture of yourself, down there . . . and i'll draw myself . . . and then we'll fold the paper and exchange pictures . . .

I remember going to the bathroom and pulling down my pants. I took a hand-mirror from the cabinet and examined myself to be sure i remembered correctly what i looked like. I had done that many times before, but drawing wasn't my forte and i had to have fresh visual images to even attempt it . . . Then i went back and drew something that looked like two eggs juxtaposed.

I was finished before he was. I sat there watching him with a smile. He was concentrating and, as usual, his tongue was sticking out while he worked. He handed me the paper, twice folded. I folded mine in the same way and handed it to him.

—When i count to three, let's both look— he said.

His drawing looked something like a bullet: a long oval shape with a curved line across the tip of it and two little circles at the other end.

—Is that really the way yours looks?— he asked.

—That's the best i can do . . . Do you want to see?— and i laughed.

I remember licking tongues with Alex, once, long ago in Sarajevo, 'to see what it tasted like,' and Braco coming in and asking what we were doing and when we told him we asked: "Do you want to try?" and he said, "Nooooo, you are both stupid!" Now Alex said:

—No, i don't want to see, this is good enough. And now we

have an assignment. We must each look at our brothers to see what they look like. Then let's draw them and exchange pictures again.

—All right, that's good, but let's swear not to tell anyone!

We shook hands and made our pact. When we exchanged pictures, a few days later, Alex said triumphantly:

—See, i told you, they don't look alike!

At first i couldn't see any difference, but then i noticed that on top of the two little round balls there were a few marks that looked like hair.

It was soon time to go back to Korčula. There were tears and kisses. When we were on board, my mother and i both held a handkerchief in our hand and waved it for a good half hour until they were completely out of sight. I saw Alex's the longest. He had made a point of bringing a blue one, to distinguish it from the others. Also, he had said he would never wave a white handkerchief: that would mean defeat, it might bring us bad luck.

5

Summer was approaching: our second Korčula summer. Some 'optimists' still claimed that the war would soon be over. Churchill had promised to send English paratroopers to help the Partisans in their struggle against the Germans. His son Randolph was going to lead them toward victory . . . Another hopeful sign came from America: it now looked as though the United States was going to come to Europe to help the British and the Russians in their fight against Germany. We would all be freed. The British came to Yugoslavia but the Americans delayed their arrival for another year.

In the meantime news from our relatives became rarer and rarer . . . Most of the ones who had been sent to concentration camps had stopped writing. We all feared for their lives. There were reports of typhoid epidemics and cholera and dysentery. Baki worried most about her son. He had joined the Yugoslav army and had been captured by the Germans. As an officer he was put in a prisoner-of-war camp, but as a Jew he was separated from other Yugoslav officers and put with Jewish officers and in that section food was scarce indeed. We occasionally received a letter from him in which he invariably asked for food. Our own rations became more and more limited. We nonetheless managed to send him packages. There was much praying that he would receive them . . .

In summer the food situation was somewhat better: the days were longer and it was possible to fish longer. At night

the fishermen could no longer go out to sea for fear that
bombers, from either side, would spot the lights and bomb
the vessels, so the fishermen had to rely on daytime fishing
which, as everyone knew, was not the best time for a good
catch. There were also fewer and fewer men available. The
younger ones had all either joined the Partisans or been taken
into the army. The Italians were not doing too well, in spite
of their claims to the contrary. Now they were taking the
older men as well. It became a common sight to see women
go out to fish with heavy nets. They did all the work now:
repair the nets, cook and clean, even work for others to make
a little money. The children were left pretty much on their
own.

One day a group of local children came over to play with
me as usual. One of them said:

—Let's go on the rocks and look for crayfish.

That was always encouraged by the adults. When we got
there, instead of looking for crayfish, the oldest boy said:

—Come here, let's go behind this rock where they can't see
us. Look at what i have.

He spoke in Dalmatian, which sounded like a song, with all
the Italian words mixed in with the Yugoslav. He brought out
a 'Nazionale,' an Italian cigarette.

—Do you want to try it?— He lit one with a match and
inhaled very deeply.

—This is how you do it: you breathe in and then you
swallow it and hold it.

—Here, let me try it.— I took the cigarette in my hand and
drew a deep breath of smoke. I was suddenly coughing and
crying and everyone was laughing. I tried again and again
until i learned how to do it without coughing. A few minutes
later i threw up. The oldest boy said:

—That's good! Now wash out your mouth in sea-water so
your mother won't smell it on your breath.


Our landlady who lived in the apartment above ours was,
in my mother's words, 'a very good woman.' She had been a

great help to my mother when we first moved there. My mother was not accustomed to cooking and washing, especially not under these conditions. There was a well in the courtyard from which we children brought water. The cooking was done on a wood-burning stove. Cooking consisted mainly of substituting. My mother, who had never cooked before—it wasn't necessary for young ladies from 'good families' to know how to cook, they would after all engage cooks for that purpose, they were trained in the more delicate art of pastry making at which my mother excelled, alas to no avail, given the circumstances— now learned to cook with surrogates: unavailable ingredients were substituted with whatever was available. Mrs. Andrić, our landlady, was very helpful with her suggestions. She would bake sardines in the oven a special way and call them 'roasted chicken' . . . Omama knew how to gather wild greens and with those my mother would make 'creamed spinach.' I used to go out in the fields with my grandmother and she would whisper her instructions in German: "The prickly ones, over there, with little white specks, those are the ones!"

One day Mrs. Andrić came upstairs to our apartment, in tears.

—What happened?— my mother asked. —Sit down.— She motioned for me to leave the room. I stayed by the door and listened.

—My son, Anton, they captured him! He is here in the prison and they are torturing him! They want him to tell where his comrades are hiding. I know because they summoned me to see. They thought that would make him tell. They don't know him. He will die first . . . They are pulling out his nails, they are burning him with cigarettes. What will become of us, dear friend?

I had often passed by the prison on my way to the beach. It was a big white stucco building, with small barred windows up high. That night i couldn't go to sleep. I kept imagining the young man sitting on a wooden chair, a bare light bulb shining in his eyes, sweat running down his temples, clenching his teeth in order not to cry, while the men were burning him and pulling out his nails. I imagined the blood dripping on the cement floor. I couldn't get these images out of my mind. These were not Germans, these were not concentration camps, these were Italians, right here on Korčula! I later learned that the son had joined the Partisans and had been captured during an ambush. The 'interrogation' lasted for months. They tried everything to make him tell where the commando was. But he never did. One day they brought his body to the house and left it there on the steps, for all to see.

My brother was studying a great deal. The Italian government had granted permission for the refugee children to take the state examination given to all children completing elementary school. If they passed, they could go on to the 'liceo' (high school), if not, they had to go to vocational school. It was clearly understood that it was very important for Braco to pass this exam: for his future, for his career, as a man. He was therefore relieved of all his duties in the household. He no longer had to set the table or wipe the dishes. All he still had to do was make his bed. I inherited all his duties.

From the very beginning of 'immigration,' as this period was referred to, it was established by my mother that everyone had to help with household chores, now that we no longer had servants. My father learned to sweep, my grandfather became the dishwashing expert, and the children were given the minor chores, as well as endless errands, perfectly timed to interrupt games as they reached their peak of interest. The women cooked; that was too delicate an activity to risk on men or children. For the time being, however, Braco was not to do anything in the house, he had an important intellectual task ahead of him. He studied assiduously, with my father's and Sonja's help. She had, after all, just finished 'gymnasium,' and some of the material was fresher in her mind, especially algebra and geometry. The subject given the greatest emphasis was Italian, the language, the history, the propaganda. He would be asked a lot of questions about fascism and its glory and he was expected to answer to their satisfaction. Otherwise none of his knowledge would be worth anything. Of course, no one in the family was too well versed in that subject. But everyone had a great deal of confidence in Braco: he was serious, he was intelligent and he 'understood the situation.' . . .

On the day of the exam he did brilliantly. My father had gone with him and he was duly proud. At the end of the exam Colonello Coronconi, there to represent the Italian government in occupied territory, asked a question, as was expected of him:

—And what do you have to tell us about the courageous Italian army in which our men are risking their lives for the betterment of mankind?

Braco stood very tall, my father recollects, in his short pants and said:

—Italians are not good soldiers. They are cowards. Germans are good soldiers. They are disciplined. An army needs discipline to win.

Colonello Coronconi became flustered. He looked at the other examiners. The principal of the Korčula high school stood up. He was a pudgy little man, with spectacles. He spoke in Italian, with a Dalmatian accent:

—My young man, you have been sadly misinformed. What you just said about the Italian army is untrue and unjust. Apologize to the Colonello.

Braco mumbled *'Scusi'* (excuse me). And so they passed him, without honors.

Soon after that incident, over which the adults laughed but pretended to be angry, we got word from the Pregers that they were sending the boys to spend a few weeks with us. It was summer vacation. We were overjoyed. My only concern was my head: it had been shaved because of lice and my hair was growing in very slowly. This was not unusual among the children of the island and so i decided to make light of it. This way i looked more like a boy, i decided, and perhaps they would take me more seriously, for a change . . .

They brought us some books, including *Pinocchio,* in Italian, which became one of my favorite books. There was also a long letter from their parents and aunt, a black shawl for Omama, medicine for Dida and to Baki they gave a box of face powder. The boys were very polite and pleased at having been allowed to travel alone. We immediately went up to the fortress to play cops and robbers. The ban against girls had been lifted some time before. One of the older boys, an islander, had said that it was more fun to play with girls, especially when you captured them, and so everyone followed this more mature view of the matter.

It was during this visit that Sergei and Braco composed their first song. It was a pastiche of the aria from *Rigoletto,* '*La donna è mobile.*' They used the same melody and the theme was still woman. It started out in Italian with '*La donna è mobile,*' followed by verses in Serbo-Croation: '*Žene su kobile*' (women are mares). The rest of the lyrics have not been preserved for posterity . . . Alex was torn in his loyalties to them, as the boys, and to me as his peer. He spent a lot of time establishing his superiority over me: he *was* older, the greatest of all status determinants.

—By all of three weeks— i would remind him.

—The fact is that i am older, that is what counts!—

He had become very attached to the word 'fact' since i had last seen him. He was also fond of measuring himself to see if he was taller than i, a less successful operation. I never let on that i noticed him standing on his toes while we were being measured, back to back. I relied on Sergei to point that out . . .

On the other hand Alex allied himself with me in his watchfulness against the older ones' persecution of the 'little ones.' He would teach me what he himself had learned from his brother, TACTICS, the masculine art. We became adept, especially in dealing with the grownups, who had a somewhat simplistic view of the disadvantages younger children had to face. We capitalized on this view. We were not bound by a sense of honor, as the older boys seemed to be, and i, especially, as a girl, was not expected to have a sense of honor. So i didn't. I lied, i cheated, i set traps for the older ones, i told on them, i teased them. I did everything i could to arouse their wrath.

This lack of respect for the rules of the game exasperated my brother. He would fly into rages and 'punish' me: this usually meant that i would be excluded from one thing or another: i would not be allowed to participate in a game; he would not tell me the joke everyone was laughing at; he would not let me into his room. He was capable of maintaining his disciplinary attitude for days. I, on the other hand, would hit him. He was strictly forbidden to hit girls. He and the other boys had their share of fights but my mother had imposed an iron rule: never hit a girl. I was therefore free to kick him in the legs with my shoes, knowing that if he ever hit me back i could go tell my mother. She generally solved this kind of dilemma by spanking us both indiscriminately. My father couldn't tolerate these confrontations. He had been dealt with very severely as a child by his mother—Prussian discipline—and any sight of violence upset him. He couldn't even stand a little shouting. This seemed ridiculous to me.

Throughout my childhood i felt that my mother favored my brother, though she disclaimed this when i would voice it. I also felt my father favored me and his favoritism pained me as much as my mother's. What i missed in my mother's attitude toward me was not affection, it was respect: she was a very demonstrative person and i never lacked physical affection. When she hugged me, as she often did, i felt her love flowing from her body into mine. But she clearly respected Braco's intellect over mine. He had to perform for acclaim, i just had to be me. As a result, he was an intellectual by the time he was eleven.

One day, shortly after the departure of Sergei and Alex, going down to the courtyard to fetch water from the well, i noticed some activity in the adjoining field. This was an area, overgrown with weeds, used only by us children occasionally. On this day, however, women were coming and going, carrying heavy loads on their heads, depositing them on makeshift tables, clearly getting ready for something. I felt the excitement of an upcoming event as i ran up the stairs spilling half the water in the pitcher i was carrying.

—Majmi, Majmi!— i called to my mother who was preparing the chicory 'coffee' for breakfast —i think they are going to have a feast or something in the field . . .

She looked out through the small window in the dark kitchen and said:

—Ya, i wonder what they are doing.

—Let's ask Mrs. Andrić, she will know. I can't wait to find out!

—Here, take this piece of nut roll down to her, i meant to send her some anyway and then you can ask her.— And she handed me a piece of the precious cake wrapped in a dish-towel; paper was as scarce as sugar.

I knocked on our landlady's door and she came to open it in her robe.

—Oh, your mother is too kind, no i can't accept that, you children keep it!

After the usual ritual of insisting that she keep the gift—in Yugoslavia it was considered impolite to accept something without at least three protests and this custom was observed even more strictly in times of war—i came to the important question of the day:

—What is happening in the field? I saw a lot of people doing something there.

—Ohhh, didn't i tell you? Today is the day of the firedance. It happens every year on the longest day of the year and that's today. We'll have a 'festa' (party) and then we'll all dance around the fire. You can even jump over the fire if you are not too scared . . .— she replied with a smile.

—Does that mean i can go too? Could i really?

—Of course! We are all invited. There will be firedances all over the island tonight and this one is for us.

The rest of the day seemed interminable.

It was still light outside when we all decided it was time to go to the 'festa.' I put on my 'good' dress—a printed silk that Baki had recut and sewn for me from an old dress of my mother's, and my new shoes, canvas sandals with cork soles; i daubed a bit of perfume from my mother's almost-empty bottle behind my ears, as i had seen ladies do. When we arrived, Braco was already there: he and some other boys were helping turn the spit on which the goat was roasting slowly. He barely looked up to acknowledge our arrival. The animal's eyes were beginning to bulge, which meant it was almost ready. The body was sweating with the little bit of fat that it had; it was a rather skinny little goat, with its ribs sticking out. It looked fabulous.

Everyone brought something: large loaves of dark heavy bread, baskets filled with nuts and berries, bowls of baked beans and 'polenta' (corn mush) and all kinds of cakes and dried fish. The men were standing around the spit, supervising the boys' work and drinking 'rakija.' The women were adorning the tables, complimenting each other on their products:

—How did you get it to rise so nicely without baking powder?

—Where did you get the pigs' feet? I always suspected you of having connections with the Colonello . . .— and they would laugh and hug each other, their faces red and shiny.

I saw my best friend, Anica, whose name was the same as mine. She ran over to embrace me. She was as excited as i was. She was an islander and had been to fire dances ever since she could remember.

—After we eat, oh i hope it's soon, it smells so good i can hardly wait, everyone will dance around the fire and then 'Starac' [the old man] will walk on the hot coals!!!— She clapped her hands and jumped up and down. —Do you believe me?— she asked with her beautiful dark eyes shining in the setting sun.

—I believe you,— i said, holding her gaze. We were best friends, after all . . .

'The old man' turned out to be a *very* old man indeed. His face was like seasoned leather, but he stood straight and on his head he wore a captain's hat. He chewed tobacco and spat further than anyone else. There were many stories about him; how he had traveled all over the world, how he had another wife and children in Africa—or was it America?—how in his youth he could run faster than other men. But the part that interested me most was about his sorcery. The older people would tell long tales about his gift: he was able to read a person's face and tell about their life in detail, he could put an evil spell on an entire family, he could make water spring from arid land. He never smiled, his eyes were bright and he always had a sweet for the children.

A group of women and men, sitting on a bench drinking heavy Dalmatian wine from a jug, began to sing. They sang nostalgic songs of those who had left and who missed their homeland: *"Ciribiribella mare moje, ciribiribella mare moje, ciribiribella mare moje, odoh u marine . . ."* It was a song about a man from Dalmatia who joined the navy and sang his song of longing to the sea. The immigrants joined in with their songs: Bosnian songs, Croatian songs. They all sang about their homes, far far away . . . Occasionally the mood would shift to a swifter melody and then there would be laughter; these were songs about the games men and women play together. Love was not only sad, it seemed, it was also funny.

We ate and ate and ate. There were continuous protestations:

—Oh, no thank you, i couldn't . . .— alternated with:

—Go ahead, eat, tomorrow we'll go back to our diet . . .

We all ate and ate until finally the children collapsed in the grass huddling together, laughing. By this time, the sun was setting. Somebody played the accordion and more songs broke out. People were sitting close to one another, arms around each other, swaying back and forth, singing. As night fell the young men busied themselves building a fire. They carefully laid down a layer of rocks, piling twigs and coals on top. The fire caught on fast and bright, it dashed into the sky.

I was huddling next to Anica: the feeling of her body next to mine, the fresh grass on our legs, the darkness all around us was delicious. I couldn't take my eyes off the fire. Then a circle formed and we all joined in. The accordionist played a 'kolo' and we danced in a circle around the fire. People periodically dropped out of the circle to rest for a while, joining in again later. The young ones never rested, they held on to each other and smiled. Their cheeks got redder and redder as the fire subsided. Finally the flames were all gone, there was just a bed of coals left on the ground. Gradually everyone sat down. The old man got up solemnly, walked over to the fire, took his shoes off, stood there for a moment, rubbed his soles with his hands. Then, slowly and deliberately, he walked across. I felt a spasm in my stomach. His arms were stretched out, his face expressionless. When he got to the other end, he rubbed his soles again with his hands and i noticed that they were unscathed. Then he went to sit down on the chair he had vacated. From then on silence reigned. People started filing out; they would bow slightly to him as they left and he just sat there gazing at the fire.

# 6

I was glad that Vito had gone to the prisoners-of-war camp in the hope that i would see him again. Later Vito said that if he hadn't been sent to the prisoner-of-war camp he would have joined the Partisans, he wouldn't have sat at home ... When Vito was leaving to go to war a friend sent him a bouquet of red roses. I said to him: "Son, go and fight!" I accompanied him to the stairs and watched him go from the window. I didn't cry. I was glad to see him go to war, to fight the Germans. Before he left i sewed a few dukats into his pants and i told him: "Son, here are some dukats, so you have them when you come back, so you have something." But in the prisoner-of-war camp he couldn't buy anything so he gave them to a friend who smuggled them out to his family for them to send food packages: they were very poorly fed in the prisoner-of-war camps, they were hungry. Especially the Jews. They fed the Jews even worse than they fed the others.

We had no news from Vito. They weren't allowed to write. I worried about him. When the Russians came they opened the doors for them and they were freed. They were hungry and they were sent into Germany to a house for released prisoners of war and they ate and ate, so much that they got sick. There had been one German officer in the prisoner-of-war camp who had been very good to them—that was a very rare case—and they went to look for him to help him, now that he was on the losing side. They found his house and the wife said that the husband had left and she didn't know where he was ... Vito and his friends said: "We want to help him. He was good to us." The wife wasn't allowed to say where he was. Then the daughter jumped up and said: "My father is working the land for the peasants over there . . ." They went and they found this German officer and they rewarded him; they arranged for him to stay in Germany, to get back into his apartment, to be reunited with his family. They helped him so that everything would be the same as before for him.

You never know how people will react. When the war started some good friends of Vito's, some German schoolmates, good comrades of his, suddenly when they would get together they changed; this one in particular, this 'Schwab,' he wouldn't even look at him . . . His father was a roof-man, every year he fixed our roof, we knew each other very well and then overnight he changed. Another friend, also a schoolmate of Vito's, a Moslem, he used to come to visit often and sit and study with him, when the 'Ustaši' came he helped me withdraw my money from the bank. We were no longer allowed to withdraw our money, but he just said: "Madam, what would you like, how much?" I couldn't believe that he was really doing it, but he did. He gave me what i was asking. I wasn't allowed to take it all out at once, only a little at a time, but he greeted me very courteously. I later heard that they killed him . . .

After Vito and the other prisoners were freed they went back to Belgrade and they were given a great welcome: the people went to welcome the Partisans, the 'Ustaši' ran away, the Serbs cheered and everyone greeted whomever they knew. A former maid of ours went out on the streets to see who was coming and when she saw Vito she shouted: "Mr. Vito! Mr. Vito!" A Serbian friend was there too and he said: "Vito, come to my house to sleep." When Vito returned to Sarajevo he didn't know where he was going to sleep. In our apartment there were already some communists. There were Moslems amongst them, who were also communists, and these communist Moslems were living in our apartment. He didn't know where to go, so this friend took him into his apartment and gave him food, but they didn't have any clothes. Then we sent some clothes for Vito from Rome. But in the meantime he found a package i had left for him. Before i left, when it all started, i put together some things: pajamas, socks, cloth, thread and all and i sent it to a Serbian family and i said: "This is only for my son, if he comes back, so he'll have something to wear." I knew the situation was bad for prisoners of war and i was hoping he would run away. And

46

so when Vito came back he found all that and in this way he had something to wear, from head to heel.

But after the war we wanted Vito to come and join us because life was very difficult in Yugoslavia. After the war there was no clothing, we had to send him things from Rome. And we wanted to be with our son again . . . So we wrote to him to go to Israel because Tito allowed Jews to get out of Yugoslavia if they wanted to go to Israel. Some stayed and some left. And so Vito went to Israel, but there were great shortages in Israel as well, they lacked food, they lacked housing. Vito told us that when he arrived there was no lodging for them so they lived in a tent and when it rained it rained right into the tent! They would go in the morning to pick oranges and there were so many oranges that they washed their hands in orange juice. But then there was no food, and insufficient lodging because Israel was still young. Now it's entirely different . . .

I always worried about Vito. When he was little he was very lively. I loved him of course, he was my 'hasherle' (little darling), but he gave me a hard time. I had to spank him once in a while . . . Wherever i went i had trouble with him. Once we went to the seashore and on the last night of our vacation i said to him: "Tonight we are going home" and i dressed him for the trip and Mr. Son fell into the sea, all dressed, combed, ready for the trip. When he came up i was there waiting for him: "Now i am going to spank you, you will see now!" "Ay, ay, ay . . ." he started crying for me not to beat him. Another time we went on an outing near a river. Who fell into the water? My son. I had to hire a carriage, leave Maja and my husband and the rest of the company and go home so that the child wouldn't catch cold . . . Because of things like that i often beat him . . .

One time something really terrible happened to him. My sister-in-law lived on the second floor and there were stairs with a banister on which the children used to slide. One day he was sliding down the banister and fell and had a concussion. For a long time he didn't know what he was saying, he kept asking: "Where am i? What happened to me? Where is daddy?" He didn't recognize us. You can imagine my sorrow . . . I had given birth to a healthy child and now . . . I didn't know if he would ever recover. Dida was on a buying trip in Vienna, he wasn't in

Sarajevo, i was beside myself with worry. It took eight to ten days for this child to begin to recognize me. He would know and then he would forget again. But the doctor slowly brought the child back on the right path. He got well but i wasn't sure how it would work out later, i was always worried about him . . .

He was about twelve when this happened. Your father's father came, as the rabbi, to visit him. And i thought that this visit meant that he was going to die, like with Catholics when the priest comes to administer the last rites before the child dies. I almost fainted. He came and he said: *"Mein Freund, was ist mit dir geschehen?"* (My friend, what has happened to you?). And poor Vito doesn't have the vaguest idea what he is talking about, nor who he is! But thank God he got better and went to school and got an education and everything . . .

When my children were little i worked all day, i wasn't with them that much. They always had somebody with them so they wouldn't fight too much. We didn't have much time with the children, by the time we got home at night they had already eaten and were ready to go to sleep. On Sundays we went with them, skiing, sledding, Dida and the children would go sledding as soon as the sledding season started. Not me. But we all went together. When it was summer we went swimming. When your mother was little she had crooked legs and she had warts on her hands when she was about fourteen, fifteen, and we discovered that when we went to the seashore this would go away. The swimming, the sea air helped a lot. They developed nicely, they grew. Today people don't pay much attention to that. Vito was short and after four weeks at the seashore we would come back and Dida would be surprised at how much he had grown. I didn't want them to be little like me. We went to Dubrovnik, to our riviera . . .

When the First World War was over they immediately instituted Serbo-Croation schools to replace the German schools. Vito and your mother went to Yugoslav schools, but i got them to take private lessons in German, in French. I always wanted them to know more than i did. We had the opportunity to educate them and to give them everything that was best . . . We had very good schools in Yugoslavia, but for advanced education they went to Austria, Hungary, to Czechoslovakia . . . In those days the children were more childish than today. Today children are livelier, more capable, independent. Before, children were very much children. They didn't know how to manage by themselves, they depended on us. And when guests came, of course, the children would go into another room. They didn't sit with us. When they were small they didn't even have dinner with us, they would eat earlier and go to bed.

As soon as my children were a little older, after they had finished the fourth grade or so, i started hiring a woman, someone with an education, to come and be with them in the afternoon when i wasn't home to oversee their homework, to take them out for walks and so on. I didn't let them go play by themselves. They went to school both in the morning and in the afternoon and when they came home from school they had a snack and then this woman would come and eat with them. When i was little nobody bothered with me, whether i studied or not and when i got married i realized my mistake and i wanted to start again and repeat school, so that i would know a little more than i know now. But it was impossible, with little children, the store, we had to work hard to cover our rent. I didn't have the opportunity. If it were up to me everybody could go and study what they want. I just wanted to read and write well and learn how to speak correctly, a little about politics, a little about what's happening in the world . . .

**7**

A year passed. When summer arrived again, the Italians were suffering heavy losses: the Partisans were gaining on one side, the 'Četniks' on the other. The U.S. and British forces had landed in Sicily. For us the situation was dangerous, the Germans were all around us ready to take over the territory occupied by the Italians. It was decided that my mother and i would take a trip to Split to inquire about the possibility of finding a way to cross the Adriatic to southern Italy, to talk to the Pregers, to find out what we should do next. We could not take the chance of being caught by the Germans. By now it was perfectly clear what the Germans did to the Jews. My father and brother would stay behind so as not to arouse any suspicion. Nobody would pay too much attention to a woman and child traveling alone . . .

When we arrived in Split, the mood in the Pregers' household had changed. Everyone was very somber; the situation was serious. Italy was our only recourse. Yes, but the problem was that the Allies were moving very slowly up the 'boot.' Were the Italians to surrender, the Germans would be there in no time. Rumor had it that they were sending troops into northern Italy, ready for the takeover.

The sleeping arrangement in the children's room was the same as on our previous visit: a mattress on the floor, the two beds, and the three of us rotating every night. We still tickled each other's soles before going to sleep, the parents still brought treats while we were pretending to be asleep, but it was all done in a different spirit: our parents were worried and that made us uneasy, our games were more routine, less spontaneous. And then the bombardments started.

Almost nightly we were awakened and rushed to the basement which had been converted into a bomb shelter. All the tenants in the building would be there, in their night-clothes, huddling, whispering, comforting the children. Sergei had become an expert at differentiating the planes by their engine sounds. He would inform us all: —That is an English plane, they are pretty accurate in their aim, so we needn't worry. They aren't afraid of flying low in order to hit the proper target.— Then there would be the whistle and then profound silence while everybody sighed with relief when the explosion followed: it wasn't us this time around! But when he said: "Watch out, that sounds like an American bomber!" people would hold each other and cry and whisper prayers and cross themselves.

One never knew where the Americans would hit. They flew very high, to keep out of the anti-aircraft range and, therefore, their aim was very poor. Sergei would occasionally go out in the yard to see the planes and the bombs. I went out with him one night: a brilliant, star-filled night with pyrotechnics all over it. The bombers were red and yellow dots darting through the skies letting out long objects, floating through the air, which landed with a bang producing a cloud of smoke and dust, followed by a huge flare. Sergei taught me how to differentiate English bombers from the American: there was the sound, of course, but there was also the shape of the planes and their flight patterns to observe. He felt much friendlier toward the British than he did toward the Americans. He considered it unsportsmanlike to fly so high taking the chance of hitting civilian targets.

We weren't allowed to stay out very long watching. Mr. Preger seemed to like doing it himself, but the mothers would urge us to come back and close the door to the shelter. After one of these excursions outside, we came back and sat down on the benches lining the walls when we heard the loudest whistle we had ever experienced:

—Mmmmamma mia, it's us this time!— someone whispered. There was much panic and shrieking, then the blast and the explosion: the whole building shook. It felt like an earthquake. But somehow nothing happened, the ceiling above our heads was still intact and nobody was hurt.

—It must have been next door— somebody said. We all went to see. In the yard adjacent to ours there was a huge gaping hole, like that carved by a fallen meteor. There was smoke and a pungent smell of dynamite, but nobody had been hurt. The bomb had missed the building. There was a lot of rejoicing, praying, thanking the Virgin Mary and we children immediately started looking for scrap as souvenirs.

One morning i woke up and noticed Sergei standing by the window. The room was still dark. I got up and went to look. I saw in the misty morning air, across the street in the schoolyard, a series of vague shapes dangling from poles. There were about ten or twelve of them.

—What are those? What are they?

I felt my stomach tighten. I gripped Sergei's arm. His pajamas felt soft. He looked at me, his sad eyes bigger than usual:

—Those are men. They are dead. They have been hung. See the red star on their arms? They are Partisans. I don't understand why they did that. There was no military tribunal or anything . . .

I couldn't take my eyes off the men, their heads bent to the side, their feet swaying this way and that in the wind. Alex was standing by me. We were all looking, fascinated. Suddenly the door opened and Mr. Preger came in. He was very upset.

—Get away from the window!— he pulled down the shade. —The Germans have arrived.— he announced, and walked out.

They left the men hanging publicly for the next few days

for all to see as a warning to the population: any disloyalty to the 'Führer' would be punished. For every German killed, ten, twenty, one hundred Partisans, if necessary, would be killed. We didn't dare go out of the house. The adults tried to evaluate the situation. Words like 'panic,' 'calm,' 'solutions' permeated their talks. The first thing to do was to get Maja and Ani back to Korčula. Then we all have to find a way out, unless, of course, the Partisans take over, which isn't completely out of the question. They are gaining momentum. More and more people are going into the hills to fight; the Germans are weakening, we'll win this war yet. Just be patient. We've made it so far, we'll make it to the end.

Indeed, a few days later, we all woke up to the sound of marching and singing. The songs were in Serbian, we heard the national anthem. We couldn't believe our ears. As we looked out of the windows we saw young men, fourteen-year-olds, sixteen-year-olds, waving the royalist flag, smiling, gesticulating to the people lining the streets. Their eyes were bright and dark. The 'Četniks' had overtaken Split, they had forced the Germans to retreat. The entire Dalmatian coast had been constantly changing hands since the Italian retreat, from 'Četniks' to Germans to Partisans, back and forth unexpectedly. It was unclear who was winning and who was losing.

A few days later passage was arranged for my mother and me and we were once more off to Korčula. I could see that my mother was very worried: nobody knew for sure whose hands Korčula was in and the 'trabaccola' had to travel through unknown waters to get there. The Germans were all around us. The chances of falling into their hands were great. Besides, they could shoot at the boat and we might all drown. My mother comforted me as much as she could: she didn't share her worries with me. One of her strong pedagogical convictions was that one should never threaten a child's sense of safety by unburdening one's fears on her. But i had overheard the discussions of the preceding days and i knew what the problems were. Mr. Preger had asked her to reflect

seriously on whether she should take the risk and she decided
yes, the main thing was to reunite the family: no matter
what, the family must not be separated. So we were off. I
remember sitting next to my mother on the bench, the boat
swaying, being sprayed by the sea, dozing, waking up in her
lap, being thrown to the floor when airplanes appeared,
looking out at the birds, the waves, the clouds, hearing
incessant whispering, speculations, feeling closer to my
mother than i had ever felt before. The journey took a whole
day, the captain had to make many detours. The Adriatic was
spotted with Germans and with mines. Finally we arrived and
we were alive.

As we disembarked, the port of Korčula was deserted.
Over the fortress, however, a blue-white-and-red flag was
flying gaily with a bright red star in the middle.

—I never thought i would be glad to see the red star . . .—
my mother said.

We walked to our house, carrying our luggage. My father
was there alone, packing. He looked at us in disbelief and his
eyes filled with tears. His embrace felt hot and sweet. He told
us that Braco and Omama were in Žrnovo, a village in the
interior of the island. They had all retreated during the
fighting and it was still safer to stay there. The situation was
so unclear, the Germans so near, they might overtake Korčula
at any time. Also there was the danger of their bombing the
port. For the time being all was well, the Partisans had
liberated Korčula, but we had to act fast, find a way to go to
a safer place. It was agreed, after some discussion, that the
children and Omama would stay in Žrnovo while my parents
returned to Korčula to work on arrangements for a passage to
southern Italy.

That night we all went to Žrnovo on mules, traveling along
a narrow dirt road to the center of the island. It was a rocky
landscape, hot and foreboding; there were goats here and
there, an occasional olive tree, and all around the smell of
musk, rosemary and hay. A hot wind, the sweet juice of
gooseberries. My father had made arrangements for us to live

54

in a farmhouse and to help the farmer and his wife with the vintage. When we arrived Braco gave us one of his rare full smiles. He was clearly very happy and relieved to see us—a little boy. The farmer took us into the kitchen and gave my mother, 'the lady,' a soft chair to sit in. He then told his wife, a stern woman all dressed in black, to make some 'coffee' for the company.

My grandmother came downstairs and sat down. There was a pot of soup cooking over the stone fireplace. The kitchen smelled good. It was dark and cool. Braco showed my mother and me our room: the farmers had given us their bedroom with windows overlooking the vineyards. The picture of the Virgin over the bed was faded and the bed was covered by a beautiful fluffy down comforter.

—The three of you will sleep here. Father and i will go back to Korčula. We must find a way to leave the country. Don't say anything about it to anyone.— my mother admonished.

I didn't like being left with Omama and i especially didn't like sleeping with her. She snored very loudly, but there was no choice this time. Braco took me outside to show me the vineyard, the grapes were hanging heavy on the vines. He started 'educating' me: this is muscat, the grape used in the sweet wine, these are the red grapes used for white wine—did i know that white wine was made from red grapes?—grapes are one of the main products of Korčula . . .

The first night was horrible. I missed my mother, the bed was infested with lice. Nobody could sleep. We all ended up on the floor and Omama finally turned the Virgin Mary's picture to the wall.


We stayed in Žrnovo for about three weeks. My parents, in the meantime, went back to Korčula to try to arrange passage.

The Allies were slowly moving up the boot. They had liberated Bari, the port on the other side of the Adriatic for which we were aiming. There was still danger that Korčula

would be bombed so it was best for the children to stay in
the country. Nights were still a nightmare: Omama's snoring,
the lice, the hard floor, the lack of air all made it difficult to
sleep. But in the daytime, life had its pleasures. Lanka, the
woman whose bed we were using, started taking me with her
on chores. I helped her feed the pigs, milk the goat and clean
the chicken coop. She taught me the language she used with
the various animals: "Pew, pew, pew, grrr, grrr, grrr . . ." Her
sounds were slightly different than the ones i had been used
to. "Animal languages vary from region to region as well," i
observed to myself.

The most beautiful memory i have of that stay is the
vintage. It was customary for friends and neighbors to gather
to help each other. On one day they all came to 'our'
vineyard. It was a very festive occasion in the course of which
work, singing, drinking and feasting fused. Everyone gathered
grapes carefully, separating them into vats by variety. There
were large juicy purple grapes and tiny little green ones: the
juices were riper, sweeter, richer than any i had ever had
before. Red-cheeked peasant boys would squirt the grape
juice at the girls and the girls would stick their tongues out at
them. Lanka would admonish them from time to time to
behave themselves with the 'guests.' When the vats were
three-quarters full the men and women would climb in to
start their dance. They would jump and kick their feet up,
holding onto each other for balance. There was singing,
harmonica-playing and, in the distance, the smell of food.

I was standing under one of the vats looking up when
suddenly a large man with a flushed face who was jumping on
the grapes caught my eye:

—That child wants to come in. Wait a minute till i get her
up!— and with that i was lifted into the softest, slushiest,
juiciest substance my bare feet had ever touched.

—Wait a minute! Wait! i haven't washed my feet.— They
roared with laughter in response: —Listen to her, she hasn't
washed her feet! What do you think we are doing if not
washing our feet?— There was more laughter and commotion

and i started jumping with them. At first i kept falling and worrying about dirtying my dress but slowly as i got used to the feel of it the jumping became automatic: it came out of my body without any effort and went straight into the sun.

On Sundays my mother and father would come visit. We sat around the fire in the kitchen to discuss the situation. Lanka held her hands in her lap and Vuko, the old man, would chew carob, occasionally sigh and remind us that nothing would ever replace tobacco for him ... I noticed that they were different when the 'gentlefolk' were there. They were shy and mistrustful, constantly watching their language. With us children they didn't seem to change. They had gotten used to us. My vocabulary had expanded. I learned that the word 'fig' referred to women's vaginas, that the expression for making love was 'mounting.' I was pretty sure my parents didn't know these expressions, that they were local.

On one of these visits my parents announced it seemed safe for us to return to town. The Germans hadn't considered Korčula important enough to waste their scarce bombs on. They were running out of war materials and they needed to concentrate on the Russian front, as well as Normandy and Italy. We were lucky once again.

In the weeks that followed an epidemic broke out in the immigrant community of Korčula: 'Bari-Bari.' Everyone suffered from it and it was the topic of many a joke. The Partisans had decided it was too dangerous for Jewish families to stay there, in constant danger of being taken by the Germans, that it would be best to evacuate them to Bari, the port in southern Italy which had been liberated by the Allies. The women, children, and older or disabled men would be allowed to go. Strong healthy men were needed by the Partisans to fight.

—There is another Bari-Bari victim— my grandfather would chuckle.

—What's the joke?— i asked.

—There is an illness called beri-beri.— Dida explained.

As usual i found grown-up jokes incomprehensible. And not funny.


Arrangements were made for the first 'trabaccola.' Crossing the Adriatic was a dangerous undertaking at this point: there were mines and Germans everywhere, but the risks were still greater in staying. The Germans were close and the Partisans were running out of ammunition. Tito's dwindling forces were depleted by the double task of fighting both Germans and 'Četniks.' Toward the end, 'Četniks' and Germans started uniting forces against the Partisans: the need for men was greater than ever. The soldiers running Korčula had no hair on their faces . . .

We were resigned to the fact that my father could not come with us. He was not enthusiastic about fighting in general and with communists in particular:

—I am a member of the bourgeoisie. There is nothing i can do about it, but at least i am not one of those armchair communists . . .— But he did admit that they were the only ones effectively resisting the Germans, so it was only fair to stay.

A big family crisis revolved around Sonja, who had fallen in love with a local young man. He was with the Partisans and she wanted to stay to join him in the fight, 'go into the hills.' Baki was horrified:

—Don't you know the consequences of such a decision? I can't leave you here alone, i am responsible to your mother! It is indecent for a young girl from a good family to go with soldiers!

Sonja sat there and listened quietly, her resolution never wavered. I watched her with admiration. Her love affair was not only passionate, it was noble: they would go risk their lives together for their beliefs. It was beautiful. I was the only member of the family who felt this way.

—You don't understand— i would be told when i expressed my support for Sonja.

It was decided that my father would talk to Sonja: he would be able to stay calm and persuade her rationally.

This went on to the day of our departure:

—You can't live with a man without being married and you can't get married in these circumstances . . . How do we know we can trust him, how do we know he won't take advantage of you?— Baki would always terminate these discussions with a definitive:

—No. No. No. I won't allow it. You are my responsibility and i won't allow it.

When the day finally came we all went to the port with our suitcases. We had to leave most of our belongings behind, the space on board was needed for lives, not things. My father was staying behind, Sonja was walking with him to see us off at the port. He was still talking to her, persuading, describing a life in Italy that would make her forget. She could pursue her studies, go to the university. He knew about love, he had been young too, but time heals all wounds. She just sat there, quietly, on the stone wall, her hands in her lap.

The farewells were dramatic. Baki was very upset about leaving Sonja, very angry. My mother and Omama were worried about leaving my father behind. Last-minute instructions covered up the anxiety:

—All right, Sonja, take care of the things we left, the sheets, silverware. Don't forget them when you leave, be sure you find the right person to entrust them with.

My father came forward, his eyes dark and sunken. He kissed his mother, who made the traditional gesture of blessing with her hands cupped over his head and the whispered Hebrew words. He kissed my brother and admonished him to be the man now, held me tight and said "think of me" in my ear. He embraced my grandfather and Baki and turned to my mother:

—Maja, you have to be strong. I will come and join you all soon.— He kissed her and she made a gesture of impatience to mask her emotion:

—Come on. Let's go. It is time to board— she said.

At that moment i knew my mother had taken command of the family. Sonja was standing in the background watching. We kissed her and tears started flowing down our cheeks. Familiar tears, departure tears, salty relief tears.

Hiding from the planes, we settled below deck in a very crowded space sitting on our suitcases. My friend Rebecca was there; her father had also stayed behind to fight with the Partisans. Our mothers were discussing the fathers' chances of rejoining us soon. After a while the captain allowed us to go up on board, a few at a time, to get some air. He was cautious not to arouse the suspicion of planes that might be flying over the boat. Sighting a crowd of people on board would give away a refugee boat. Rebecca and i were walking around deck, arm in arm, looking at the albatross following us; many years later, when i read Baudelaire, the image would appear in front of my eyes of watching these awkward, majestic birds follow us on our flight to freedom. We were speculating on their nature when we heard a motorboat approaching. Korčula was still in sight. We saw a small boat coming toward us fast with a red-star flag flying over it. The captain ordered everyone below deck. The whispering began, speculation after speculation. What was wrong? Are they Partisans? Is this a German ploy? Did they change their minds, decide we should not undertake the journey?

We heard the motor stop, an anchor thrown overboard. Eventually the captain came to the aperture at the top of the stairs and made the announcement that we were turning around, heading back to Korčula. Our feelings were mixed. We didn't know what had gone wrong, but at least we would have a chance to see my father and Sonja again. As the boat docked we saw three Partisans, with berets, red stars and partial uniforms, coming on board. They went straight toward an elderly couple. I remember their greying hair and lined faces, man and wife, huddled together, going down the gangplank. As soon as they were out of earshot the questions began. And the speculations. My grandfather came toward us:

—They are collaborators. The captain told me. They are going to be shot. That leaves room for two more people.

So my father and Rebecca's father, the two oldest men left behind, were able to come with us to Italy.

It took us two days to cross the Adriatic. We had lost a lot of valuable daylight time in the exchange of passengers so that we had to stop for the night at Lastovo, an island southwest of Korčula which we knew to be in Partisan hands. I remember the stop clearly. We children were unleashed as soon as we stepped on ground after all those hours of confinement. We ran around wildly while the grownups set up sleeping quarters in two large halls with stone floors inside the building where the Partisan headquarters were. We immediately took to the vineyards, heavy with late-ripening grapes. We played hide and seek and ate a lot of the fruit. My brother suddenly exclaimed:

—Oh! We shouldn't be eating. Today is Yom Kippur!!! I forgot!

I felt a tinge of guilt, looked up to the darkening skies half expecting to see an old man with a white beard waving a finger at me, but then i replied:

—Well, these are unusual circumstances. We are not held to the talmudic laws in unusual circumstances. Don't you remember?

During our stay on Korčula not only had his formal education been more carefully tended than mine, but also his Hebraic education. Soon he would be thirteen, after all, and become a man: he would be entitled to read from the Torah at his 'bar mitzvah' and, war or not, my father had carefully instructed him. I also got Hebrew lessons, so i wouldn't feel left out or jealous, but my father's Hebraic instruction, like his chess, algebra, writing, reading, or history instruction was much more casual toward me: i was, after all, 'just a girl' and an education wasn't so important for me.

At nightfall, we all gathered in the two halls and my father read evening prayers. The Partisans gave us some soup and bread and we lay down on the floor and fell asleep.

We were awakened very early before sunrise by the captain who urged us to board the 'trabaccola.' The most difficult part of the journey was ahead of us, crossing the Adriatic, and we couldn't afford to waste any daylight. I remember little of the journey, except that it was long and filled with anxiety. It came to an end that evening: when land was spotted, everyone rushed up to the deck and started waving frantically. English and American flags came slowly into sight: "They are red, white and blue, like the Yugoslav flag," i thought to myself. "That is a good omen . . ."

## 8

When all this started we couldn't believe it was really happening. We heard about it but we couldn't believe that it would be bad for everyone. An Austrian who went from Vienna to America wrote us to pick up and flee to America, but Dida didn't believe him. He put the letter away, he didn't believe it. I thought differently. I thought: "Run away!" I saw that there was not much hope here. I saw with what cruelty they started, but i still didn't think that it would be the way it was. When the Germans and the 'Ustaši' first came to power we thought: "We have always worked honestly, nothing will happen to us." Intelligent people couldn't believe that such evil could exist. They just couldn't believe it.

Once in 1938 i was at the baths for a cure and there were some women from Germany there. They weren't allowed to move about much, they were restricted, but one of them told me she couldn't complain yet, that they still could walk around. But then it got worse and worse. After that people started fleeing from Germany and they came down to Yugoslavia. They told us. We heard from them. When the Germans first came we heard on the radio that Jews are untrustworthy, that they cheat people, everything bad . . . Then we weren't allowed to have a radio or a young maid: the maid had to be forty or over. We were not allowed to be on the streets after six or seven, we weren't allowed to buy food until ten o'clock in the morning, by which time almost everything was sold out. But a good Serbian woman bought me some chicken when i asked her. She bought me some chicken, she bought me some eggs, we weren't allowed to buy these things.

We didn't think of leaving until they started taking people to the camps. Dida didn't want to leave even then. He said: "Nothing will happen to me, i didn't do anything bad to anyone." My brother was in a camp with his son. They were in this room and some Jew was hiding, i don't remember how or why, but i know that the 'Ustaši' came in and said: "Is anyone hiding in this room?" So my brother said: "I guarantee with my head that there is no one." And they searched and found the man, took a gun and killed my brother; his son shouted: "Don't, that's my father!" Another gun and they killed him too.

In a year they liquidated too many Jews in these camps in Yugoslavia. But there were also good people who helped them get out of the camp. For instance, my sister-in-law's brother sent a lady and she got her daughter out of the camp. The mother was also supposed to get out, the 'Ustaši' were going to let her out too, but she forgot something in the room and once she went back she couldn't get out anymore . . . There were also Jewish children who were saved by the priests, they were gathered up and sent to the priests and they took them in. When the war ended, the Jews wanted these children back, but the priests said that they saved the children and they had to save their souls as well and they didn't want to return the children to the parents. . . .

There were many ways by which people saved themselves. In one family the 'Ustaši' came and picked everybody up. One woman in the family jumped through the fence and ran away. In another house one man succeeded in going up to the roof so that they didn't know that he was there and they didn't take him. Another family who now lives in Israel had this happen to them: when the 'Ustaši' came for them, the woman jumped out of the window and she broke her leg and they had to amputate her leg. She still lives in Israel with an amputated leg. But very few people saved themselves this way. Very few.

The 'Ustaši' came at midnight. They weren't allowed to shout so that people wouldn't find out how these Jews were taken away, in the winter. They got them out of bed, in pajamas, they didn't allow them to get their shoes on or anything, people went to the camps just like that. You can imagine how they suffered, how they got sick, how they died. We were very surprised that the Croatians were so friendly to the Germans. They used to say that they were an old culture, Bosnia and

Herzegovina, that the Serbians were less cultured, but we found more protection with the Serbs. The Serbs helped me, but also that Croatian doctor helped us escape . . .

When we arrived on Korčula, Dida no longer had any shoes. So we bought a pair of wooden shoes and he wrote to a Serbian friend in Sarajevo, a man who lived next door to our store: "Dear brother, send me shoes, a shirt, underwear," to such and such an address. We asked him to send it to a Croatian location. Then we hired a Croatian woman and she brought us the mail and the packages and this Serbian man sent my husband everything he asked for. When i got out of jail i went to the house of this Serbian family who had kept some of my things for me and the woman let me take a bath there. She said to me: "You can come whenever you want, just don't say your name when you call me on the telephone, say you are 'Micika.' " When i called her i said: "This is Micika, can i come?" And she said: "Come!" The Serbs helped the Jews a great deal during the 'Ustaši,' as much as they could, but it was very dangerous for them . . .

On Korčula the inhabitants behaved unusually well. They were Dalmatians and they were better than the Croatians in Croatia. We went through difficult and sad times, very difficult times. By the time we came to Korčula we didn't have a shirt to change into. Your father gave Dida one of his suits to wear, but that wore out. Everything tore, the stockings tore. Fortunately it was warm there and we dressed simply. We ate poorly because we didn't have any money. If we had been able to bring out some dukats we could have bought food on the black market. But it was still very nice among the Italians. At least we could buy a few sardines . . . If we had stayed under the Germans we would have already been in the camps. The Italians weren't too strict. If someone was found on the streets after curfew, five o'clock, they weren't too strict, they didn't lock them up.

The 'Korčulani' (inhabitants of Korčula) behaved very well with the Jews. They knew we were Jewish and those who had money gave their laundry to be washed by the peasant women, they bought things on the black market and that way the peasants made some money from the Jews . . . They welcomed us warmly, they didn't turn anyone in, they didn't persecute anyone. There were also Jews who didn't have any money but for them those who did set up a 'mensa' (soup line) and whoever didn't have any money could go there for a meal. There were students on Korčula from rich families who were sent and left without any money. They helped move people and that way they earned a little money. These students formed a group and they went to cut wood for all of us for very little because none of us had much money . . . They were fed at the 'mensa' and that way they managed.

My niece Sonja was one of these students. Her mother and younger brother were taken to the concentration camp and she got out. She was seventeen and all alone in Split, so i sent for her to come live with us on Korčula. But it was very difficult for me to have her because we didn't have enough food for ourselves . . . "How will i feed her?" i asked myself. Besides, she was in favor of the Partisans, she was a communist sympathizer. When we were leaving for Bari i wanted to take her along, but she wouldn't go. When she came she had brought some jewelry her mother had given her to take with her and this jewelry we didn't touch. When she said she wouldn't leave with us, i cried a lot because it was very hard for me . . . And so i left her the jewelry, a sheet or two, and she stayed and we left.

When the Partisans came, they helped us run away, to leave Korčula. The Italians were leaving, there was no food on Korčula and the Germans were near. So the Partisans allowed us to go by boat, the older people and the children. Your mother came to ask us to take you with us so she could save the two of you, as they weren't allowed to go. Dida said: "We'll take them." You can imagine our sorrow, to leave the daughter and take her children! We didn't know ourselves where we were going. After that the situation changed so the parents were allowed to go also. I was very happy. On Korčula we were in great danger because the Germans were in Split, not very far . . .

We all went to Bari on a fishing vessel, a 'trabaccula.' The trip was very difficult . . . We saw German planes, but the Partisans protected us. We sailed for a while, then we had to get off the boat because the German planes were all around, so they warned us not to walk around, to lie down, to hide under branches, so they wouldn't see us. When it was dark already, then we went out and the Partisans let us sleep in their apartments. But they themselves didn't have much. Some of us, those who could afford it, had taken a little flour, a little oil, and the Partisans said: "You are going where there is food and we don't have

66

any. Leave that here." And so we left them what we had. And we went on.

When we arrived in Bari we were taken to 'Via Carbonara, a place for refugees that the English had set up, where they fed us. We all slept together, men, women and children, all in the same hall. When we arrived in Bari the English offered us tea and cakes. You can imagine how good it felt to us to be greeted and to be given refreshments!

# ITALY

1

As we landed in Bari we were greeted by a spectacular bombing attack. Sirens screeched through the city, anti-aircraft crackled in the night, flickering like fireflies, planes dived and climbed again, their bombs emitting sinister whistles, splashing waterfalls through the air. I wasn't frightened. I assumed survival in the face of death. I amused myself below deck by conjuring images of Italy's geography: a slanted boot floating on top of blue water with Bari on the uppermost part of the heel. Sicily was under its toes, like a soccer ball ready to be kicked, Sardinia lay on the other side of the leg, isolated, distrustful of its foreign neighbor.

This welcoming attack was the first of many to follow: the Germans, having razed Messina, were now intent on destroying the other major port liberated by the Allies. After an hour, we heard the long wailing siren, announcing freedom of movement. Young men in khaki uniforms met us as we disembarked. Some wore large, slanted berets, others wore very small kepis sitting miraculously on the sides of their heads, some others wore full hats with visors: those were officers, i realized. One young man turned to Braco and mumbled something, sounding like he had a mouthful of mashed potatoes. I made a gesture of incomprehension with my hands and he laughed: he had a nice open face with pretty white teeth. He reached for a thermos hanging from his belt and filled a cup with warm liquid which he then handed to me. It looked like coffee and milk but it didn't taste like it, it was sweet and slightly astringent. The soldier handed me a flat, dry cake with zigzag edging. I bit into it. It was delicious. When my mother tasted the warm drink, in turn, she laughed:

—This is tea, English tea, with milk in it . . . It's good for you, it will warm you up! These poor children . . . they don't know anything . . . but now we'll catch up!

She was in very good spirits.

As we walked along, carrying our bundles, one of the men accompanying us explained how the modern part of Bari was built like New York: all the streets were straight and ran perpendicular to each other so it was easy to orient oneself. Many years later when i saw New York and they said that it was the only place that was built on a grid pattern, i countered: "No it isn't, what about Bari?" and they said: "Bari, where is that?"

Being in a new country, with beautiful sounds and buildings, just before my birthday seemed appropriate: i was starting a new life at nine. According to Braco uneven-numbered years were lucky years and, in many ways, it was true for me; this was 1943 and i was meeting Italy!

We lived in a furnished apartment, my mother, father, brother, Omama and i. Baki and Dida lived nearby in a home for refugees. We spent a great deal of time with Omama: it was a mutual babysitting arrangement, she being quite disoriented by the change of geography and language, while we children were in need of adult supervision, or so our parents thought. She told me stories of her childhood in Frankfurt, of children being beaten if they didn't obey, of being locked up in dark closets for lying, but also of outings in the beautiful forests, and she hummed sweet childhood songs.

Once when we were walking down a street, she wearing black clothes as usual and i skipping along listening to her talk to me in German (she had regained use of her native

tongue, now that we were free), we heard an exalted cry
behind us:

—MAMMA! MAMMA!

As we turned around we saw a thin Italian soldier running
wildly towards us. He approached Omama, took her in his
arms and twirled her around, kissing her and hugging her all
in a flash. Tears were running down his unshaven face.
Omama stiffened, trying to shake him off, repeating the one
word she knew in Italian:

—*Prego, prego* . . .

As the young man realized what had happened, he put her
down gently and started sobbing and excusing himself. He
was returning from the Russian prisoner-of-war camps, he
thought she was his mother. He didn't know yet whether his
mother was still alive, he was looking for her. He had been
told that his house had been bombed . . . We smiled and i
said:

—*Auguri!*— That was a handy word which held many
meanings, used to wish someone good luck.

Life under 'freedom' was not very different from life
under the fascists. Italian was still the principal language,
bombings were even more frequent, our future was still un-
certain. However, my father started working for the first time
since we left Sarajevo: he got a job with the English port
authorities, doing some kind of paperwork. It was this job
that caused him to almost get killed and my mother to have a
'collapse of nerves,' as it was called. His office was in a
wooden barracks and the day of the bombing attack, a bomb
fell on it, hitting the side where he usually sat; fortunately he
had just walked away from his desk and was standing in the
other half of the structure, but we didn't know that until
much later.

When the sirens started, we ran down to the shelter as
usual. My mother, Omama, Braco and i prepared ourselves
for a long wait, permeated with explosions, sobs, cries, silen-
ces. The shelter was stuffy and dark. I could taste the damp-

ness. It was hard to breathe. It was crowded with people from the streets; this was a daytime attack and the streets had been bustling. The Germans were bombing more and more in daylight. People said that was a good sign, a sign that they were losing: they were risking more of their planes and lives in a last desperate attempt to win the war. This last attempt lasted for another year and a half . . .

Latecomers told us that the attack was concentrated on the port.

—That's where my husband is!— my mother said.

There were comforting sounds from the women:

—*Signora, si calmi*— and they would cross themselves.

The men analyzed the situation. Among them there were always optimists, looking for good signs in the midst of disaster: they were the nurturers of hope. Omama was murmuring prayers in Hebrew, adding to my mother's aggravation. Braco was stoical, but his face was yellow. When all was quiet and the sirens sounded the signal that it was over, the men went up inquiring from one another on the streets where the damage was, what houses had been hit, which barracks in the port. The ambulances started wailing. One man said that Barracks 12 was hit. That was my father's barracks. My mother looked at us:

—Braco, you and i are going to the port. Ani, you stay here with Omama.— And they left.

What seemed like hours later, my mother and brother came back and with them was my father! He looked gaunt, he explained what had happened. My grandmother was sobbing, my mother was angry (she always got angry, after strong emotion, just as i do now). My father looked as though he had done something wrong and my heart went out to him. I thought to myself: "I will never be like that with a man when i grow up. How insensitive of them! Don't they realize that he almost died, that he is scared . . ." And so i held his hand and he squeezed mine; i felt our secret pact solidifying.

Afterwards, there were many days of my mother lying in

her darkened room, of doctors' visits, of quiet. Baki and Dida would take us for walks, looking very worried. Omama looked flushed and hurried around the apartment intermittently whispering advice in German to my father. She cooked the meals; i hated how watery and overcooked the food was. I missed my mother. When i went to her room, she looked unhappy, distant, in pain.

—What's the matter, is something hurting you?

—It's women's problems; i am bleeding all the time and they don't know why, but don't worry, Anči . . .— and she'd smile. When i kissed her now i sometimes felt that i was the mother and she was the child.

Then one day, she looked better; she was sitting up in her bed, propped by two large pillows, wearing a light blue bed-jacket that a neighbor had crocheted for her. She called Braco and me in: my father and she had decided we would all leave Bari and go to Sicily where it was safer since it had already been all bombed out . . . The familiar, soothing atmosphere of packing began to spread almost immediately. My mother was activated by the preparations: she, as usual, became the organizer, Braco and i the executors. There was an old Yugoslav saying—"What you don't have in your mind you have in your legs"—which Braco adapted during the packing period to: "What Mother doesn't have in her mind, she has in Braco's legs." And it was often repeated thereafter as a 'bon mot.' There were endless errands to run:

—Go back to the cellar and get some rope.

—Please go to the store and get half a liter of oil.

—Go tell Baki to come to dinner earlier, i need her to help me with the trunk. She is the best packer in the family.

Telephones were a visible part of my childhood, if not an active one. I had memories of the dark green telephone we'd had in our apartment in Sarajevo as a mysterious, forbidden instrument. Like many of the muted memories of our life 'at home,' that too had become a symbol of 'peace.' Since then we had never had a telephone of our own, nor did any of our friends or relativies. So the children's legs replaced its function. During the packing and cooking—we had to prepare enough food to take us through at least a week of traveling— my father and grandfather inquired about trucks going to Reggio di Calabria, the southernmost port in Italy, from which we would take a ferry to Sicily. Railways throughout Italy had been badly damaged and the ones still functioning were used solely for troops and armaments.

When it was all organized, the seven of us climbed into an open truck with our belongings. We sat down on the wooden benches along the sides; the back remained open until all the soldiers got on, then they shut it with a rail. Some of the soldiers sat on this back railing. They looked tired and happy. We were part of a long caravan of trucks transporting Italian soldiers back to their villages in southern Italy and Sicily. For them the war was over: they were going home to their 'mamma' or to their 'fidanzata,' sometimes to both. Some were wounded, all of them looked thin and frayed, but they were singing, joking and ready to play and do tricks for us: they seemed very happy to see children again.

During the next days of travel we all got to know each other intimately. Occasionally one of the Italian soldiers would take me on his knees and tell me about *his* little girl. They told many stories, some of which i couldn't understand, but through them i started learning Italian, or what i thought was Italian: actually it was mostly 'Calabrese,' the dialect of Calabria, and Sicilian. The journey from Bari to Reggio, the toe of the Italian boot, took five days. We traveled through remote regions, the smell of woods all around us. These were arid forests, not green like the ones i remembered from 'home': the branches on the trees were grey, thin and withered like old men's arms. The roads were bumpy, dirt and gravel; the older people complained from time to time about the cold, the wooden benches, the lack of protection, the fear of having our few possessions stolen. I was very happy with our new adventure.

The soldiers were very affectionate with Baki and Omama:

they joked with them as they did with us and seemed grati-
fied when they got them to smile. Baki spoke to them in
'Španjolski' (Spanish-Jewish dialect) and they spoke back in
their dialects, but somehow they seemed to understand each
other. I soon realized that she was telling them about her son
who was a prisoner-of-war in Germany and asking them
about the conditions on the other side, in Russia. They
would all shake their heads. She looked worried. She even
told one of the men, Ugo, that he looked like her son, Vito. I
didn't remember my uncle very well. I looked at Ugo and
from then on Vito's face became Ugo's face.

Then we arrived in Reggio di Calabria. We immediately went
to inquire about the ferry to Messina, Sicily's mouth. We
didn't have to wait long. Soon we were on a boat once again,
a larger one this time; it even carried a tank. It felt good to
smell the sea air once again, although the atmosphere had
altered considerably since we had left the Adriatic: the
clouds hung very low, there was almost no motion in the air.
We were told that meant that there were great winds
approaching us from Africa, the dreaded 'scirocco,' perhaps.

When we landed in Messina we saw a city before us that
was completely flattened. It was all white. The inhabitants
moved about furtively, dressed in black for the most part,
with somber, suspicious faces interminably looking through
the rubble of their homes. Ironically, the only structure still
erect in the principal piazza was a statue of King Emmanuele
of Italy, whom the Sicilians never even recognized as *their*
king. To many of them Sicily was not part of Italy, in spite
of the statues, it was SICILY, the independent head of the
old empire . . .

In Messina we saw a great many American soldiers: they
cruised around in their jeeps, smiling at us. They often
stopped and inquired about our papers, but they were
friendly and it seemed to be just an excuse to talk to us. I
noticed that many of the jeeps carried signs under their wind-
shields that said: SICILY ROME — BERLIN AND HOME.
We all discussed the meaning of the sign and were quite

cheered by it. Americans were definitely going to help us defeat the Germans. The soldiers were especially friendly to us children; they gave us our first Hershey bars for which we learned to say "sank-u." My mother seemed pleased that the children were finally getting their due—chocolate . . .

We said goodbye to some of the Italians who had traveled with us, whose journey had come to an end. The men had a brief meeting. My father and grandfather came back with the results: the drivers advised that we drive around the clock. They said it would be dangerous to stop at night in the Sicilian countryside: the Mafia had taken justice into its own hands once again during the war and there was no telling how they would appraise us, as enemies or friends! In either case they would lighten the weight of our possessions . . .

The caravan started its slow, winding journey along the coast of Sicily toward Palermo. There were about eight trucks following each other. Whenever one got delayed, the whole convoy would come to a stop. These stops were welcomed by the old and the young: they could stretch their legs and we could run, throw stones or just m-o-v-e! I have many memories about this part of the journey. Much of it took place at night. The air smelled sweet; there was much intimate talk, sharing of fears, sharing of hopes. I remember events through the haze of sleep; dream and reality fused into one.

Ugo particularly stands out in my mind. He and Baki had developed a special relationship: she treated him like a son, worrying about his catching cold and whether he was getting enough to eat, while he treated her like a mother, making sure that she got a comfortable seat, helping her off the truck, guarding her while she went behind the bushes . . . He talked to her about his mother. I was beginning to understand what he was saying: mainly it was about his hope that she was still alive. He had enlisted in the army even though she had begged him not to go because he had the notion that he should go fight for his country. Now he knew that she had been right, that staying home is better than fighting, much better for everyone. Why did they fill the schoolchildren's heads with all those ideas, patriotism, heroism, bravery ... "Those perverts," he called them and he got red in his face. At night he sang lovely soft songs that sounded like wolves' calls.

There were many sweet moments of reunion: as we arrived in small coastal villages the inhabitants came out of their houses, their eyes searching for a son, a husband, a brother. Sometimes they found him: he would jump down from the truck and there would be sobs and embraces and the younger children would turn away from him, refusing to kiss a stranger, and he would cry and the men would cry and the women would cry and sometimes we cried on the trucks watching them. They gave us jugs of water for the journey, they brought huge loaves of bread out of their dark kitchens to slice off chunks for us. Occasionally they handed small red apples to the children and that, for me, was always a very special treat.

At night Ugo often sat on the wooden ledge enclosing the back of the truck. Lying on the floor, awakened by the frequent bumps from the unpaved road underneath us, i would hear his Sicilian songs—Moorish, melancholy, passionate songs. I would lie there with the smell of the dark-olive army blankets mixing with the smells of people's feet and the breath of sleep. Occasionally the sound of a hawk or an owl pierced the air. Omama whispered her Hebrew prayers and my grandfather emitted his loud, generous snore. I felt cozy, at once protected by my family around me and aware of the unfamiliar countryside through which we were winding our way.

There was something in Ugo's countenance that predicted what was going to happen. He seemed more melancholy than the others. Even though he played with us, his smile was a song to sadness. I looked at his face, at his light brown eyes, at his beard and i would say to myself: "He is beautiful."

—Anica, *come si dice 'mamma' in jugoslavo?* (How do you say 'mamma' in Yugoslav?) That was his favorite joke. I always answered:

—Mama.

Then he would say:

—*Vedi che siamo fratelli dopo tutto* ... (See, that proves we are brothers after all ...)

He sometimes let me sit next to him on the wooden ledge at the back, reassuring my mother that he would see to it that i didn't fall over. He talked to me about his 'mamma'; he was worried something had happened to her during the bombardments, that she no longer was alive, that all his months of prayer in the Russian prison camp hadn't helped to protect her. Then, suddenly, his mood would lift and he would exclaim:

—My mamma and i are going to go dancing on Saturday night!

Other times i would sit on the bench next to my mother watching the convoy snake behind us. Sicily reminded me of Korčula, a larger, more dramatic version. Even the air was more extreme; as it entered my lungs it felt dryer, hotter, more perfumed, thicker. Silence in the Sicilian mountains seemed heavy with meaning; i watched for clues in the faces of 'our' soldiers. My parents mainly worried about bandits, while to me they seemed like a minor aspect in the general mystery of these mountains, volcanic mountains, barren on one side and thickly wooded on the other, depending on their exposure. Winds whipped through them and the sun beat down on them from dawn to dusk. The elements seemed more brutal here than in Dalmatia: i felt Africa in the air.

And then it happened, without warning. I was startled out of my sleep as the truck came to a bumpy stop. The night suddenly filled with confusion:

—What happened? What happened?

Nobody seemed to know. I thought: "A bombing attack." But there were no planes. The trucks were lined up, drivers talking excitedly to each other with their hands. My father and grandfather went off on their usual mission of inquiry. My mother told Braco and me to sit still, not to go anywhere, her policy being that the children should stick by her in moments of danger. I looked around for Ugo. I noticed that people were gathering around something by the side of the road, near the back of our truck. It was a bundle, covered with an army overcoat. The men were shining flashlights on it. I focused my eyes in the darkness and saw it was a man, lying very still. It was Ugo. I knew it before anyone said so. He had fallen off the back of the truck and the truck behind us had run over him in the dark. He was dead. His village was going to be the next stop.

The rest of the trip was very quiet. When we arrived in Ugo's village i remember noticing there were vineyards in the surroundings and toddlers running around without pants. We stopped in the square, next to the water fountain. They took his body and laid it out in the middle of the piazza. The priest came with his large black hat and laid a cross on Ugo's belly, over the American army coat he had been wearing. A very small woman, dressed in black, was kneeling down, next to his face, sobbing. Baki was crying:

—Once again the order has been reversed: the old live, the young die— she said.

2

Palermo was a metropolis. As a capital, it had all the buildings that distinguish such places from other cities. The opera house was my favorite, round and majestic, welcoming and forbidding at the same time, like the churches. The boulevards were lined with trees, opening onto large piazzas with extravagant fountains in their centers. We even saw some cars on the streets and streetcars and taxis. The shops tried to look as though they had something to sell. One in particular attracted my mother's and Baki's attention: in the middle of an otherwise empty window it displayed a pair of nylons. They saw shades of fashion in that single pair of stockings that totally escaped me.

—Nylon is the new fabric, it is stronger than silk.

—It may be stronger, but it doesn't look as fine— my grandmother replied.

The 'Allies'—the allied American and English liberation forces—assigned us to a recuperation center. We were classified as war victims, in need of special care and attention, so we were shipped off to an elegant villa on the outskirts of Palermo, near the small town of Monreale, famed for its cathedral. This was a former private clinic taken over by the Allies for returning prisoners of war and refugees. It was located in the 'Conca d'Oro' (Bowl of Gold), named after the golden oranges and lemons that lined the sloping hills. We arrived in November as the fruits were ripening.

I was beginning to notice that Italian stressed a dimension that Yugoslav didn't: it emphasized shape, smell, light, color. The sound of a word often conveyed its meaning directly; that was a great help to me as i was learning it. I looked at the scooped countryside and the word C-O-N-C-A resounded in my head. The 'bowl' reflected the shape of the oranges; everything was rounded off. Even the volcanic mountains in the distance had a softness to their edges. The light was sharp and produced bright orange sunsets. Sicilians seemed to avoid light whenever they could. There were cave dwellers all around us: people whose houses had been bombed out, who had taken shelter in the natural caves of the rocky hills. They seemed quite at home there, cooking spaghetti on coal stoves outside their caves, laughing. Their laughter stopped whenever they saw us approaching. We were foreigners. They didn't differentiate between Germans, Americans, soldiers, civilians, or mainlanders for that matter: even the Italians from the peninsula were foreigners to them. Never laugh in front of a foreigner seemed to be their motto.

Life in the clinic settled into a comfortable routine. We all had beautiful, spacious rooms with verandas overlooking the orange groves. Through my windows i could see storms approaching far on the horizon. I learned to recognize the smell preceding a Sicilian tempest before any clouds were in sight. The dogs always gave their signal before anybody else. We all ate our meals together in the main dining room. Good, substantial meals, with pasta to start. There was meat at each meal and the spaghetti had holes in the middle through which we learned to suck air; grownups were constantly reprimanding us for the whistling noises we produced. Lovely, slippery spaghetti 'al dente,' dripping with oily red sauce. And parmesan cheese sprinkled so thick that it formed mounds on top. We had ice cream, oranges, pastry, chocolate. Life was good.

I started going to school, walking with the other children every day, up the hill to Monreale. The cave dwellers watched us as we passed by and slowly began to nod at us. We were often cautioned not to talk to strangers, not to accept anything from strangers. Most of all, never to go with strangers. Baki was fond of telling me kidnapping stories:

—When i was about your age— she would begin —the gypsies stole my mother's best friend's son. He was just a baby, sleeping in the sun, outside her window. She never saw him again. She almost died of sorrow.

As we walked to and from school we thought of these stories, but paid no attention to them. One day we even accepted a ride from an old man chugging up the hill in his little black 'Topolino' car. We felt very brave and a little scared. My friend Rebecca and i just got in and he took us to school with a smile. He deposited us in front and wished us a good day. The school was dark and musty. We recited many prayers.

Rebecca was my best friend, a year older than i, dark and serious. She had freckles and a younger sister whom we ignored. The garden around the clinic was large and the paths were covered with white pebbles. The trees and bushes were carefully clipped into regular patterns: it was an 'English' garden. Rebecca and i walked around by the hour, arm in arm, our sandals crackling on the gravel. We never stopped talking. She told me about her mother and father, how she had heard them making love in the other room. They thought she was asleep. Her father would laugh loudly, her mother would sometimes get angry and sometimes tease him. They seemed to enjoy it.

Rebecca's father was tall and had a moustache. He pinched my cheeks a lot. He was not a 'professional.' Rebecca was not exactly the kind of friend my parents would have picked for me, but what could they do! She was polite and seemed more sensible than her mother and so it was all right for us to be friends. She told me that she saw her father's penis sticking out one day when she was looking through the keyhole. It looked funny. Her mother was laughing, so she must have also thought it looked funny.

—Did you see them do it?

—Well, i couldn't exactly *see* them, but i heard them . . .

—What is there to hear?

—I don't know how to describe it. Just noises.

—Like what?— i pressed her for details. —Make the noises.

She started groaning and growling and laughing. The men passing by, as they strolled in the garden discussing the war, looked at us with discomfort, even distaste, i thought. Of course, they didn't know what we were doing. They probably thought we were 'just playing.'

We were constantly warned about the dangers around us: "Don't talk to strange men," they said over and over again. Baki was especially apt to say how men seemed sometimes kind and fatherly with young girls, but they just wanted to . . . We were never told what the danger actually was, but it was intimated that it had something to do with virginity. I grew up with a feeling that i was a delectable green fruit, especially tantalizing because i hadn't ripened yet. They talked about my innocence. I never felt innocent, i always felt wise and worldly. I didn't like girls who were naive and who blushed or got embarrassed. Boys weren't queasy. I liked that. Rebecca was like me, even wiser, i thought, and i liked that about her.

Sometimes dangers materialized and then i would think twice about making fun of the adults' warnings. One day, as we were playing in the back of the clinic, my brother and i came upon a live hand-grenade. He picked it up, at first not realizing that it was live. We were used to finding empty ones: they were standard toys in our childhood. But this was the first live one we had ever found. As soon as he realized that the pin was still in, he told me to stand back and very slowly he put it down on the ground. We looked at it for a second, the red plug staring at us.

Then we ran and told my father, who got very excited. He went and told the other men in the dining room:

—My children just came upon a live hand-grenade! They could have both been killed! We must do something!

Three young Slovenian men, playing poker, put down their

cards and said they would go. They were the cooks at the clinic. They were fresh out of Italian prisoner-of-war camps, used to dealing with dynamite. When they came back they were laughing:

—The children can play safely again. We dismantled it. See this?

They showed us the shell. One of them came over to me and let me look at it in his hands. His name was Stefan, he told me.

I was learning to recognize real danger from false danger. Outside in the dark it was easy. When it came to man-made objects i still had a lot to learn. One day, in the garden, i was sitting on the bench reading a love comic book. A man about fifty years old, whom i had seen before at the clinic but whom i didn't know, came by and sat down next to me.

—What are you reading?— he asked.

I showed him the magazine without answering. He sat there for a while. I felt distracted. I found myself re-reading the same page twice.

—Would you like one of these?— he asked me, offering me a small yellow box filled with little white shiny squares.

—Oh, thank you. But no, no thank you— i answered.

He extended his open palm toward me with one of those white squares sitting on it. He urged me to take it with his motion. I thought to myself: "Hah, you think that i am dumb, that i would believe that this medicinal-looking object is candy . . . No candy has ever looked like that! He thinks all children are idiots. Well, we are not. I know what it is: arsenic! You are one of those men Baki told me about who go around poisoning little girls." I felt proud of myself for being so alert. In my most polite manner i said:

—I am not allowed to eat between meals . . .

Irrefutable argument. Many years later, i encountered the same white pills in the same yellow box, in Rome. They were Chicklets!

Baki's room was one of my favorite places to visit in the clinic. It was large and sunny, like all our rooms, but hers was cluttered with pieces of cloth, pins and thread. She had established a small business: she had set up a sewing machine and was always busy working at it. Young men in the clinic who needed something altered or fixed came to her and she would fix it for them, for a small fee. Men, in her opinion, were clumsy. Their hands were too gross to handle a needle and thread. And there was no reason why they shouldn't pay for the service!

—They all have money in their pockets. It is better they spend it on their clothes than on drink— she often said.

She was resuming the trade of her youth and with the money she earned she was setting up a secret fund, as she used to have at home. A fund of her very own. For emergencies.

Baki wanted to teach me how to sew. She gave me lessons every day for half an hour. I liked visiting with her, but i didn't have any talent for sewing. I was always pricking my fingers or making the stitches too large.

—A girl must know how to mend. Here, i'll show you, come here!

I tried to please her, but i just didn't have the patience to pay attention to what i was doing.

—You'll be sorry when you have children. Who do you think will mend their socks? Mending is an art. It takes patience. All you want to do is run and be in a hurry. What for? We'll never have maids again, those days are over no matter what your mother says. I have seen changes before. After a war life never goes back to the way it was. Anyway, it's better this way . . .

Omama's room was altogether different. Darker, more austere. It was smaller too, since she lived alone. She spent many hours each day praying. She had her things all neatly put away in bundles lined up on the shelves. She tied everything up: letters, documents, all sorts of scraps, even food. She was very moody. Sometimes she greeted me with a big smile and gave me a sugar cube. At other times she would scold me for writing on Saturday, for not praying enough—

almost nothing was permitted on that day.

Life was settling into a routine.
—Is this 'normal' life?— i asked my father one day.
He smiled sadly:
—Yes, this is normal life. We have food, you can go to school, we are free. Soon i will work again, then it will be even more normal!
What my father was going to do became the focal topic of conversation. He was forty-three years old and here he was, a Yugoslav lawyer in emigration, an alien in Italy. What could he possibly do for a living? All he wanted to do was to practice law again. He missed the discussions, the dialectics, the feeling of helping others.
—I'll take the Italian exams and practice once more, don't worry— he would tell my mother as she expressed her anxiety about our 'livelihood.' For the moment we were being taken care of by the Allies, but that would soon come to an end. Then we would have to fend for ourselves.
—And what about me— my grandfather would say —i am not old iron yet, like you seem to think!
He was the tallest member of the family and as he made these pronouncements he would stand erect and show us that he still counted.
—Well, right now we must all concentrate on learning Italian. Without the language none of us can do anything— my father would reply.
—But this is all just temporary— my mother would interject —the war is coming to an end. Hitler is losing, everyone says so, he can't hold out much longer. The Allies are working their way up the boot, very nicely. They'll be in Germany in no time, just watch! Then, we'll all go *'ohm*.
She said 'home' in English, not pronouncing the 'h.'
—Sicily, Rome, Berlin and home!— i would sing to them.
My father nodded, but there was something in his eyes that expressed doubt. Baki said:

—It will never be the same, everything has changed. You saw those Partisans, they will be in charge now. *They* will tell *you* what to do, not you them!

She looked victorious.


My brother spent many hours in our room, reading and studying. He was in 'gymnasium' and, in spite of language difficulties, already doing very well. Latin was one of his favorite subjects:

—It's a *logical* language— he was fond of saying —not like Italian, which is sloppy and emotional. Imprecise.

—Italian comes from Latin, in case you forgot— i said with growing impatience.

Then i usually walked out. I often went downstairs to the main lounge to listen to the radio. I liked Italian songs. I liked the Italian language in general. It was full and light.

—When we go to Palermo we'll go to the opera, you'll see how beautifully they sing there . . . and the costumes . . . the sets! You'll like it!— my mother had told me.

One day, as Rebecca and i were sitting around the lounge, listening to the radio, one of the cooks came in—one of the Slovenians who had dismantled the hand-grenade. He smiled at us. We smiled back. He said:

—You look bored.

—You are correct— Rebecca answered.

—Now, let me think. What would interest young ladies?

He stood there, his hand under his chin, in mock concentration.

—I have an idea!— he said after some thought —Would you be interested in some 'caramelle'?

We looked at each other. What a question! We both loved Italian hard candies, with those pretty wrappings depicting the fruits.

—Yes— we said in chorus.

—Well, come along! What are you waiting for?

We followed the man up the wide marble staircase leading

to the third floor where all the bachelors had their rooms. I looked back to see if anyone was watching. Rebecca whispered to me:

—Do you think it's all right for us to go with him?

—Of course! Why not?— i said with feigned nonchalance.

As he opened the door, i saw a room flooded with sunlight; there were three beds, covered with grey blankets and books and magazines strewn over them. The bathroom door was open and i saw Stefan sitting on the closed toilet seat, shaving. He smiled at us and motioned for us to come in.

—First things first— said Mate, the man who had brought us there, — these young ladies wish to have some 'caramelle.'

He brought out a packet of candy and offered them to us ceremoniously:

—Are we in the mood for orange or rasberry or strawberry today?

—One of each, thank you— we answered and we all laughed.

I went over to Stefan and watched him shaving. His face was covered with lather. He was using a straight-edged razor. Rebecca stayed with Mate.

—That looks like fun— i said —is it?

—Yes, in a way, although i don't think about it much. Do you want to try?

Stefan offered me the razor.

—Oh, i don't know how to do it, i wouldn't want to cut you!

—Don't worry, just watch what you are doing. You are handy, i can tell. Here, sit on my lap, it will be easier that way.

He put down his razor and helped me onto his knees. As i straddled him, we faced each other for a moment, smiling. His teeth looked yellow next to the shaving cream. I could hear Rebecca and Mate playing behind me on his bed, near the door.

Stefan picked up the razor and showed me how to run it

down his cheek, in a straight line. His skin was brown and smooth. He showed me the lather on the razor: it looked like salt and pepper mixed together. He handed me a soggy rag:

—Wipe it on this.

I took the razor and ran it down his cheek.

—How is that, does it hurt?— i asked him.

—No, no, you are doing an excellent job, you are a first-class barber!

The bathroom was airy and warm. The window was wide open and the sun was shining on us. It was very pleasant to sit like this, with my legs taut around his. While i was concentrating on the shaving, he put his hands on my hips and ran them slowly down my thighs. I kept working on his face. After a while i became aware of his hands between my legs. At first, they just lay there, quite still; then his fingers started tickling me. It felt good. I wanted to pee.

—What about your chin? That looks hard.— i asked.

—Just pull the skin like this— and he pulled on his cheek.

Slowly his face was becoming exposed. His hands were soft on my crotch. He kept rubbing me and i was laughing. After a while i felt a delicious tingle go into my navel, like a shiver:

—What are you doing?— i asked him.

—Oh, nothing, just playing. You pay attention to what *you* are doing!

Suddenly there was a commotion behind me.

—Anica, let's go. We must go now— Rebecca's voice was determined.

I put the razor down and climbed off Stefan.

—Where's the fire?— he said —what's the hurry? My barber hasn't finished!

—I want to go now. Thank you for the candy— Rebecca replied.

I looked at her. She was standing by the door with her hand on the doorknob. She looked frightened.

—Yes, thank you very much— i said to Stefan —and thank you for letting me shave you.

—Come any time— he smiled at me. His eyes were shining.

—They are little babies, they want their mommies . . . said Mate mockingly.

As we went out, Rebecca was walking fast ahead of me, toward the staircase. She skipped the stairs, two by two. That was hard to do, going down; we usually only did it going up.

—What's the matter, why are you in such a hurry?

—We shouldn't have gone. Let's just get downstairs before anyone sees us!

When we got down Rebecca told me that Mate had 'tried.'

—Tried what?— i asked her.

—You know what . . .

—You mean . . .

—Yes.

—Stefan touched me down there. Do you think he was trying also?

—I don't know , but i do know that Mate tried. I don't think we should tell, do you?

—Are you crazy? Of course not!

It was my policy never to tell grownups anything they didn't already know.


We walked into Rebecca's parents' room and found them sitting around a small round table playing cards with my mother and father. The room smelled of perfume and cigarettes and vermouth. It was a nice mixture of smells. Our parents interrupted their game and looked at us:

—Where have you been?— asked Rebecca's mother.

—Oh, nowhere— i started saying.

—We were just playing . . . on the staircase— said Rebecca.

The parents picked up the evasiveness in our answers like trained detectives. A series of questions started coming at us in rapid succession. After much mumbling, Rebecca finally blurted out that we had gone to Stefan's and Mate's room for some candy. Both sets of parents became very agitated. Rebecca's father stood up and looked quite red in his face under his moustache:

—What could they possibly want of these children? What went on? I insist on knowing the truth!

He was huffing and puffing a great deal in between words. It was decided that we would all return to our own territory and that each family would discuss the matter privately.

Once we were in my parents' room i assured them that nothing unusual had happened, that i knew that i shouldn't have gone there, but that no harm had been done, that i wouldn't do it again, that the men had been very nice to us, that Stefan had let me shave him even, and besides that we had only stayed a few minutes . . . I thought it best not to mention the candy. The 'not eating before meals' rule seemed to apply to the whole day. Anyway i was used to fitting the truth to my parents' needs. I thought the incident would end there.

The next day, however, i learned from Rebecca that when she told her parents what had happened, her father became so upset that he stormed out of the room, looking for Mate. She didn't know what was said but she gathered that he reported the incident to the director of the clinic.

—What did you tell them happened?— i asked Rebecca.

—I just told them what happened, what do you think i told them?

—But what *exactly* did you tell them?— I felt impatient with her.

—I told them that we had gone up because they had invited us to have some candy and that when we got there Mate had tried to embrace me . . . that he had wanted to lie on the bed and touch me all over . . .

—Why did you have to tell them that? You know they wouldn't like that!

—I felt that what we had done was bad. I was scared.

—You idiot!— i said and i walked off.

I was very angry with Rebecca. She was making a big thing

out of nothing. And now the parents, of course, were making it even bigger. I was worried about Stefan. I didn't want him to get into any trouble. At dinner that night it was announced that Mate would no longer be one of the cooks. He had been dismissed for 'certain reasons.' The next day it was reported that Mate was missing. Three days later his body was found at the bottom of a cliff.

# 3

I was born under the Austro-Hungarian rule, but my parents, they were born under the Turkish rule. They dressed as Moslems: my mother wore a veil, she continued wearing it even after the Austro-Hungarians came, she was used to it. My father, he wore a fez . . . In their time, the men and women were separated. Life was not easy for them. My mother had ten children, two died. There was no electricity, they used gas light and the house was always filled with smoke, your nose was always filled with smoke. Everyone had either candles or petroleum lamps and we had to clean the glass cylinders. We were very careful with them, we worried a lot about fire, we watched carefully over the children. In the winter we went to bed early because there was no light.

There was no order under the Turks. In the middle of the night 'Hadjilojo' [a bandit] would come and wake everyone up and ask for dukats. If we said: "I don't have any," he answered: "I'll be back tomorrow and if you don't have any I'll kill you!" That was it.

But Austria did a lot of good things, brought progress. While the Moslems were calling for 'aksham' (evening prayer) from the mosks, Austria built schools, trains, businesses. I don't think we had trains before Austria . . . The people were satisfied, not the Serbians, they weren't satisfied, that is why they killed Ferdinand. When Austria came, they brought modern ways so that women didn't have to have so many children. Life became easier, they brought those rubbers for the men to use . . . But still if a boy was born that was a great event, if a girl was born it was just a . . . pisspot!

The Austrians brought electricity, they brought the electric streetcar, before that it was horsedriven—they paved the streets, not all of them, but some of them. Under the Turks, there was no asphalt. When i was a child and my family went on vacation we all got into a large carriage pulled by two horses and in this carriage we put our down quilts, our cushions, dishware and luggage. They would pack it all in and we would sit on top and ride like that all the way to the village where we were going to spend our vacation. We didn't go far, an hour or two away.

I was born in Sarajevo. My father had a store with his brothers, a wholesale store for Turkish goods: 'čakšire' (bloomers), 'gunje' (blankets), all kinds of Turkish goods. The old man, my grandfather, left the store to his three sons, but then they split up. They paid my father off and he opened his own store, a smaller one, retail, also for Turkish goods. My mother didn't work, she stayed at home. But it didn't go too well for my father, so we moved to a smaller town, to Bijeljina where my father started another store, for the peasants. It didn't do too well either: there were eight of us, one person couldn't feed eight children.

Then, in Bijeljina, we bought a nice little house, we had a cow, my mother learned to milk the cow and she sold the milk. We got along, but there were no luxuries. As the children were growing up, my mother said that there was no future for them in Bijeljina, so we went back to Sarajevo. She found jobs for my older brothers, one in a lumber mill and the other in a store. After a while the eldest brother opened his own lumber mill. He did very well, the business flourished.

I was the eldest daughter. I was named after my father's mother so that my father loved me more than my younger sister who had my mother's mother's name. That was some sort of tradition: my father loved my eldest brother most because he was named after my father's family, while the younger one was named after my mother's side. And that is how it went in many families, more mine, more mine. But still, the men were always first. When the food came to the table, the men were served first, then came the women. The women addressed the husband in the polite form ('vi') and the husband addressed the woman in the familiar form ('ti'). The woman was second rate and the husband was the boss in the house. When the husband came home, the best was for him, he came first, then the children. And it was the same among the children: we fought and the boys would beat us up.

My mother was a very smart and a very good woman. I got along fine with my mother. I have good memories of my childhood, it was good and after a while there were riches in the house. We didn't have beds, instead there were benches all around the room, they were called a 'minder,' Turkish style, and there were pillows on them to sleep on at night; in the daytime, the pillows were picked up and that's where we would sit, high up. We cooked on the stove, with coal or wood, but mainly with coal. And to heat the house, when i was little, we had very nice earthen stoves that we heated with wood. There was such a stove in each room. On the floors we had rugs, woven locally: there was a weaving place where they made national Yugoslav rugs. I knew a lady in Mostar who wove these rugs, very nice ones, i remember, and she would weave first to the right, then to the left, right, left, right, left. In the factory I think they wove the same way.

My maternal grandfather had a brick factory. Houses were made out of bricks. When they started to build a house they began in early spring and they would work until August, September, weather permitting; they put the house under a roof and during the winter they let the house dry, if it was several stories high. It took about a year to finish. From May to November they would work on the roof and then again in the spring they would finish it. Only the rich had brick houses, the poor, they lived in rented rooms, they just had one or two rooms. The poor lived in a different section of town and there were cheap apartments there built under the Turks, more primitive.

Austria introduced good schools. There were German-Hungarian schools and Serbo-Croatian schools. There were also parochial schools run by the nuns, dressed in black and white. I went to the German nuns' school and then to the Serbo-Croatian school. The archbishop tried to convert the Jews, but we didn't. Some did and some didn't: Dida's brother did, his mother didn't. I liked the nuns' school better because they spoke German and because we sang and played nice music. We studied singing, they played the piano and it went: "AAAAAAAAAA, EEEEEEEEEE," it was very gay. I went to school until the seventh grade, after that i didn't like going anymore. Instead, i started to sew. We weren't doing so well anymore and my mother sent me to learn how to sew. So i sewed. I sewed until i was married. I went to Vienna, that was like going to the university because Vienna was a bigger city and that is where you went to learn how to cut, how to make more modern patterns. After i came back i sewed for another couple of years and then i got married.

My mother was more intelligent than my father, she did everything: she took us to Bijeljina, brought us back from Bijeljina, she saw that there was no future there, my father didn't see as much as my mother did. But my mother didn't even know that she was smarter, she was so used to thinking that the husband is everything in the house and that she is second rate. My father loved my mother very much, but he didn't ask her for her opinion in the store. He worked alone, she didn't participate. My parents lived well together, but after we grew up and heard him scolding my mother we would protest because we saw that he wasn't always right, that in many ways she was more just than he. So my late father said to us: "When you were little i said what i wanted, now you don't allow me!"

My mother kept kosher, but she had many Turkish ways: she wore the veil and she didn't mind having to hide herself, she was brought up that way. But when she unveiled herself she was happier: she preferred to be able to go out, to see people and so on. She cooked very well, she ran a good household, very neat, very clean. She was very good to us children, she encouraged us to get ahead, to learn new things. She could read and write in Hebrew, she wrote her letters in Hebrew. My father wrote both Hebrew and Serbo-Croatian. But amongst themselves, they spoke 'Španjolski' (Spanish patois spoken by Sephardic Jews) and with me also, we all spoke 'Španjolski' at home. There were mainly Sephardic Jews in Sarajevo, before Austria. The Ashkenazim came with the Austrians; they were given more important positions and the Sephardic Jews were envious so they put the Ashkenazim in prison when the Austrians left and Serbia came into power. They kicked the Ashkenazim out and didn't allow them to take anything with them. They were given eight days to leave Sarajevo; the natives were allowed to stay but the merchants born abroad were driven out. My husband was an Ashkenazim but he was born there so he was allowed to stay. Also, he spoke 'Španjolski' because he had worked in a Sephardic store and had learned it.

My father had this store and he sold to the Moslems; he got along well with the Moslems, my father did, but i didn't. I knew Moslems, they came to our store, under Austria, but we didn't like them. The women would come and they wore the veil and they would steal under the veil so that you couldn't see them. My mother and father got along well with the Moslems, very well, but when Austria came it changed, the Moslems never liked the Austrians, but i was for Austria. I didn't like the Moslems because they weren't good customers. A Moslem didn't spend any money, he lived very modestly. They had their own stores on the Čaršia (Turkish bazaar in Sarajevo). When you went there you could see them sitting on the floor, crosslegged, working on copper, pounding and carving. Beautiful things.

The Moslems and the Jews lived well together. When the 'Ustaši' came, the Moslems helped the Jews a lot, some even took them into their homes ... Even those who went with the 'Ustaši' were good with the Jews. They would come home at night and tell those families they knew: "Be careful, they are coming for you tomorrow!" And they took them into their homes, they helped them. Of course they also got some money for it, but they came of their own accord to tell them and they saved as many as they were able to. One lady was hidden by the Moslems for five years and when the war was over she was freed. But they weren't allowed to help the Jews, it was very dangerous for them, it was strictly forbidden. All in all the Moslems and the Jews got along fine, very fine: they are similar by nature and even their customs are similar.

4

When we had sufficiently 'recovered' we left the clinic and moved to the city, to Palermo. Another Yugoslav family we knew had found a pensione they liked and we moved in. It was run by a large, beautiful woman who looked like an opera diva. Her name was Signora Ciupella and it suited her perfectly: she reigned over the pensione like a Verdi queen. Her staff consisted of a sad, ragged maid whom she mistreated mercilessly and her handsome eighteen-year-old son whom she abused and adored.

Signora Ciupella presided over the meals, with her son Giulio sitting at the other end of the long dining room table. Our two families, the guests, sat on either side facing each other, while the maid ran up and down the table dishing out the spaghetti and bowing every time she was yelled at for not having done this or that ... We all drank red wine poured from a pitcher, the children's mixed with water. My mother didn't agree with the policy of giving children wine to drink.

—But signora— Signora Ciupella argued —the children *need* a little wine for their blood. Look at how pale your son is!

My mother looked at my brother and wondered whether this Ciupella wasn't right, after all. But how could she be? Alcohol is bad, very harmful for everyone. But still, with this diet of daily pasta, perhaps it was necessary. One must adopt the customs of the country, that was my mother's theory, there was always a basis for them. Besides, the fruit was good, the figs, the apricots and even the salad, once you caught all the worms.

The 'pranzo,' the midday meal, left us weak and ready for bed. It consisted of several courses, heavy 'minestra' (soup, pasta or rice dishes) to start, followed by fried eggplant or fish and syrupy desserts. I loved the meals and the talk. Signora Ciupella had a way of making current events sound like the fulfillment of old prophecies. She stressed her Sicilian identity; the Italians, the mainlanders, as she called them with disdain in her voice, got what they deserved. Whatever gave them the idea of following a crazy lunatic like Mussolini? There were no fascists in Sicily, it seemed. Later, as we moved up the boot, we discovered that this was a widespread Italian phenomenon: nobody had ever supported fascism, they were all avid resistance fighters. Occasionally there would be a 'nonno' (grandpa) in a family who would quote 'il Duce' with reverence, but he was considered 'rimbambito' (senile), he didn't know what he was saying.

Signora Ciupella spoke Italian to the 'foreigners' but to her son and to her maid, she spoke Sicilian which resounded like curses through the corridor of the pensione. I would listen to her through the door of my room scolding her son. She often humiliated him in front of everybody, calling him a ne'er-do-well, throwing his report card at him with disgust. Giulio, his full lips curled, his hair slightly disarrayed over his forehead, looked melancholy. I admired him. He suffered well. He occasionally smiled at me. In my mind he was an artist, a philosopher, a genius. His mother didn't understand him: he couldn't be bothered with the dull assignments he was asked to perform in school. I understood him.

Whenever Giulio displeased his mother she would punish him by locking him up in his room, without any meals. To me that seemed a monstrous act of barbarism. At times like that i thought my parents were right about how 'primitive' these people were . . . In the evenings, after a typical meal of soup and polenta, Signora Ciupella 'received' visitors in her bedroom: she lay on her bed, resplendent in an assortment of nightgowns, a silk quilt draped over her large body, propped up on several lace pillows. As people entered, she extended a pudgy hand and the men would kiss her rings, like the Pope's . . . She would point to a Florentine chair, uncomfortable in spite of its carved wood and brocade splendor, and warn them to be careful how they sat in it, lest they disable its wobbly legs even further. Around ten o'clock, having washed up in the kitchen, the maid would come in and kiss her hand good night. Signora Ciupella would give her hand distractedly while pursuing her conversation with the visitors; the maid bowed and left to go to her dark, damp room in the attic, free until six o'clock in the morning.

When Giulio came in, if he was in her good graces, she would motion to him to sit by her side on the bed. If she was angry with him, she would ignore him and he would remain standing looking awkward and lanky. Whenever i saw him standing like that on one of my brief goodnight visits to the sacred bedroom, my heart went out to him. "Poor, misunderstood poet . . ." i thought to myself. I calculated in my head: "I am nine years old, he is eighteen, that's the same difference of age as between my mother and father . . ." I would make it up to him, the cruelty his mother showed him, i would show him that not all women were like that.

One day Giulio was absent at 'pranzo': Signora Ciupella looked more proud than usual, her fists on the table, her breath filling her bosom. He was being punished in his room. She had daubed a bit of extra rouge on each of her cheeks and her eyelashes glistened with blue mascara sending dramatic highlights into her sparkling green eyes. I decided the moment had come, my chance to prove my devotion to Giulio. As each course arrived, i slipped some food into the napkin on my lap: some bread, a piece of thin 'bistecca' (beef steak), cheese, fruit. I didn't think he'd care if he missed the mushy zucchini, with pieces of even mushier tomatoes swimming in them: i could hardly swallow them without retching. Ciupella would get red in her face if the children didn't eat everything on their plates and she took it out on the maid:

—Look how 'schiffoso' (disgusting) your food is, *even* the children won't eat it . . .— she stressed as though children were lower on the evolutionary scale.

When the meal was over, i took my little bundle to the bathroom, next to Giulio's room and hid it under a towel while i went to get a broom, a basket and some rope. I wrapped the napkin around the food, like the Italian workers do, with four corners tied into knots on top of each other, then laid it in the basket. I took the broom, stuck it out the window and knocked gently three times on Giulio's window. He would know that was a signal. I leaned out the window, quite far, and looked down the six stories for a minute: "I am risking my life for him," i thought to myself. When he heard the knocks, he opened the window. We looked at each other. I put my finger on my mouth and motioned him to wait. I then brought the broom in, lay the basket with food on top of it and once again i leaned out, balancing the goods very carefully. Seeing his hairy arms sticking out of the window thrilled me. He took the contents off the broom with one hand and held on to the brush with the other, signaling me to wait. A moment later the basket came back with this penciled note in it: "Anica, you are a treasure— 'tesoro'—. You saved my life. I will never forget." I took the note and stuck it down the front of my blouse as i had seen the 'primadonna' do in the opera and rushed out to put the basket and broom away before anybody noticed they were missing. I hummed: *"Un perfido amore . . ."* A few days earlier i had gone to see *Lucia di Lammermoor,* my first opera, at the Palermo Opera House.

Outside of our 'pensione,' in the meantime, the war raged on. It was the summer of 1944. The Allies were slowly working their way up the Italian peninsula. Braco had hung a large map of Italy in our room and on it he showed the progress of the Allies by pinning red and blue flags on the cities being liberated by them. He put black flags on the cities that were still in German hands. He read the papers every day and changed the positions of the pins. The lower third of the boot was all blue and red. When Cassino fell, we celebrated. When Anzio fell, we celebrated again: the road to Rome was now clear. These had been among the bloodiest battles of the war, with heavy Allied losses. For us it meant that soon we would be going north, to Rome, the free city, protected by the shade of the Vatican.

One of Braco's favorite games was playing airplanes. It consisted of making paper airplanes out of newspapers, preferably *The Stars and Stripes,* and drawing English emblems on the wings. Then he would climb on top of the armoire in our room to fly them down on strategically placed books which represented buildings and military installations. The city he was most fond of bombing was Berlin. These were no ordinary bombs, these were incendiary ones, capable of burning down a whole city. He thought the Germans were showing great courage to fight against such odds but they had made some fatal strategic errors. The invasion of Normandy had assured the American forces' victory, while the Italian front was closing in on them from the south. The Allies had just landed in southern France as well. Mussolini, fighting in the north of Italy, was suffering mass defections. The end of the war was near:

—No doubt about it!— Braco would exclaim, after an especially successful bombing raid in our room.

Sicilian summers are hot and dry. When the scirocco hits, the population disappears. I remember walking in Palermo one day and noticing the city was unusually quiet. The natives could always tell when the wind was coming. They would close their shutters and their windows and gather in their dark rooms until it was over. The wind started like a caress at my feet; by the time i had reached home it was whipping my elbows and the dust burned my eyes: "Never go out to the seashore when the scirocco is coming," the Sicilians warned us. We learned to study the weather before going to Mondello, the beach town outside of Palermo where our friend lived.

We visited her often and my mother would sit and talk

with her in the shade of an oleander tree in her garden, while we changed into our bathing suits in her house to go swimming on the beach. She was a beautiful woman, proud of her high, smooth forehead. She didn't have any children and her husband was a prisoner of war in the German camp where my uncle was. She seemed to be waiting for him to come back. When he did, years later, they found that they couldn't live together anymore, their lives' experiences had separated them. She used to take my chin in her hand and say:

—Don't wrinkle your brow, you will get wrinkles . . . They are a woman's worst enemy.

I would laugh. The idea of wrinkles seemed preposterous, nonetheless every time i wrinkled my forehead i thought of her and still do.

On the days we didn't go to Mondello we visited the monuments of Palermo. The architecture was varied, reflecting Sicily's glorious past.

—This is good for the children's education— my mother would say.

—The best way to study history is to visit its relics— my father would add.

The guides often started the tours with the well worn phrases: "Sicily is the archaeological museum of Europe. Palermo is the pearl of the Conca d'Oro." And indeed it was. The city was situated on a beautiful bay, encircled by mountains. The Conca d'Oro, from which we had just descended, was the plain between the city and the mountains. The guides would tell us about the Cyclops, the one-eyed giants who used to inhabit Sicily and who worked for Vulcan, under Mt. Etna. My mother explained that was mythology, not history, but to me they were the same.

"Palermo was founded by the Phoenicians and then conquered by the Carthaginians."

—The Phoenicians were Semites— my father would say.

As we walked through the ruins i would imagine what Africa was like. *Casablanca, Tunisi, Algeri,* these were familiar sounds from the news reports, but to me they were like exotic birds. I felt as though i was taking long journeys to those shores while walking through the rubble. The guides spoke with surprising freshness in their voices. They were called 'cicerone,' after the great orator; and true orators they were, instilling enthusiasm into their listeners about Sicily's past: "Then the Romans conquered Sicily and then the Goths . . . Everybody wanted us, can you blame them?" The guide's eyes would twinkle with pleasure and pride. "Starting in the sixth century Sicily was ruled by Byzantine emperors and by the Arabs and then in the eleventh century the Normans took it and built these beautiful structures that you see here."

While i was learning about the Normans' building skills and of their conquest of Sicily, the Allies were landing in Normandy: 'Operation Overlord' took place on June 6, 1944. The Yugoslavs drank a toast discreetly that afternoon in their rooms at the pensione Ciupella. Two days earlier Rome had been liberated.

Discussions of our departure began:

—We must wait to make sure there are no retreats. Let them reach Florence, at least, or Pisa, before we go— my father said.

—There are not going to be any retreats. The Germans are finished. It's about time!— my grandfather replied.

—Let's start packing slowly and then when it is time to go we'll be ready— Baki said.

—So here we go again . . .— my mother said.

But there was levity in their voices.

Before we left i took a secret walk with Giulio. I told him about my calculations around our age difference, that nine years for a man and a woman was about right. He seemed not to understand. I persisted:

—I will think of you every night before i go to sleep. When you finish school, you will come to Rome. We shall meet in front of St. Peter's, all right?

He agreed, uneasily. He wanted to talk about the soccer teams. Sicily was a better team than Lazio, the Roman team.

—Of course!— i said distractedly. I squeezed his hand a little and he smiled. When we left i gave him a kiss on the cheek and he seemed pleased. I wrote to him from Rome, but he never answered. I suspected that his mother had intercepted his mail.

We traveled to Rome by truck, as usual, a long and tiring journey. We saw many bombed-out villages, wounded soldiers, children with limbs missing, their heads bandaged. There were big holes everywhere, right in the middle of the road sometimes and we often had to wait until the men filled them with earth before going on. There were also American jeeps with smiling blond soldiers on them, distributing their Hershey bars, chewing gum, peanuts—'American nuts,' as the Italians called them—. They seemed glad to see children and we were glad to see them. They smiled and lifted their hands to us, forming Churchill's 'V' for victory with their two forefingers.

We passed through Anzio, a disaster area: the rubble had not yet been cleared. There were buildings sliced in half, the walls exposed, with pictures still hanging, kitchens with stoves and chairs, the wiring hanging loosely like disarrayed hair on a pillow. We saw a child's bed, with a cross over it, remnants of normal life. There were pictures of the Virgin in every piazza and women dressed in black gathered around them, bringing fresh flowers, praying. They exclaimed in bewilderment: "Madonna mia! Madonna mia!"

5

I want to tell you how Dida and i met. That's *very* interesting. We used to go to dances, but then it was different than today, there was no such thing as going with an escort or something like that, instead you go and sit. The young men come and look at this one and at that one. Then they come and ask for a dance. This was during Austria. So we went to dances and i danced. I was a *very* good dancer, especially the waltz, yes! And Dida would come for me very often because . . . i danced the waltz beautifully and now whenever i hear the waltz, it's always so painful for me . . . The orchestra played the waltz and i didn't like Dida! He had ears like this . . . I liked others, but here he comes, poor me! Here he is and we sit and he comes and puff! I was very light on my feet and i danced very nicely and this dancer was always bothering me, yes he bothered me.

In Bijeljina i had a different suitor but that one left me: his mother wouldn't let him take me because i had no money. It was always like that, the mothers would interfere, or someone else. And so that one left me. I was very unhappy, that hurt me very much. But after a year or two i started dancing again. And . . . there is this dancer who is always bothering me, he is bothering me, but still somehow we fell in love and then he got a better position in the store where he worked, he became a more important man, he was the head of the store, and i then opened my eyes a little and i thought to myself: "This is a good match, he loves me, it's a good match."

That is how we started, but there was never any walking around together, we would just see each other on the street and he would greet me and that was all. We spoke a little. When i went to his store to shop i liked for him to wait on me and so on, but there was no walking on the street together, that didn't exist in my time, in your mother's time it existed. One day at a dance an acquaintance of ours said that we were a good match and he went to see my mother to tell her that this was a good match. He asked Dida if he wanted to get married and Dida said he didn't even know how to make buttons, that if he loses his job he doesn't know if he'll get another job, that it wasn't so simple to get a job.

And so Dida started talking to me about that, that this man told him to get married and that he said such and such. Sometimes he came a little to the house and we would talk down on the stairs or we would stand at the door; so i said: "I'll continue to sew if i get married, i'll continue to sew." He says: "You don't have any money." I answered: "Who said that i don't have any money?" I had a thousand five hundred dukats . . . Eh, when he heard that . . . he loved me! He was about twenty-five or twenty-six at that time. He still didn't have a livelihood, but he wasn't dumb, he was very smart. And so we took each other.

The wedding was *very nice.* I was never extravagant, i just wanted a little suit, not a bride's gown. But the wedding was unusually large because he knew a lot of people. And then, after the wedding, people came to the house for a wedding reception. And then the young couple who was going on a trip would go to the station with all their closest relatives, brothers, sisters, the whole family, all of them went with you in carriages to the station and there the groom would treat everyone to what they wanted to drink. When we went on our wedding trip we first went to Vienna, then to Budapest and so i was dead tired; instead of staying in Yugoslavia, on some small island to get some rest, we had to go see this and go see that . . .

In those days there was no such thing as not being . . . a girl . . . a virgin. No girl had been with another man before she got married. That was unheard of, un-heard-of, for a girl not to be a virgin! The first man i saw was my husband. I never knew another man. I knew them, but i didn't have contact with them. Not just me, it was the same for this woman and that woman as well. In my time it wasn't common for women to have outside affairs, Austrian women yes, but not the others. But with the next generation it started; there were quarrels, but they didn't get a divorce. If a woman had a lover she did it secretly so the husband wouldn't know. Austrian women were very modern. It was known that this one was the girl-friend of that one and so on. It was known. But we didn't approve of that.

As to my husband, i don't know if he had contact with other women, but i think he did. He ran around Vienna. Before he knew me, of course, yes he did. In those days there were public houses for men and they paid by the hour, but they didn't go to public houses when they were married. If someone had a friendship with a neighbor . . . that i don't know. What i do know is that Dida went to Vienna on buying trips and that in Vienna there was theater, night clubs and they went to them. There were operettas, very nice ones, *The Merry Widow*, i saw it in Vienna when i went. There was also a nightclub in Vienna with some very modern women, lively ones. It was called "Maxim's." There were some very beautiful women there, 'animir dame,' who played instruments, who sang and, of course they gave themselves for money . . . only he never told me about it. Some had . . . intimate . . . there. Not in the same hall, but they got to know each other there. They sang: *"Ich liebe alle Damen und ruf Zju-Zju, Lu-Lu, Mi-Mi!"* So they called these ladies by their first names, they were so intimate that they called them by their first names. I saw that in this operetta.

I was glad to see it, but i didn't know that my husband also went! One day he told me he had gone, after he came from a trip to Vienna, he told me he had gone to Maxim's and then i knew what that was all about. That always bothered me . . . I usually went to the seashore with the children and he went to Vienna during the buying season. After the children were grown, Dida went alone on summer vacations, he said we couldn't leave the store without one of us being there, so i stayed, but this bothered me a great deal. He used to go to Frantzbaad, a resort for sterile women and men with weak hearts. He had a weak heart, so he went there for a cure. It was customary for men to go alone.

I went on vacations also, but i went to rest. In the afternoons i would go to a concert, i liked having company, but it never occurred to me that i could look for a . . . man! Once when i went with the children, a gentleman tried with me, but i didn't want to . . . That was considered tactless. If it became known that a woman went with somebody else, the husband had a right to get a divorce and vice versa.

On Sundays i liked going for long walks. In the winter i would dress myself warmly and leave the house at nine o'clock and come back at 12:30. The cook was in the house and she would cook the midday meal, so i would go for a walk around the Poligon, the mountain near Sarajevo. That was my greatest pleasure. In the afternoons we would go to the theater or the movies or for another walk, with Dida. He liked to go to Hairo, a very beautiful piece of property owned by a Moslem on top of the mountain. He made good Turkish coffee and that is where people who liked to walk met. We usually went there and met our good friends and sat and talked for a few hours.

We often went out for dinner on Sundays, the cook's night out. There was a man there who had been to America, a Yugoslav, and in America he had learned to make hamburgers and we often went to 'The American's.' He made 'ražnjići' (skewered lamb) and 'ćevapćići' (little hamburgers) and we liked that very much. We met our best friends, the men would talk business, a little about politics, but mainly about business and the women would talk about the maids, the children, the house and so on. These were Dida's closest friends who later perished under the Ustaši.

Maids were not hard to find. The best ones came from Slovenia, they were very hard working. We didn't pay them much . . . I always paid a little more so they would stay because if i didn't and the neighbor found out that she was good she would offer her more . . . But now i see that they weren't paid enough, that we expected too much from them. If we had guests they had to work until ten at night, or eleven, wash the dishes, serve coffee, all for the same pay. Now it is much better. In America they only have to work eight hours and if you want more, pay more. With us they worked every day, from morning to night and they lived there. On Sundays they worked in the mornings and had the afternoons off.

I gave my maids two hours off on Mondays if they wanted to go buy something for themselves. I heard that from an Austrian customer of mine, that they gave maids a little time off for themselves, but that was not customary. On Mondays one would go, not two at the same time.

The next Monday the other would take off so that there was always somebody at the house. At our house they ate the same food as we did, but in some rich homes they gave the personnel different food, they gave them heavier food.

I had a maid during the First World War who was very good and in the mornings—we didn't have gas and heating—she had to make a fire to heat up the house. One morning the fire wouldn't light so she threw a little gas on the wood and it spilled on the linoleum which caught on flames and she started burning. She cried so loud that i thought the Serbs had come . . . She shouted. My husband flew to her, wrapped her in a rug, took her to the hospital. She was badly burnt. Before she left she told my husband to call me. She said: "I have twenty-five dukats in such and such a place, please take care of them for me." I took those twenty-five dukats and my husband took her to the hospital. Before dying the priest came to confess her as is usual so he asked her whether i had required that she start the fire in this fashion. She said: "No, my lady is good, i did wrong." Not long after she died i took those dukats to the court. Dida said: "You have to take that to court so her family can get it." But the court, since it was wartime, paid in paper money and not in dukats—the dukat was worth much more than the paper money—but i had given it as she had asked. My soul was clean.

When i was a young girl nobody told me about anything, but when mother became a young woman we told her about menstruation. I had a very good woman in the house, a so-called governess and when mother got her menstruation she ran to my room and Vito ran after her and i told the woman to explain it to her and right away i went to buy what was needed to take care of it. But about having children, we didn't tell them about that. No. When i got married that was the first time i saw a man naked. Nobody told me . . . I even reproached my brother's wife for not telling me because the first time that hurts a lot. So she  said: "Nobody told me either."

We knew more or less what was going to happen, but we didn't know how it would go the first night. We wanted to get married and he wanted to get married, so we went to the Temple and got married and then we went to live together, it came by itself. With my daughter it was different. She didn't ask me about such things, the daughter was

112

more intelligent than i, better educated, she read; if she needed to ask something she didn't ask me, she got advice from the doctor.

There were instances where the husbands . . . with the maids, and then the maid gave birth. But it was all kept secret, the woman would keep it secret. They would liquidate the child, how i don't know, but they didn't keep the child. One of our friends had several sons and this one son had relations with the maid and the maid gave birth; she brought the child to the young man's house and his mother had many children. She was a fun-loving woman. "Come on, rock him!" said the maid. And the mother took the child: "Rock him!" she sang.

But then she nonetheless gave the child back to his mother and probably with money it was all covered up. At our house, thank God, that didn't happen. There was another case: he didn't have any children, he had relations with the maid and when the maid gave birth he wanted a divorce to marry the maid. So the wife said: "Bring the child, i'll accept him!" But he didn't want to and he went with the maid. There were cases like that, but not too many.

In my time life was much more peaceful than now. If we quarreled, my husband and i, it was about jealousy, i didn't have any other reasons to quarrel. I was jealous. He was very cheerful, very gay, he joked with all the women, paid them compliments, but at home he didn't do that and that bothered me. I used to say to him:

"If you know how to pay compliments, do it in the home, the same way. For your own wife, a little compliment . . ."

But i didn't know how to steer him. If i had known how to explain to him a little better what hurt me he would have been careful or he would have cajoled his wife a little as well. He was gallant with me also. I was more tight with money. When we went on summer vacations he would say: "How much do you need?" I answered: "Give me ten thousand dinars." He would give me fifteen thousand. I saved five and put it in the bank. And when the Ustaši came, i didn't have the right to take the money out, just five hundred dinars and so all was lost. I had my hidden money that he didn't know about.

I loved him very much and i always tried to cook what *he* liked. If i asked, "What would you like to have for lunch today?" the next day it was on the table. That pleased him a great deal. I watched over him very very much. But then more and more that crazy jealousy started to interfere and we were less careful with each other. I would say: "Why don't you joke with me as well?"

I didn't want him to tell me i was beautiful or something like that, why should he? I am not beautiful, but he should know that i am a good housekeeper, that i keep the house well, that my children were very neat and polite, well educated and that when i had to leave them i left them in good hands. When i came home from work i always bathed the children, he would go out a little, to visit a friend, to talk, but i would stay home. I never allowed the maid to bathe my children. And i would give them their dinner and they always went to bed early. So i wanted him to compliment me for that. And i would reproach him and he kept silent and then usually we didn't talk to each other for two or three days, and then we would get together again and slowly all was fine again.

We quarreled about silly things. And then we would make peace and then we wouldn't fight anymore. He thought that he is everything and that the wife must do as he says. That was the custom. He thought he knew more than i did. Yes, he thought that he is smarter than i. He was smart, but i had many good ideas, in many things i helped a lot. When things were on the brink i said: "Let's start like this, let's do like this."

He listened and it went forward nicely. Yes, he listened about many things, we worked together a great deal. I always believed that women are equal to men, that it should be that way. But it wasn't.

**6**

As we approached Rome i became aware of a special excitement prevailing on the atmosphere around me. The light changed its quality and in the evening, just before sundown, the countryside started to look like a stage set. The colors were highlighted, dark greens muted with greys, dramatic skies, streaked with purples and oranges; aqueducts curved majestically between the cypress trees, ending abruptly, purposeless. When i saw Rome, i experienced an emotion i had never felt before: it was love at first sight.

Rome welcomed us; it was a warm, friendly city, its people looked kind. And it was intact. It had not been bombed much, thanks to the Vatican. Both the Germans and the Allies had heeded its sanctity. This, in spite of the shortage of food and other vital goods, was a sign of peace and a preview to normalcy. I loved everything about Rome, its symbol—the wolf suckling Romulus and Remus—, its narrow streets winding around each other, its mixture of architectures, its ruins. Ancient, weathered ruins, caressed by many hands, not like the fresh ones we had seen along the way, filled with death.

Our family, all seven of us, aged nine to sixty-five, arrived in Rome, baggage in hand, our eyes wide open. We were immigrants and there were many like us, searching for familiar faces. Other Yugoslav families had preceded us and a circuit was established through which new arrivals were told of all the others so they could help one another. We were now joining a new contingent of Yugoslav Jews, mostly from Zagreb, who had fled to northern Italy where they had been interned by the Italians. They had been in Italian concentration camps where, while restricted to the grounds, they had nonetheless been treated humanely. According to rumor, Mussolini had tried to appease Hitler with these 'campi,' but the Germans had been quite dissatisfied with the results. After the Italian armistice the people had to hide and flee, lest they be sent to Auschwitz, Buchenwald, Treblinka . . .

Many of them hid with Italian families, some in the Vatican, some in churches and monasteries, some in convents. There was much talk among the reunited friends:

—Italians are good people, they don't like violence.

—They were the 'enemy' and they saved us, while our 'friends' turned us in.

—Italians are family people, they worship their 'mammas.'

—*La mamma e la pasta . . .*

Everyone was cheerful, relieved to be alive. The Italians' love for their countryside, their history, their operas, their sunshine, their buildings, their cities, their past, was contagious. We were all feeling it. Mussolini had dreamed of sailing his fleet through the Mediterranean—'mare nostrum' as he called it after the Romans—but the people just liked going to the beaches and swimming in it.

Some friends told us there was an apartment in their building which was situated in the Parioli district of Rome, the modern section, toward the outskirts, near the Tiber. The apartment was on the first floor of a new building at the end of a street called Via Ruggero Fauro. There were a few more buildings after this one, then the road turned to mud and there was open country, a small pine forest, the river . . .

—A heaven for children— somebody said.

—Yes, but is it safe?— my mother inquired.

—Of course it's safe, we are all safe now! The war is over for us. Our worries are over. All we have to think about now is whether the children will remember to come home on time for their meals— said our friend, Mrs. Dilinger.

We took the apartment. It was quite elegant, with a mirrored coffee table in the living room.

I was given a room that faced a courtyard in which the family below kept chickens; the rooster woke me up every morning. My window sill was a favorite resting place for pigeons. I was surrounded by bird sounds. Omama got the room across the hall from mine, a rather dark room which she filled with prayers as soon as we arrived. My parents' bedroom was large and beautiful, with an all-mirror vanity in front of which i spent many happy hours dressing up when my mother was out. We even had a bathroom with warm water, sometimes, and a separate toilet for the maid. The living room was spacious, facing the street, with a console radio and deep armchairs. Since there was no separate room for Braco, he slept in the living room and that became our battleground: he claimed his territorial rights over the radio when we were alone in the house. It was 'his' room. The battles over this issue were to last for our whole stay in Rome. They were known to be loud and violent.

I was approaching my tenth birthday in Rome, the free city. I was fond of saying in those days that to me more important than food or shelter was freedom. My brother laughed at that:

—It is scientifically proven that one cannot live without food or shelter.

—You can live without shelter.

—In the tropics perhaps, but not in the rest of the world.

Our arguments led nowhere.

My mother and i walked around the city, looking. She was mainly struck by how empty all the stores were:

—Look, there is nothing in the windows, there is no merchandise in the stores. I wonder why the shopkeepers don't just go home.

—I suppose it makes them feel more normal to spend their days in their stores— i speculated.

—I think they are hoping for a long-overdue delivery. But,

in the meantime, what am i going to cook today? That is the
question. We can't live on noodles, after all. I have two
growing children . . .

She would go in that vein, seemingly forgetting that one of
those growing children was walking right at her side, quite
excited by what she was seeing and not at all concerned with
the midday menu!

Each time i saw the Colosseum, it was like the first time all
over again. I looked at it from the outside, its roundness
welcoming me as i approached. Its thick walls spiralling
around each other seemed ready to embrace me. Arched
openings in the walls made the structure look like a piece of
swiss cheese, or like some very fine pastry, beautifully
folded. Once inside i was amazed by the size of the arena. As
i walked along the stone benches i imagined the spectacles
below. Men, women, children being devoured by wild lions,
struggling bravely, fighting, protecting each other. Huge
crowds of fat Romans, their togas flying in the evening
summer air, laughing loudly, spitting seeds from their
mouths, the red grape juice running down their beards . . .

In the middle of October, just before my birthday, i went
to school for the first time in Rome. I was assigned to the
fourth grade of elementary school. After that i would have
one more year before taking the state exam for admission to
the 'ginnasio,' high school. I felt shy and uneasy, but as soon
as i arrived in the dark, musty classroom i realized that the
other girls were just like me and that we would be friends.
The boys, on the other side of the room, looked younger
than the girls, in their short pants and dark blue aprons. We
all wore uniforms over our clothes, to hide the differences
between the poor and the rich. I thought that was just.

The teacher looked like a caricature from a Dickens novel.
She had fine ringlets pasted all around her forehead. It
became a subject for speculation among her students, in the
course of that school year, how she kept them in place. They
looked wet, but we realized the shine in them came from oil

on the hair. After months of careful observation, we concluded that she didn't wash her hair and that was how they stayed in place. She always wore the same grey dress which was too loose on her, blousing hollowly over her chest and hanging unevenly over her large slim body. Her eyes were grey, like her dress, and i mainly remember her standing behind her desk waving the ruler to tell us to be quiet and do our work.

There was no heat that winter in Rome and every morning i took a warm bottle to school with me to hold in my lap while i sat in the ice-cold classroom. I liked feeling the warm glass in my hands while listening to Signorina Cichetti read us verses by Carducci, her favorite poet, or describe Garibaldi's struggles to unify Italy, his brave wife Anita at his side. I soon learned that she was Italy's second heroine, ranking in popularity right after the Virgin. My name in Italian was Anita and i was told i should be proud of my namesake.

Signorina Cichetti was well known for her fierce punishments. Once or twice i was caught talking and then she sent me to stand in the back of the classroom, my hands up in the air for five, ten minutes at a time, until she declared that i could put them down. If i showed any strain she would prolong the agony. I stood there against the wall, with my aching arms, thinking of German tortures. This barbaric custom made me question the Italians' reputation for kindness. When i told my parents they too were horrified, but they didn't let on: the teacher's authority was not to be questioned in front of the children.

I sat next to a girl whose name was Maria. She lent me a book which opened new vistas for me. It was the first really long book i ever read; its title was *Via col Vento (Gone with the Wind)*. I thought it was a masterpiece, passionate, vast, beautifully written. Margaret Mitchell had moved me by her description of America's internal struggle between the South and the North.

—It's the same situation here in Italy, you know?— i said to Maria.

—Great writers, by definition, are those who are capable of presenting universal themes through human situations— Maria answered, mimicking Signorina Cichetti's voice.

We were reading *Gone with the Wind* in secret. It was not considered appropriate literature for us. They thought we should read Kipling, Jack London, Pascoli. Scarlett O'Hara became our heroine. Like millions of other young women, we measured our waists against hers.

That year we went to St. Peter's Square on the 31st of December, before dark, the curfew having made the usual midnight celebration impossible. The crowd gathered and the Pope blessed us from his balcony, predicting the end of the war and peace for the world in the coming year. I had heard criticisms of the Pope, rumors that he had collaborated with the Germans, but i liked his message and most of all i liked being there with the Roman crowd watching him extend his hands over our heads, the Michelangelo dome glistening in the setting sun.

While i was deciding whom i liked better, Rhett Butler or Ashley Wilkes, the German forces collapsed and on May 7, 1945, they signed an unconditional surrender. All of Europe celebrated. People crowded the streets, embracing one another, filling the city with songs. For us the war was over. The Pacific Ocean was on the other side of the globe . . .

Another event had touched us deeply that spring. One day on my way home from school, i stopped as usual at the kiosk on Viale Parioli, looking for the new issue of my favorite love comic book, when i noticed the huge headlines on the Roman dailies:

PRESIDENTE ROOSEVELT MORTO (President Roosevelt Dead)

L'AMERICA IN LUTTO PER IL SUO PRESIDENTE (America in mourning for her President)

ROOSEVELT DEFUNTO (Roosevelt defunct).

Tears spurted out of my eyes, much to my surprise. I felt

the historic impact. I ran all the way home, down the hill, rushing to tell my mother. I had always associated Roosevelt with Churchill and Stalin, and i needed to know what my mother thought would happen next. She interrupted tossing the salad as i told her the news and said distractedly:

—The balance of powers has been disrupted . . .

Later that spring there were cherries on the street stands, another sign of peace to me. I brought some home:

—For me it's not going to be peace until we are all back in our house, with our things— my mother said.

We spent our first summer going to Ostia, a beach town outside Rome, by train. It often took us many hours to get there since the train had to stop frequently for track repairs. We played with the Italian children on the train, tossing paper balls at each other, inventing word games. A general feeling of gaiety prevailed, optimism was in the air. Even the little worried war orphans, with their shoeshine kits, came to Ostia with us for a swim. They picked up a few customers on the way. The beach was deserted, with white sand and shallow waters:

—Here we can walk on water— we used to say as we waded through the gentle waves.

The water was warm and we found many lovely shells intact for our collection at home.

The Pregers had also arrived in Rome by this time and had settled near us in the Parioli district. The four of us—Sergei, Braco, Alex and i—resumed our friendship on the way to Ostia. Sergei and Braco were the heads of the expedition, Alex and i the adjuncts. Everything we did had a military flavor. Our ranks were determined by our ages. I occasionally attempted to break that pattern, being more interested in Sergei than in Alex all of a sudden, but these maneuvers were discouraged by the adults:

—Play with boys your own age— they repeated frequently without any explanation.

The boys played soccer a great deal and sometimes i played with them just to show that girls could, but it didn't interest me. I preferred to lie in the sun and read the serialized love stories which i bought every week as soon as they appeared. What made the situation passionate, it seemed, were impediments: the parents opposing the union, the woman getting consumption, the man being mortally wounded. I dreamed of such adventures happening to me, minus the tragedy. That didn't seem a necessary ingredient. The boys scorned love, or pretended to, all except Sergei who also was interested. But in general the company of boys was less appealing to me than in the past. They seemed less observant than girls, not as mature.

Our upstairs neighbors' son, who was fifteen, practiced tap dancing every evening in his room, over mine. Fred Astaire was his idol and i briefly considered following in Ginger Rogers' footsteps, but i didn't like the music that went with it and soon gave up that career. He attended the French lycée. His parents talked to mine about sending us there as well. My parents were dissatisfied with the education Braco was receiving at the Jesuit school he attended:

—They are indoctrinating him.

—What do you mean?— i asked.

—They study too much Latin and Greek— they replied diplomatically.

The official policy in my family was never to openly criticize Catholicism, but to avoid it as much as possible.

—The French are more modern, more progressive; i think it will be better for the children— my mother said.

—But that means they have to learn another language, these poor children— Baki interjected.

Baki and Dida lived at the other end of town and every Sunday Baki would put away her sewing and cook a Yugoslav meal for us all. Our education became the main topic of conversation over these meals.

—The more languages they know, the better— my father said.

—I agree with you— my grandfather added —languages are more valuable than money these days . . .

122

And so it was decided that we would be sent to the French lycée. I was happy with that decision. The school looked much nicer from the outside than the one i had been going to. It was situated in a pretty white villa, surrounded by gardens, near all the embassies.

It was in the garden of this patrician villa that i learned how the great verses and ideas of French poets and philosophers could apply to me. Inside the classroom we resisted as much as possible the information being imparted to us, but once we were free to move and to talk, to do what we wanted with it, we immediately adapted it to our interests. The best part of school was 'la récréation.'

When the recess bell rang in mid-morning we ran out unleashed, the boys and the girls in separate directions: the girls' side was a pretty French garden, with pebbled paths and flowers, the boys' side was an open area where they played soccer. Once in a while the older boys and girls broke all the rules and met each other through an opening in the hedge, touching hands or looking closely into each other's eyes. We discussed these girls' behavior in great detail. Some thought they were 'loose,' others considered them 'adventuresome.' Mainly in my age group we walked arm in arm along the paths and played games. One of our favorite games was pretending we were important military men, deciding how to win the war. I always played General de Gaulle.

The next four years, the postwar Rome years, form a joyous kaleidoscope in my memory: my intellect and my senses developed simultaneously, in harmony with each other, almost imperceptibly. All that had transpired started to make some sense, to be ordered, to be explained. I would walk through Piazza Venezia, for example, and see the balcony from which Mussolini, 'il Duce,' as he was still referred to, had pronounced the speeches that we had heard through loudspeakers on Korčula. Suddenly i understood how he had inflamed the people's imagination: encouraged by the simplicity of the surrounding Venetian architecture and the expanse of the square below him, filled with cheering crowds, standing there alone on the balcony, he must have felt taller, august even. Small wonder that he had forgotten the epoch and mistaken himself for a Roman emperor! The fact that his words were being transmitted by radio to remote parts of the world, to us on the island of Korčula, must have seemed unreal to him, but the impact he was having on the people below him was not; after all, the Romans are fond of being addressed from balconies.

7

At home life was ordered but not harmonious. The battle between my mother and my grandmother raged on. Now that the war was over, Omama resumed her religious practice with renewed vigor. My mother refused to go back to a way of life which was interrupted by the war; she refused to keep kosher. She viewed my grandmother's religious fervor as fanaticism, it made her hate all religions. Omama held her ground, feeling persecuted. She walked all the way to the synagogue every Saturday through the Pincio, the vast pine forest in the middle of Rome, refusing to ride the bus on the Sabbath. The quarreling between the two women was vociferous, followed by long periods of heavy silence. They would both look to my father for arbitration. He would shake his head, torn between his mother and his wife.

My father worked with the Allies, distributing the new drugs, penicillin and sulfa, to Italian pharmaceutical companies. He also associated himself with an Italian lawyer in the hope of one day passing state exams and once again practicing law. The likelihood of our returning to Yugoslavia was diminishing now that it had become communist, under Tito's leadership. Over espresso and cake in each other's living rooms, the Yugoslav community was busy discussing the pros and cons of returning to their native land.

—The Yugoslavs will never change— was one side of the argument, —all will go back to normal, you'll see. The Serbs

125

will quarrel with the Croats and both of them will quarrel with the Bulgarians, just watch . . .

—No, no— answered the other side, —nothing ever goes back to the way it was. It's going to be communism from now on and everyone will have to roll up their sleeves. Perhaps it's better this way . . .

In the meantime there was optimism about the new prosperity brought in by the Americans. The professionals were in a worse position than men who had trades so the latter chided them about it, getting even for having been snubbed in the past:

—So, just show them your diplomas, Herr Professor.

Every Saturday afternoon we went either to the opera or to the movies. I had seen Shirley Temple tap dance and smile on the screens of Sarajevo before the war:

—You have dimples like Shirley Temple— they used to tell me.

I would look in the mirror and see no similarity. But now, after several years of not seeing any movies at all, we approached going to the 'ci-ne-ma,' as the Italians said with open vowels, with great enthusiasm. Braco, Sergei, Alex and i discussed movies at great length and it was decided that Italian movies were terrible and American movies the best. As a result of this error in judgment we forsook *Open City* in favor of *For Whom the Bell Tolls, Casablanca, Great Expectations, The Best Years of Our Lives, Brief Encounter, The Postman Always Rings Twice, The Song of Bernadette, The Spiral Staircase* . . .

I liked going to the opera almost as much as going to the movies because there, too, passion prevailed. We sat way up, near 'paradise,' as the upper tiers were called, watching *La Traviata, La Bohème, Il Trovatore, Aida.* Every time one of those short, paunchy fathers would pace across the stage, gesticulating fiercely to his much larger daughter, forbidding her to see her beloved, my friends and i laughed and laughed and the people around us looked at us with disapproval, making 'tsk, tsk' sounds with their mouths. But when the love arias were sung, especially the ones following the death of one of the lovers, i would wipe away a tear or two with my handkerchief, mimicking the prima donna. The music moved me, but not the drama.

Italy recovered slowly under the Marshall Plan. The shops filled up again and life gradually became more comfortable. We were still, in large part, living on CARE packages from America, distributed through the relief agency, UNRRA. I always looked forward to picking up our ration and taking it home to examine what was in it. There were mysterious cans with English words like 'meat 'n vegetables' and wonderful creamy soups, but mainly they contained spaghetti.

—The one thing we have, that's what they send us— Baki said every time, shaking her head.

—They are trying to send us what they think we want— my mother would defend Americans, —they know that Italians live on 'pasta,' they don't know what we have and what we don't have. When you have everything it's hard to imagine what others need.

My father befriended several American soldiers who would come home with him for a home-cooked meal. They always brought us presents, canned goods of all kinds. One day we opened a can that contained golden slices of a fruit i had never seen before. I tasted it and thought of it as 'celestial':

—Do you like it?— the soldier asked. —It's pineapple; how do you say that in Italian?

We didn't know.

—It comes from Hawaii— the soldier explained.

—Awayee— i repeated after him, —very nice!

We also received clothing allotments. My grandfather was working at one of the dispensing centers and he looked out for good quality items for us. He felt like he was back in his store in Sarajevo again. He would finger the material of a piece of clothing and say:

—Oh, yes, this is 100% wool, i can guarantee it!

127

This is how we became acquainted with American taste. The clothes were usually bright in color, some that we had never seen before. There were chartreuse blouses and chartreuse dresses and even the slips were chartreuse. My mother would shake her head but i thought that that color was very strong, interesting, *modern*. What i didn't like about these clothes is how nothing fit well. Even pullovers of the right size were shaped in such a way that they were baggy and i had to soak them in boiling water to make them tighter. But it was a relief not to have to wear Braco's outgrown shirts any longer; i was tired of wearing boys' clothes!

Braco was studying English, reading the *Stars and Stripes*, put out by the American occupation forces in Europe, and *Time* magazine, shipped in from the United States. He was preparing for the future. It was through these publications that we learned of the atomic bomb, of Hiroshima, of Nagasaki. The impact of those events took many years to fully reach us. Now the war was officially over everywhere, but the atmosphere around me didn't feel like peace had been described to feel.

My first year at the *lycée* consisted of going to the class for foreigners, with children from all parts of the world, studying French with Mlle. Blois, an old lady who lived alone and was very religious. I helped her with her coat at the end of the day, i brought her apples and flowers, i was polite and sugary to her, while laughing behind her back. But i liked her: she seemed lonely and intelligent and she didn't seem to think there was anything wrong with either foreigners or Jews. That wasn't true of all the teachers.

I liked French, i liked its sounds and i learned it easily. It became my 'literate' language, although i rarely spoke it: Italian was still the spoken language among my friends and Serbo-Croatian at home.

—But in French it can be said more *precisely*— Mlle. Blois would tell us. While she didn't claim that the French were superior to other nationals, she did claim the superiority of the French language over other languages:

—*"Tout ce qui n'est pas clair n'est pas français"*— ("All that is not clear is not French") she quoted in an emphatic tone of voice. She read Chateaubriand with great feeling; he was her favorite author, she liked his 'religion of nature,' but to me he was rather empty.

'Empty' became my favorite word for a while. I liked ideas to be 'thick,' at least that was what Cara and i had decided together. Cara was my friend, my best friend. She was a month younger than i and she was already in Braco's class. I admired her for that and it helped in arguments with my brother over how stupid girls were, especially girls my age. She was French but had lived in Italy since childhood.

Cara lived in the center of Rome in an old building with a wide marble staircase that was totally dark, even in the middle of the day. Whenever i went to visit her the concierge would ask me where i was going and i never knew whether to give Cara's name or her stepfather's name or her grandmother's name. It seemed to me always as if a great many people lived in her house, a large apartment with many mysterious, closed doors. I loved going there. There was an air of bohemia, of intellectualism, of internationalism, of work and freedom all mixed into an interesting atmosphere for our secret games. Every wall was covered with etchings and paintings, most of them dedicated to one or another of the inhabitants of the house.

I loved Cara. She was smart and she had wonderful freckles all over her face and her eyes were green-grey, she was just about my height and she was cuddly. We walked around Rome arm in arm by the hour, laughing together, telling each other how much we meant to one another, how there was never going to be another friend 'like you.'

—Do you think grown-ups have best friends?— i asked her one day.

—My mother does: Jacqueline— Cara answered.

—Yes, but she never sees her!

—That's just because she lives in France and my mother lives in Italy, but she still tells her everything when they see each other.

We had established the criterion for friendship to be telling each other *everything*.

—I don't think so— i would argue —she probably doesn't tell her about your stepfather, what they do, how it is between them and all that.

—I am sure she does— Cara would insist, faithful to the concept of eternal friendship.

—Well, anyway, we can't conclude anything *logically*— i said and we both laughed, —unless, of course, you plan to ask her . . .

That seemed like the best joke of all. Then we would run off and pretend to be late for an appointment with a lover.

This was our favorite game: we played each other's lover, taking turns being the man or the woman, not caring too much which we were since we played them both the same way:

—In any event, when we grow up, we will still be each other's best friend, no matter what.

—More important than the lover or the husband?

—Yes, why not?

—Yes, why not!

And then we shook hands. Once we even pricked our fingers with a needle and exchanged blood.

—Now we are bound by blood ties— Cara said.

Among our Yugoslav friends there was one boy whom i befriended. His name was Boris; he was an only son, adored by his family. His father was a doctor, 'our' doctor, and his mother, a large beautiful woman, worked with her own mother, taking in sewing, like my grandmother. Boris had been afflicted as a small child by a dislocation of his right hip and, following a series of unsuccessful operations, had been left with a fused hip joint. He walked with a limp and his family felt that, due to the war, they hadn't done right by him. The doctor, especially, felt responsible for his son's condition.

I liked Boris even though he was spoiled. He was handsome and he liked me, both admirable qualities. His passion was music; Beethoven was his favorite composer. He was going to become an orchestra conductor. We took long walks through the Pincio on Sunday afternoons during which he would talk to me about the subtlety of a certain passage, the passion of such and such a movement, the mastery of Toscanini, his idol. I went to concerts with him, with much encouragement from my parents, but i was bored. The music came alive when i visited him in the course of one of his frequent bed-ridden periods: he would be propped up on large feathered pillows, the Victrola turned up to its capacity, conducting with a ruler. As i watched his upper body move with the music i would begin to feel it in my body as well. His mother or grandmother would look in periodically, bringing us sweets, and he would motion them not to interrupt. The *Eroica* was his favorite symphony, but to me the emotions expressed in it were somewhat embarrassing, exaggerated, overstated.

Boris was a little in love with me, or so his mother said to mine. I was flattered, but i knew it would be best if he thought of it as just a friendship: i knew i couldn't reciprocate. Not because of his leg, of course, i would explain to Cara, but because there just wasn't any 'electricity' between us. We were fond of that expression; it seemed mysterious and precise at the same time.

Alex was jealous of my friendship with Boris. He was also contemptuous of him because Boris couldn't play soccer. He pretended it was pity, but i knew it was contempt. I was less and less interested in playing with Alex, i much preferred Sergei's company. That made Alex sad; he told his mother who in turn told my mother who then reminded me that Alex was my friend, not Sergei. That was one of the many idiotic aspects of adults: *they* told us who *our* friends were, or tried to. Their reasoning was: Sergei is too old (which was exactly what i liked about him) and therefore it wasn't healthy (non sequitur) to be with him.

Sergei and Alex also started attending the *lycée*. Sergei was in the older group, with the seventeen- and eighteen-year-olds. The girls seemed incredibly glamorous to me, tall, beautiful, 'sexy'—the word had just arrived in Italy from America and they were trying it on, like a new hat, their voices throaty and melodious, imitating Anna Magnani. They came from all parts of the world, daughters of ambassadors, and some Italians who couldn't adapt to the antiquated Italian system of education. They seemed self-assured, teasing the teachers, laughing, wearing rouge in spite of regulations against make-up. The most beautiful of them all was a thin mulatta, the daughter of an African tribal chief, who wore her hair African style, on top of her head, making her even taller than she already was. She later joined the Martha Graham dance troupe. As Sergei started flirting with them, i considered him the most sophisticated man i had ever seen. He had a sweet smile and a gentle manner. He was considered a 'gentleman.' He was always in love, sadly in love. I liked talking to him and listening to him tell me who he was in love with that week. His mother kept a close eye on him, as she did on the rest of the family.

On Sundays we went sightseeing, as we had done in Palermo. My parents befriended an American captain whose name was Crystal, Captain Crystal; i liked his name. He was from New Jersey and he missed his family: we became his substitute family. He came to see us frequently and took us out in his jeep, his corporal acting as our chauffeur. We would all climb in on top of each other and go visit monuments. This is how i first saw the 'Terme di Caracalla'—where we later saw *Aida* on a beautiful summer night—the thermal baths built by the mad Emperor Caracalla outside Rome. We also visited the Tivoli gardens, with waterfalls sparkling like gems on the pebbled paths. We drove down the Via Appia Antica, the mother of all highways, on a jeep, bumping along the cobblestones: the marriage between Americans and Romans, between past and present, was being consummated in harmony.

I wished we didn't have to listen to the boring explanations the guides were so fond of providing, but i liked walking through the Forum and finding Roman coins:

—They scatter fake coins on purpose, to attract tourists— Braco would whisper to me.

I had started a coin collection, but i was never sure whether they were real or fake. Another favorite monument of mine was the tomb of Vittorio Emmanuele because it was white and gaudy, but most of all because it was called 'the wedding cake of Rome.' Having never seen a wedding cake i imagined it looked like that, with a horse whose belly had a trap door large enough to let a person hide in it.

One day Captain Crystal came over and told us that he had called home on the telephone and that he had talked to his two-year-old daughter whom he had never seen:

—What did she say?— my mother asked.

They communicated through a combination of German and Yiddish, with a smattering of Italian.

—She said: "Daddy! Daddy!"— and he imitated the sound with a loud EHHHHHHH, EEEEEEH.

—Ohhh . . .

—Yes, she said Daddy, but i could have put a cow at this end of the line—MOOOOOOOOO—and she still would have said Daddy!

I imagined the little girl looking at a picture of her father in uniform and then looking at a picture of a cow grazing in a pasture, saying "Daddy, Daddy" both times.

8

That summer i had to make up the grade i had missed while studying French in the class for foreigners. I spent many hours in the dining room, translating Latin into French, French into Latin. Braco sat in an armchair in the living room, 'his' room, reading *Time* magazine or listening to concerts or soccer games on the radio. When i was particularly stuck i went to him for help. There were endless quarrels. He didn't like being interrupted all the time, he felt i never tried to do the work on my own. Instead of just giving me the answer, he would pose questions, guiding me to find my own answer, like a grown-up! Under the guise of pedagogy, he would lock me out of the living room for entire afternoons. I would pound on the door and he would remind me, in an exaggeratedly calm voice, that the door was made of glass, as if i weren't made aware of it enough by the reflection of my angry, frustrated face staring back at me from the silvery mirrored panes.

The 'logic' of Latin escaped me. I didn't like having to memorize all those declensions and conjugations, and then, the worst ignominy of them all, i had to start all over again with innumerable exceptions. That was called 'logical'! History and geography i liked somewhat better. Napoleon reminded me of Mussolini, but i liked Josephine. She wasn't pretty, but she carried herself well, from what i could see in the illustrations of my history book. I tried to imitate her posture for a while, straightening my shoulders, but i never quite succeeded. When Braco would finally concede to open the door, i would kick him on his bare legs with my shoes. He rarely hit me back; he would simply take my hands and hold them behind my back and slowly lead me out of the living room, locking the door, assured in the knowledge that i couldn't kick *it* since it was made of glass. When i couldn't stand it any more, i went out into the streets of Rome, quickly forgetting my sorrows.

One day, while walking through the *Piazza Santiago del Cile*—the streets in our neighborhood had South American names: *Via Panama, Via Rio di Gianeiro, Via Buenos Aires*— i met Sergei. There we were, in front of the ice-cream store, talking, the sound of churning cream behind us, under the shade of the multicolored awning, in the Roman August heat.

—May i offer you an ice cream cone— he asked me, with a bow.

—Yes, thank you very much.

—Lemon?— he asked with intimacy.

He knew my favorite flavor! Or rather my former favorite flavor. I nodded my head. He was standing very close to me as we licked the whipped cream off the ice cream, looking at me, smiling:

—You should wash your neck— he said suddenly.

I was crushed. That was his intimacy!

—I wash it, what do you think! It's not dirty.

—Yes, it is. Look under your chin, in the mirror, when you get home.

We parted soon after that and as soon as i got into our apartment i ran to the bathroom. Indeed, it was true. I was deeply humiliated. Obviously i was a child to him.

That summer we took a vacation, our first since the war had started. We went to Florence, to museums, walked along the Arno and crossed the Ponte Vecchio. I didn't like Florence, Rome was my city. The rivalry between the two cities was well-rooted; as with soccer teams, one had to make a choice, or so i thought. The Florentines recognized my accent as Roman. Those who cultivated the language of Tuscany, the language of Dante as they referred to it, were snobs in my opinion. I prided myself on my collection of Roman curses, gestures included. My ultimate goal was to talk the language of Trastevere, the poorest but also the oldest section of Rome. *"Te possero ammazzà!"* (May you get killed!) i said, opening my mouth wide. *"Pezzo di stronzo!"* (Piece of turd!)—that was practically poetry in its assonances. *"Fica!"* (Cunt!), *"Cornuto!"* (Cuckold!), *'Figlio di puttana!"* (Son of a whore!). The gravest insults were those directed at mothers: Italian men and boys would immediately engage in fights if their mother's name was insulted. The sight of young men fighting, with one trying to separate them, was common. There was shouting, crowds gathering, cheering for one side and the other. Their method of choosing sides was very subtle, according to regional allegiances, family ties, neighborly bonds, all transmitted through differences in speech inflections. But the fights rarely looked serious, the violence was somewhat manufactured through exaggerated gestures and facial expressions. They mostly looked like they were hugging one another. The men of Italy often did hug one another. So did the women. And the children. There was much kissing on both cheeks, in the streets, in the homes, the hands moving in harmony with the mouths.

When i turned twelve my formal education began. I entered the *cinquième,* where we had different teachers for each subject. French was the most important area; we had to memorize endless verses and write perfectly organized compositions. Art consisted mainly of drawing oranges that ended up looking like apples and vice versa. I also started studying foreign languages. I chose Italian because it was easy for me, taught by a Corsican woman with a French accent, and English because my parents said that was the language of the future, taught by a Frenchman with a French accent. English was hard.

Whenever i went to Cara's house her mother insisted on speaking French to us instead of Italian:

—You need to practice, you'll never feel comfortable unless you use the language, you should speak it to each other!

She treated me like a daughter and i liked that. She was French and wanted her daughter to maintain her French heritage. Her own mother, Cara's grandmother, was a beautiful Russian who had fought with the Bolsheviks in the 1906 revolution; after its failure she fled to Italy and married Cara's 'nonno' (grandpa), a dashing archeologist who periodically came to visit. The grandmother gave Russian lessons in her room to serious-looking men and women: the women never wore any makeup and the men all had briefcases under their arms. They looked like spies.

—Did you get any more visas?— Cara's mother asked me.

—Yes, we obtained one to Argentina the other day— i replied.

—Ar-gen-tina— she said, pronouncing it in Italian with open vowels and rolled 'r,' —that would be nice for you, it's still a Latin country. I think it is important for you that you be in a Latin culture. The Anglo-Saxons are too complicated, too cold. Now i must leave you, señoritas— she said and went out laughing.

The previous week we had been granted a visa to South Africa. We had applied for immigration papers all over the world: Palestine, Australia, Canada, various South American countries, the United States. My parents had decided not to return to Yugoslavia after Tito had established communism in our country. There were endless discussions among the Yugoslavs:

—They are putting all the professionals in prison. Some people disappear, never to be seen again.

—You know what that means . . .

—We would be considered 'bourgeois,' as if there were anything wrong with that! The peasants are running the government while the educated people work the soil. The world is turning upside down.

I said to Cara:

—I just hope we can stay in Italy, i don't see why we have to go anywhere. Eventually i am sure we'll be able to buy some papers . . .

—In this country you can buy anything you want . . .— she replied with cheerful cynicism. —Come, let's go to my room!

Once in her room, we would close the door and start talking. We told each other everything. I talked to her about my problems with Braco.

She liked him and sometimes defended him:

—He is the best student in our class. He is very intelligent and . . .

—What use is his intelligence if he won't even help me with my homework!

—Maybe you don't know how to treat him. You have to learn how to handle men, you don't just say anything that comes into your head, you have to prepare a strategy.

—I don't want to use strategy with my own brother, wait until you have one!

Cara had told me that her mother was expecting a child.

—So far you have been lucky— i continued, —but your days are numbered.

—Perhaps you are right; i can't help it if i have a 'cotta' [crush] on your brother— she laughed.

Then we would go on to other topics:

—Did you start *Madame Bovary*?— Cara had lent me the book. I nodded.

—Did you get to the part where she takes on a lover?

—I am not sure, do they tell you? How do you know? I hope my French is good enough to understand what is happening.

—You'll know, don't worry. It's a realistic novel.

My parents encouraged me to read French novels to improve my vocabulary. When they saw me reading authors like

Flaubert and Balzac they would wonder if such books were appropriate for me. I reassured them that my teachers had recommended them. It was just a small lie. Actually Cara's teachers had assigned them to *her* class and since she was a month younger than i, it meant i too was ready for them.

—Do you read the descriptions or do you skip over them? I sometimes skip— Cara said.

—I read them. They are long and a little boring, but i like postponing the good parts. Anyway they make the action more alive, i like to be able to *see* what is happening. That's why i like movies. When Emma Bovary goes to the ball i can imagine the chandeliers, the evening gowns, the music. Then, when he kisses her hand, the gesture seems somehow richer.

—Yes. Isn't her marriage dreadful? Imagine living with a man who is ugly. Ugly *and* stupid. I think all marriages are awful. I am never going to get married.

—Oh, you will change your mind! But I agree with you, i don't want to have an awful marriage either. I would only marry someone if i were sure that we loved each other passionately.

—What if the passion doesn't last?

—If it doesn't last, then i think one should leave. No matter what. Start anew, in another country. I would take my bundle and leave.

—Your child and your bundle?

We had just seen Paulette Goddard in that very predicament.

—Yes, my child and my bundle.

Braco and i started taking Spanish lessons that winter, just in case we decided to go to Argentina, or to Venezuela for that matter. There was even talk about Chile as a possibility for us, like the piazza near the Pregers' house: '*Santiago del Cile,*' i would say to myself as we crossed the square on the way to Sergei's and Alex's house, after our lessons. When we arrived there we would have a snack, usually consisting of bread and butter with sour milk to drink. Then we would decide what games to play: either the boys would set up their lead soldiers on the dining room table and hold soccer tournaments, or we would play ping-pong doubles on the same table. Sometimes we played poker, for money. We pretended to be playing for beans, in case the parents walked in, but it was understood that those beans represented *lire.* The poker games were quite tense, but they were my favorite. They generated the most excitement. I didn't have a 'method,' but i sometimes won through 'instinct.'

One day we were playing like that and i had to go to the bathroom. It was a rather large and dark room, painted blue-grey, with high ceilings and inaccessible cabinets. After peeing i looked at the toilet paper that i had used to wipe myself with. I don't know exactly why i looked, perhaps i always did, without thinking. I wondered about that afterward. There was some red on it, just barely. I felt a great sense of exhilaration all of a sudden. This was it! I realized i had been waiting for this moment. The conversation i had had with my mother about menstruation, way back on Korčula, flashed through my mind. I couldn't remember what she had said, but some of the girls in my class menstruated and they were always talking about it. I looked in the mirror and observed myself carefully: "Do i look any different?" I composed a nonchalant face and went back into the dining room.

—Alex— i said, —do you know where your mother keeps the cotton?

—Why do you need cotton?

Braco and Sergei raised their heads from the magazines they were reading and i thought i detected a faint smile on Sergei's face.

—I have a callous on my toe— i answered, returning Sergei's smirk.

As i followed Alex into the bathroom i thought to myself: "I mustn't discuss this with a man." Alex climbed on a stool and got a small round ball of cotton for me from an upper cabinet. I knew that it was too small, but i decided not to ask for more, for fear that it might give him a clue. I had no idea about how much one used, but i knew it was more than that. After he left, i pulled down my pants. I remembered that at the ballet one day Cara had told me that ballerinas wore it 'inside.' I put it inside my pants and pulled them up with the little piece of cotton in the middle, between my legs. A new feeling of well-being invaded me: i held a voluptuous secret. For the rest of the afternoon, every time i turned my thoughts to it, i experienced pleasure. I was eager to go home, to tell my mother. I thought of calling her on the phone, but i decided to save it, so that i could tell her in person.

As Braco and i walked home, my whole being was concentrated on the warmth between my legs. It felt cozy. I treasured my privacy and my joy. When we got home, i went into the kitchen. My mother was peeling baked peppers. She asked me how the afternoon had gone and, after a brief reply, i whispered:

—Come into the bathroom with me.

—Ahaaa!— she exclaimed. My mother always seemed to guess my thoughts.

We walked down the corridor, past Omama's room, in silence. I locked the door behind us.

—What is it?— my mother asked.

—I think i am menstruating.

She smiled and hugged me. —Let's see.

I showed her the little daub of cotton. It had a few drops of blood on it.

—Yes, you are!— my mother exclaimed, —my little girl is a big girl now, a woman— and my mother laughed and hugged me again.

Then she sat down on the edge of the bathtub and took my hand:

—You are not worried about it, are you?

—Oh, no, i just didn't want it to show.

—Don't worry, i'll give you all you need. How do you feel?

—A little tired, i think, but fine otherwise— i answered. I wasn't sure if i felt any difference.

—Wait a minute. I'll be right back.

When my mother returned she said:

—Look, i bought this for the occasion: here is a little belt you wear.

She handed me a piece of pink elastic and showed me how to wear it. Then she gave me a pouch made out of cloth:

—Inside of this you stuff rags to give it extra strength. She handed me two safety pins and showed me how to attach the pad to the belt.

—And here is a spare one, to change with.

I had some questions but they all seemed silly. How do you know when it's time to change it? How do you know when it's over? I decided not to ask her, just to wait and see.

—Shall we tell 'tata' [daddy] — my mother was asking, —i am sure he would like to know!

—Yes, tell him, but not when i am there, just him, no one else. Don't tell Braco.

As i left the bathroom i felt that i was walking funny. I went to my room. That evening my mother asked Braco to set the table. When my father came home, i heard my mother talking to him. He knocked on my door:

—Come in.— He came in and hugged me. Then he held me by my shoulders and looked at me:

—My little Anili is a woman now. Congratulations!

We shook hands. "It's the twelfth of May," i thought to myself, "and i am twelve. That's easy, i'll always remember the date that way."

# 9

There was a girl in my class whose name was Clea, a very pretty name i thought. She was two years older than i and a great beauty: she looked like Elizabeth Taylor, we all agreed, at least those of us who had seen *National Velvet*. I told her her eyes were just as 'velvety' as those of Elizabeth Taylor. She seemed pleased. She was Swiss and she spoke French and Italian fluently in addition to German and Swiss-German, her native language. She seemed very accomplished and sophisticated to me.

Monsieur Brillaume, our professor of English, had a crush on her, treating her with all the courtesies due to a lady, while the rest of us he treated like vermin. That too impressed me about her, that she could get the teachers to treat her with respect. She was calm and composed and her handwriting was very neat. I speculated a great deal about her and talked to Cara who didn't seem to like my interest in her:

—You are not going to betray me, are you?— Cara asked.

—Oh, no, *never!* You are my best friend, forever and ever!

Since Cara lived in a different part of town and Clea in my district, we often met on the tramway going home. After a while we started waiting for each other and walked together. Boys buzzed around her like flies; she didn't even seem to notice, but i did. It was fun going home with her, there was always someone following us . . . She was friendly to me, she seemed to like me. One day she asked:

—Are you Jewish?— She had a nice direct manner about her.

—Yes. Why do you ask?

—Oh, nothing, i just wanted to know.— then, after a while she added:

—My mother said that you probably were, that you were Jewish refugees, most likely.

—You've told your mother about me?— i asked, feeling pleased.

—Of course i have!— and she laughed at the question.

I felt uneasy about this conversation. It was all right to be Jewish, now, my mother had told me, and while i should never volunteer the information, if anyone should ask me about it, i shouldn't hide it. I had been so used to hiding it throughout the war that i still had the feeling there was something wrong with it. And besides i didn't feel Jewish . . . Now with Clea i sensed that it wasn't completely all right, at least as far as her mother was concerned; that made me sad. I thought about it all the way home. "I guess i really want her as a friend," i said to myself, "my second best friend!" Then i went into the café near my house to buy a lovely 'maritozzo' (cake) brimming with whipped cream.

When i started menstruating i told Clea and she turned out to be very helpful. She told me that she had some Swiss pads which one could just throw away when they were soaked with blood, one didn't need to wash them. She said she would get me some. She had a very modern and well-informed way about her; she thought it important to be 'practical' in life.

—The Swiss are very advanced— my mother said when i told her of my new discoveries. Then she asked:

—What does her father do?

That was a standard question whenever i made a new friend.

—He is an engineer.

This information met with approval; Cara's mother was

144

divorced, that was a bad start, but to compound it she was now married to an Italian psychiatrist. That was definitely suspicious. A Swiss engineer seemed much more 'solid.'

One day, to my great delight, Clea invited me to come to her house. My mother said i could go. I dressed with great care: my new navy blue dress with the silk bow that my grandmother had just finished sewing for me, and navy blue suede shoes to match. Then i took the 'filovia' (wire-bus) up into the hills, to the Monti Parioli, where Clea lived. This was the most fashionable section of Rome, with private villas surrounded by large gardens and a view of the city. The Romans claimed they could always spot a 'pariolina,' a girl from Parioli, by the way she spoke. *Caaara,* they would mimic, prolonging the 'a' and gurgling the 'r.' But Clea wasn't like that. We had already decided that we didn't like snobs.

Clea lived in a large apartment building with balconies winding around the whole front and side of each apartment. There were flowers on each floor and brightly colored awnings. The entrance was marble and glass, the elevators were spacious and soundless. A maid opened the door: she was young and pretty, wearing a black uniform with a white apron and a little starched crown in her brown hair. She showed me to the living room. At Cara's house we never went into the living room since that was the doctor's consultation room.

The 'salotto' was not very large, the furniture was simple. Modern. There were small engravings on the wall. A light breeze was coming through the curtains over the open balcony door.

—You must be Anica.

Clea's mother's manner was stern. When she smiled, however, her large white teeth made her seem friendlier.

—Ciao, Ani.— Clea came in and shook my hand, —this is my mother.

—Yes, obviously— Clea's mother said and left the room.

—You'll get used to her.

Then Clea took my hand and led me down the corridor to her room. The house smelled fresh. Clean smells. Polish. Flowers. The maids had their own quarters; the kitchen and the laundry were completely separated from the rest of the apartment.

Clea's room was beige and rose. She kept it very neat. We sat down on her bed, covered with a beige brocade bedspread with little antique roses woven into it. The afternoon went in a flash. We talked the whole time. At four o'clock we had a snack with Clea's brothers, both younger than she. When we went back to her room she said:

—They are actually my half-brothers. My mother remarried and her new husband adopted me when i was little, that's why we all have the same last name and we feel just the same as if we were true brothers and sister.

She said all this in a very natural tone of voice, but i sensed that it was a delicate topic and that i should not ask for any more explanations. She would tell me when she wanted to.

Before i left she showed me her prize possession, her diary. She kept it in her night table, under lock.

—I have been keeping a diary since i was nine. I have never shown it to anyone. I write in it every night before i go to sleep, the way some people say prayers. Do you say prayers at night?

—Not anymore, i used to.

That year i had decided to stop praying at night. My father had taught me Hebrew prayers and, when i was little, he would come and say them with me before going to sleep. That had been pleasant, but now i had to decide for myself; it was time to choose. It felt daring to stop, but it seemed hypocritical to continue since i didn't really believe in God. But i hadn't said that aloud yet.

The following Monday, at school, Cara asked me:

—Did you go to Clea's house on Saturday?

I was stunned. How did she know?

—Yes. How did you know?

—Feminine intuition . . .— she said and walked away.

That incident made me uneasy. I knew that Cara was hurt but at the same time i felt that i had done nothing to betray her. I told my mother about it that night. She said:

—She is jealous.

In my family whenever the word 'jealous' was used, it had a tone of finality to it, as if its meaning were perfectly clear; everyone seemed to understand it, to a nuance. They often said when i was angry with Braco, for instance, "She is jealous" or "Don't be so jealous." Baki always recounted how Maja, when she was little, was jealous of Vito.

—They called him 'hasherle,' little darling— my mother would explain in a mocking voice. It was assumed that brothers and sisters were jealous of each other as if it were a law of nature.

By the time this incident occurred i had already pondered a great deal on the subject of jealousy. I didn't think it *had* to exist between brothers and sisters . . . In movies they always made the women seem jealous, but i thought that probably men were more prone to it. Wasn't Rhett Butler's anger at Scarlet prompted by wild jealousy? What my parents called jealousy during my quarrels with Braco, i called injustice, yet i recognized that they were right in part. I didn't like it that it was always he who was praised for doing well in school. During meals there were often comparisons made between his grades and mine. That irritated me. They didn't seem to be interested in the circumstances, they just looked at the results.

Whenever a 'serious' subject came up they would ask him what he thought.

—How do you think the Allies should deal with the Germans now?

—Do you think they will establish a Jewish state? They say they will because nobody else wants all those Jews going to their country . . .

If i objected to their not including me in their discussions they would say:

—How can you talk about something you are not informed

about. Read the papers, then we'll discuss it.

That also annoyed me. I could never find anything interesting in the papers. There were endlessly boring articles which stated simple things in very complicated ways. I had my own opinions and i knew what was happening in the world, i had a 'sense' of it, but that didn't seem to count.

My parents, on the other hand, praised me profusely for 'being a good helper.' When their friends came to visit on Sunday afternoon, i would pass around the coffee cups and the pastry tray. The ladies smiled and complimented my mother on her cakes and on her daughter. The men often said:

—Such a pretty little helper— and they would pinch my cheeks.

My mother looked at me and smiled.

—You are smiling now— the man from upstairs said, —but one of these days she will give you plenty to worry about!

Everyone laughed. Braco, sitting in a corner, got a funny look on his face. It made me sad for him.

It occurred to me at about that time that the quarrels between my mother and Omama were caused by jealousy. I decided that the only way to handle this bothersome emotion was to examine it closely and find out what it was. In school we were reading Racine, Corneille, Molière. We had to memorize their verses and recite them in front of the class. I had been in a play, *Les Précieuses ridicules,* in the role of the maid and had acquired a liking for the 'alexandrin,' the twelve beat verse so in vogue in the seventeenth century. Our professor of French explained:

—Tragedy is based on the conflict of passions; it is your task to uncover which ones are at work in any given play. There are five principal passions: maternal love, filial love and carnal love, all interrelated; and then there is ambition and jealousy. Whenever you see any of these in conflict with each other, like in *Andromaque,* who is torn between her love for her son and her love for her husband, you are confronted with an explosive situation.

These ideas reverberated through my mind as i started to examine the dynamics of jealousy in my own life. "Is this what they mean by 'thinking' in French?" i asked myself.

That night when i went to bed i thought of Clea and Cara. Clearly Cara was still my best friend, but i was sorry that she had looked so pained. I was annoyed at her for walking away from me, i would have liked to talk about it. My thoughts about Clea were lighter, more pleasant: she was so calm and wise about life, but most of all i liked the deep look in her eyes.

I was lying on my back, thinking, feeling sleepy, not exactly sleepy but still wanting to close my eyes, aware of my body. It felt full. My breasts were growing. I touched them. They didn't fill my cupped hand. "I wonder if i'll have large breasts. Mother's are pretty big, but she doesn't seem to particularly like that. I think i would rather have small breasts, to feel freer." It seemed important to be agile, to be able to run at all times. As i touched the tip of my breast a little shiver went through my body. I turned over, with my cheek on the pillow. I rubbed it against the pillow. My arms were folded under my breasts. A new, delicious feeling was invading my whole body. I closed my eyes. I let my body move, very slowly, in rhythm, like a samba only more slowly, more like a rumba. I felt my hips gently moving, with my buttocks rotating in the air, pushing my pelvic bone into the mattress. I moved my legs, but not my arms. I was smiling. A little tingle went through that place, for which i had no name, where a few hairs had appeared. I kept on moving. The tingle grew in breadth, slowly radiating down through my legs, up through my ribs and arms, into my face. It wasn't exactly a 'physical' sensation, it was more like a very gentle electrical discharge: "I wonder if that's why they call it electricity?" i said to myself before going to sleep.

We had a maid whose name was Pina. She came every day to help with housework and the meals. She lived with an ailing mother and seemed very pale; my mother cooked liver for her, to build up her blood. Under the guise of helping her with the housework i spent many hours listening to her. She told me about her 'fidanzato': she loved him very much, but she didn't know when they would be able to get married. He was unemployed.

—*Oh, signorina, basta così* [that's enough]! I'll make you think that love is all sadness, it's not. Last Sunday we went to the country and we picked great big bouquets of wild flowers and brought them to my mother who said: "Bless you children, you are bringing mother nature to my bed to heal me." While running through the fields, deep in tall grasses, he came up behind me and threw me off balance. We rolled through the hay and the flowers and i felt like a fish . . . It was wonderful, signorina!

—What else did you do?

—What else?— she was laughing.

—Yes, tell me what else. Did he kiss you?

—Oh, come now, that's enough, we are not getting our work done, give me a hand with the wax instead!

Everything Pina told me remained engraved in my mind. She seemed to have learned a great many cures and truths in her village while she was growing up. She told me that when a woman is menstruating she should never touch plants or they would die. We were watering the geraniums on the living room window sill, picking off the brown leaves when she told me that.

—Oh, i just touched them, now they'll die!

I worried about this for days; i watched the geraniums every day for signs of death, but they survived and flourished instead.

Before my thirteenth birthday my mother asked me, as usual, 'to make a list.' On top i put: 'silk stockings.' Clea never wore socks or—horror of horrors!—kneesocks, she always wore silk, or to be more exact, nylon stockings. I became very aware of my socks, how inelegant they were. I had a skirt that was similar to hers, plaid, cut on a bias, mid-calf in length, just right, but its effect was ruined by my short socks. No matter what i did, i still looked like a child. I wanted to look like a glamourous woman; i even started wearing ties with my blouses. I had been invited to some afternoon parties where we danced to the latest records—"Begin the Beguine," "Besame Mucho," "Stormy Weather"— and most girls wore silk stockings.

On the day of my birthday we had the traditional family breakfast: coffee with whipped cream and 'kugulhuf,' baked by my mother, streaked with chocolate. My seat was decorated with greenery and flowers. My father, in his robe, my brother already dressed for school, were waiting for me, ceremoniously, to sit down. When i opened my presents and found a pair of nylon stockings, in their box, just the right color, with dark seams, i was overcome with love for my mother.

Clea went to dancing school and taught me all the steps she learned. She would bring the phonograph to her room and play her favorite records, American songs sung in Italian. The tango was the most complicated. She would first demonstrate the steps and then assume the lead; we would take long strides through the room, our hips touching, our faces staring ahead, side by side, our arms stretched upward, pointing the way. As we reached the end of the room she would dramatically twirl me around and we would repeat the same steps in the other direction.

—Just call me Rodolfo, Rodolfo Valentino!— she would say.

Then, one day, Omama received her visa for the United States. Everyone was outraged. Because she was born in Germany, it only took her two years to receive an entry visa; the rest of us, having been born in Yugoslavia, were still waiting. I was delighted: it meant we were staying in Italy. Nonetheless it did seem to us that Americans were using some strange criteria for deciding whom to let into their country. The Germans, who were the enemies, had a more favorable quota than allies like ourselves. We were all puzzled. My grandfather explained:

—An American at work told me that the quotas are based on the makeup of the American population: there are more Americans of northern-European ancestry and that is why they favored the Germans. Southern Europeans, Italians, Greeks, Yugoslavs, all have very unfavorable quotas.

—But there are a lot of Italians in America, i am told— my father said.

—I am just telling you what he told me. That's all i know.

I had always felt that the southern Europeans were more fortunate, they laughed more easily, they sang, they danced. The English, the Norwegians appeared to be more melancholy; i had just seen *Hedda Gabler* at the theater with Cara. But all that mattered for the moment was that we were staying in Rome.

# 10

During the First World War it wasn't bad for us, nothing like the Second World War, it was just very difficult: with personnel, with food, more and more difficult all the time. There wasn't enough food, fewer and fewer goods all the time. The yardage goods which we sold in our store came from Austria, but during the war everything was needed for the army so they took all the fabrics, chiffons and all. People wove by hand, the factories couldn't produce enough.

For us, it was easier with the Austrians. When the Serbs came they said: "Austrians have to leave: those who came with Austria or with Hungary—they called them 'koferaši' because they came with their suitcases—out!" Dida was born under Hungary, in Virovitica, and so he too was driven away. We had sold the store, we were allowed to sell, but we weren't allowed to take the goods with us. They wanted to send him away also, but he was able to prove that he was born Yugoslav, so they didn't send him away.

He was in the Austrian army during the war. He didn't serve in Sarajevo. He had a weak heart then, he suffered from over-ventilation, so they transferred him to Sarajevo, to the commando, and he was a telephonist there. When the commanding officer needed to make visits, he would go with him, in a carriage, to the president, to the bank director, to the major . . . Since Dida knew everyone he would sit on the carriage, next to the driver, and lead: "Here is the World Bank, here is Director Berković . . ." The major was very fond of him, he was a Serb but he was in the Austrian army, and he would always take Dida with him whenever he needed to make calls.

In the meantime i ran the store and the children were small so they stayed home, and the maid, when she could, would take them to the park. But it was very difficult with the maids, very difficult, because then the maids worked for the army and they were paid better there. It was also difficult with food, but it wasn't too bad for us because Dida knew people and we had money, so we bought under the counter without them knowing. In the army there was a man who delivered milk and sometimes by paying a little more he would get us meat.

My brothers all served in the army, they all went to the war, but they all came back alive. One was wounded and they wanted to amputate his leg, but he didn't let them, so he kept his leg. When Ferdinand was assassinated i wasn't in Sarajevo, i was vacationing in Split with the children, but i remember when the coffin went by, near the seashore, on the way to Vienna. I remember seeing Ferdinand's coffin, from a distance, being carried to Austria; it pained me a great deal.

My people were Sephardim and my brothers, one was Sephardic and another had an understanding that he was Sephardic and Ashkenazic at the same time. . . The Sephardim accused the Ashkenazim of having taken the better positions, that Ashkenazim were presidents, that they wanted to take over. There were fights. Sephardim had Ashkenazim put in jail. One day there was a big reception so my older brother bought a ticket for my mother to go to this party given by the Sephardim. My younger brother was against it and said: "Mother, you can't go to the reception!" He didn't like it because the party was just for Sephardim and against the Ashkenazim. Another big Sephardim who was against the Ashkenazim, a doctor of law, a bank director, married a very rich Sephardic girl and she wanted to be equal, so he said: "I want to play first fiddle." So they separated and he who was a great opponent of the Ashkenazim nonetheless married an Ashkenazim girl, without any money, this time! He saw that money wasn't everything and he got along very well with her. But then the 'Ustaši' came and they took him; they always took away first those who were in high positions, so they took him, then they took her and the son and everybody . . .

A cousin of this man's, also a lawyer, had a secretary in his office with whom he had intimate relations, so she got pregnant and he had to marry his secretary. When she gave birth, the same day, his father died and he went to the funeral and he didn't go to see the child because

everything was waiting downstairs, the carriage, the rabbi, everybody.
When the 'Ustaši' came they took him and the son and this poor woman
went crazy with sorrow for having lost her husband and her son. She
was Serbian but the son was Sephardic. Such cases happened during the
'Ustaši' . . .

After the First World War it was very difficult for us, very difficult.
It wasn't as difficult for everyone as it was for us because my late
husband was like a 'shwab' and the Serbians didn't like 'shwabs.' His
name was German because he came from the Austrian side. When my
brother came back from the war he started his own store, yardage
goods, new materials, silks, things he had never seen before and he
started to sell on credit, that was new. He hired some salesmen and sent
them to smaller towns and started offering goods on credit. He made a
lot of money that way, he did so well he bought a house. His son didn't
want to go to school so he went into the store with him, but his
daughters studied; one became a doctor and the other finished gymnasium. His family was very well off, then came Hitler and the devil
took everything. Some ran away and some perished. His son perished,
he was taken into the army and the 'Ustaši' captured him and they took
him and sent him off.


During Austria i traveled a lot, during Serbia i also traveled, to Italy,
but then they reproached me for spending Yugoslav money in Italy, for
not going to Yugoslav baths . . . I used to go to Italy with the children, i
liked Italy, it was very nice, i liked it *very much*. Španjolski is very
similar to Italian so it was very easy with the language.

It was customary with us for young girls not to talk to men of
another religion, to heterodox men. My sister was very beautiful and a
Jewish officer who was serving in the army stood in front of our store
and talked with my sister; he was a lieutenant. And my brother went by
and saw his sister and he called her into the store and gave her two good
slaps in the face. The older brother had many privileges, he was
supposedly smarter, we called him, 'hermanu,' anyway my sister when
she got two slaps in the face said: "That's a Španjol, that's a Sephardim
for you!" And my brother left.

When i got engaged to Dida, we loved each other, my brother said:
"To each his own." They thought it wasn't good for Sephardim and

Ashkenazim to mix, yet all those who had Ashkenazic husbands lived well; it was known that those were better marriages than just among Sephardim because the Ashkenazim were more cultured, more political, a little better, while the Sephardim were big Bosnians—primitive—so they treated women differently, not so well.

All my sisters married Sephardim except one. And then, it was believed with us that one should consult the eldest brother and the eldest sister as well, so that is why my sisters thought that i was smarter than they, i wasn't though. When they grew up they got an education, one was a teacher, she was very smart. I would tell them this or that from time to time but i didn't boss them around.


Dida and i were not political, we didn't care about politics, but things went well for us under Austria and when Serbia took over it was very difficult for us, in the beginning, until the customers got used to us. But the late Dida was very handy, very friendly, he knew how to satisfy customers, how to offer cheaper prices than other stores, than Serbian stores. They very much believed to each his own, that the Serbs should go to the Serbs, not to Catholics or Jews, rather each to his own. And Dida knew how to sell inexpensive goods, how to come and help, wait on them so that slowly, slowly the customers got used to our store as well.

During the war we bought a house on Skenderia street, a very nice house, and we moved in, but that was at the beginning of the war, after that we couldn't have done that; if we hadn't bought the house, probably the money would have gone too. When the Serbs came, the currency changed and that way we lost money. Your mother was insured for 2,000 dinars and these 2,000 dinars came to very little in the new currency, there was nothing left.

It was very difficult for us, very difficult. Maja's insurance is worthless, there are the children to take care of, the goods we had in the store were no longer in fashion. The styles changed in women's underwear: brassieres came in, short underpants, slips. Before the war the dresses were long, but then that changed also and they became shorter, but we also wore long skirts and when we went on the street, we held the trail, in our hand. After the war the dresses were shorter.

I remember when short hair came into fashion! It started from abroad, from Austria. . . . One lady went to the baths and came back with short hair. I was surprised, so she told me: "You will all have short hair." When i went abroad i noticed that everyone had short hair and that i looked strange, but i didn't dare to cut it because of my husband, i didn't know what he would say . . . So i came back again with long hair, but the fashion caught on so fast that i had to cut my hair. The men had long whiskers, and i didn't like whiskers. But then, the fashion changed with them also and they started to cut their whiskers and one day my husband surprised me when he cut his whiskers without asking me, but i was glad. By the time i cut my hair he knew that it was fashionable and so he didn't say anything about it, he knew it was time for me to cut my hair.

Then: it was fashionable to wear locks on the face with short hair, but i didn't want to cut my locks so i put on false locks without my husband knowing; he thought it was my real hair. And once, at my mother's house, as we were laughing and sitting around nicely together, he said: "There are women who have false locks, my wife has real ones, look!" And he pulls my locks and i am left with just one . . . He got so scared, so frightened! And so i took off the other one too and i got angry and he kept quiet and that's all.


After World War I, dresses were worn very tight, and after World War II, when we were in Rome, another fashion began, longer and wider skirts, so we all started wearing them. After each war the fashions change. After World War I we wore short skirts. And then, there were great balls, the women's society ball was the most elegant. We sold a lot of dresses for those balls and we went, the late Dida and i. We danced the waltz—as i told you we got to know each other through the waltz—and we danced the quadrille. The men all wore 'smokings' (tails) or tuxedos and, of course, gloves; both men and women wore white gloves, without gloves one wouldn't go . . . And we sold feathers in the store, long feathers were in style. And then some American dances came in after World War I; i didn't know much about America, but i knew the dances.

In my time we didn't use much make-up, i just used powder on my face, but even that was considered unusual. The men didn't like it if the girls used face-powder. The late Dida didn't like powder and when we got married i asked him to go down to buy me some powder. He said to me: "I never liked powder and now i am going to buy it . . ." But i continued to use powder. And when you were little, you and Braco would come with your governess—we had you over every week for lunch—and one day you went to the bathroom, you opened the powder and you put on as much powder as you could and when you came out you can't imagine how you looked! So the *'fräule'* motioned to me with her eyes to look at you. When i looked i had something to see! And you sat there and ate, all powdered up and your dress was full of powder, yes, yes . . . But i didn't use any other make-up, i didn't like it, just powder. I liked jewelry, but i didn't wear it to the store, i liked having it for certain occasions. The late Dida bought me some nice pieces during the war; when it was possible to buy it cheap and good, then he would buy it.

Then: it was modern to wear a corset, to pull it very tight in order to have a narrow waist, a high corset. It was difficult to wear, but that was the fashion. It was designed so cleverly that you could take hold of the two strings, yourself, and pull them, you didn't need any help. And then after the First World War, i believe, that fashion passed; after that it was much better: brassieres, girdles, short underwear, after that we were much freer, it was much more pleasant, there is no comparison!

My interest in fashion developed because i learned to sew and, as i studied sewing, i followed fashions. So that when i came into the store having fairly good taste helped me a lot because i knew both what was fashionable and what was tasteful, for that time. In this way i could help the clients; with us it wasn't customary, like now, for the clients to go, to look and choose by themselves. Instead, she came and she wanted something for a dress and she didn't know what, so we would show her and show her and we had to make an effort to hit upon her taste. We kept fashion magazines in the store and we would pick out a fabric and immediately look at the fashion magazine for a coat, so that the client could see. There were no good ready-to-wear articles, they didn't fit, not like now. So it was nicer to make things to order. There were certain customers who always wanted me to wait on them because they agreed with my taste. The late Dida was very clever and a good salesman, he inspired confidence in the client, they trusted him for his honesty and they trusted me for my taste.

As for me, i was always dressed very simply, i liked good things, but simple ones. One client, i remember, told me one day that if she had a store she would wear a different dress every day! But i didn't have the wish to wear something new every day, no, no, on the contrary, i was fairly modest. In the beginning i sewed for myself, later when we were doing better it no longer paid for me to sew and i went to a seamstress and then, when we were doing even better, then i ordered dresses from Vienna because i wished for greater knowledge than mine, a better cut, better workmanship. When i wanted something special i asked Dida to bring it for me from Vienna. Other people followed French fashions, but we were mainly oriented toward Vienna: when the Austrian women were there, under Austria, there was high fashion, great balls, and the people followed high fashion, but mostly from Vienna, mostly from Vienna . . .

At the lycée, they managed to pack in an enormous amount of information between 8:30 and 12:30, when school let out. Some of it seemed very tedious: in geography, we had to memorize endless names of rivers, 'départements,' oceans, while in French we had to abide by strict rules of composition; first one had to make a plan and follow it, then one had to remember to use appropriate tenses and moods of verbs, and most of all one was never to use the pronoun 'i,' one had to use 'on' instead, the third person neuter. My grades hovered between passing and failing in several subjects.

There were two categories of girls in my class, those who were serious and attentive, who studied, didn't cheat and didn't give parties, and the others who were frivolous, who flirted with the boys, followed fashions and movies and developed elaborate methods for getting by. One of the more popular cheating systems consisted of pinning answers to our slips and during exams, we lifted our skirts and looked up the information while the teacher, walking up and down the room monitoring, would avert his eyes with due modesty. I got caught twice, once in natural sciences and once in geography. The first time i was given a warning, the second, they sent me in front of the dreaded 'conseil de discipline.' We had been asked to draw a map of the United States from memory and i made the mistake of handing in a perfect map, traced the night before from an atlas which i had pinned to

my slip and exchanged at the appropriate moment. I couldn't
deny, when questioned, that i was incapable of drawing a
perfect map from memory.

—The perfect crime consists of drawing an imperfect map—
said Clea in an attempt to lift my spirits as i was waiting to go
in to hear my punishment.

There were seven teachers sitting around a long table with
the director at the head. I stood in front of them all, my
hands behind my back. The questioning of the facts behind
the crime was thorough; then i was asked to step out, so they
could deliberate. I went to the bathroom and peed. When i
went back in, Mlle. Corrari, my teacher of Italian, read the
verdict:

—Mademoiselle, you will be expelled for three days. Your
parents will be notified. You will be expected to do all the
work that you miss. Should this occur again you will be
permanently expelled. You may leave now.

As i left, my heart was beating very fast. My friends
greeted me with warmth and reminded me how lucky i was
not to have to come to school for three days. And anyway
the main thing is to risk!

Special status was awarded to those of us who went
through this ordeal; while our names would be stricken off
the 'tableau d'honneur,' the official gold-framed list of those
pupils who deserved to be named on the honor rolls, they
would be put on the student oral list of popular martyrs.
When i went home my parents' response was remarkably
moderate: i was forbidden to go to the movies for a month.
After about ten days even that ban was overlooked.

My life outside of school was becoming increasingly filled
with promise. Every day now i would walk home with Clea,
very slowly, arm-in-arm, pretending not to notice the flock of
university boys following us. Some had Vespas making elaborate gyrations in the middle of the boulevards for our
benefit. Others just walked behind us, never talking to us, but
occasionally we would get a bouquet of flowers addressed to
us, anonymously. One day i threw such a bouquet out the

window thinking that the sender was standing around the corner waiting for my reaction. Refusing such an offering seemed consistent with my attempt at fulfilling the 'femme fatale' role.

But most of the time Clea and i talked to each other, oblivious to the boys. We were flattered by their attention, especially since they were from the university, but other things were on our minds. We discussed Dr. Jekyll and Mr. Hyde at great length, we even enacted them. Did we all have a good and bad side? Were there impulses buried in each of us that would prove to be evil and deadly without our knowing it? Such questions preoccupied us although we usually decided that we didn't have such buried instincts. We rewarded ourselves for being so noble by treating ourselves to a 'maritozzo.'

When Clea and i parted, most of the boys went her way, except one, Vincenzo. But i didn't pay much attention to him, i suspected him of having sent me the flowers, but my mind was fixated on Sergei. He was growing up and looking very handsome. He shaved regularly now. He confided in me. He fell in love every other week and talked to me about his new flame; i would look at her in the school yard and try to see what she had that inflamed him so. Usually i saw it; he picked girls who were not necessarily beautiful, but they always had something beyond beauty alone . . . I respected that in him. They never seemed aware of my watching them; to them i was just Braco's younger sister, a mere child.

One rainy Saturday afternoon when both Cara and Clea were busy i called the Pregers, looking for something to do. Sergei answered the phone:

—*Pronto.*

—*Pronto, ciao Sergei, come va?*

We spoke Italian with each other; our Yugoslav was getting rusty, we reserved that for the parents.

—Are you looking for Alex?

—Yes. I was thinking of coming over. What are you doing?

—Nothing much. Do come over! Alex isn't here, he went somewhere with mother. In fact nobody is home except me— he said casually, —but you can still come over.

—All right— i replied without hesitating. As i hung up the phone i thought to myself: "This is good luck, it always happens when you least expect it!"

—I am going over to the Pregers— i said to my mother as i was leaving.

—Don't forget to come home by seven, for dinner— she replied.

—Yes, yes, it's always the same thing . . .— i stopped myself. I didn't want to get into an argument about these maternal reminders. I didn't want her to ask me any questions.

When i got there, he opened the door for me with a sweet smile. He always looked at me with a deep look, but this time there was special intimacy in it. Somewhere we had gotten the message that boys and girls were not supposed to be home alone together. It was never said, but it was understood. And we knew why. That added to the excitement of the situation. We walked down the corridor in silence. I noticed that one of his shoulders was higher than the other, he was bent to the right, with a characteristic slouch. I imagined him at forty, with a suit on. He was wearing a short sleeved shirt with a wool pullover over it. We went to his room.

It was a pleasant room, facing a courtyard. The light was grey, a Roman winter afternoon light. He sat on his bed and i sat on a chair by his desk. It felt like a boy's room.

—What's new?— i asked him.

—I want to show you something and get your opinion.

He got up and went to his bureau and brought out a small package. He opened it and inside was a blue jewelry box which he then handed to me. Sitting on the little satin pillow was a filigree silver butterfly. It was light and shiny, almost

transparent. I had a strange feeling that perhaps he was going
to tell me that the present was for me, but at the same time i
knew it wasn't.

—I like it very much. It is really pretty.

—Do you think a girl who is about sixteen would like it?

—Of course! She would have to be an idiot not to like it!

—It's not too young for her, is it?

—Oh, no, it's very grown up! It looks precious . . .

—It is real silver, after all.

The main criterion for jewelry, kid jewelry versus grown-
up jewelry, was its authenticity. Clea and i had decided
together that fake jewelry was vulgar.

—It's a present for Aurelia— Sergei said solemnly. I looked
at him and told him that it was a wonderful present. Very
special.

—She likes you, you know— i said.

—How can you tell?

—There is no way to describe how i can tell, but i just
can . . .

The afternoon went by in a flash. We talked and talked
and talked. He talked and i listened, to be exact, asking him
questions about his 'cotta' (crush) for Aurelia. He thought
she had soul and soul was the most important element in a
woman.

—I thought legs were— i teased him.

—She also has legs— he said and we both laughed.

Listening to him gave me the impression of participating in
real love affairs, not just imaginary ones like the ones i
explored with Cara and Clea. Sergei treated me like a friend
who could understand. We spent a very pleasant afternoon
together.

We suddenly heard some footsteps in the hall.

—Is anybody home?

It was his aunt. When she came into the doorway she
looked at us sternly.

—What are you doing?— She looked suspicious. —Is nobody else home?

—No. Alex should be home any minute.— Sergei's voice was beginning to get tense.

—I am going to call your mother, Ani.

She walked out of the room. Sergei and i looked at each other, shrugging. Ten minutes later the doorbell rang. We all went to the door. My father was standing there in his blue winter coat. He took his grey felt off and greeted Sergei's aunt. Then he looked at me. His eyes were darker than usual, shining, somewhat sunk in their sockets.

—Get your coat.

We walked down the stairs in silence. It was almost dark outside. The air felt damp. I caressed the marble ledge on the buildings as i walked by. I liked feeling the smoothness interrupted by the roughness of the porous parts.

—So what happened, Anili?— my father asked. His voice was soft and intimate, the special, conspiratorial voice. I felt relieved. It was going to be all right.

—Nothing happened.

—But you spent the whole afternoon with Sergei. Alone.

—Yes, i thought Alex was going to be there when i went over— i lied.

—His aunt said you must have known he wasn't there, he had a dentist's appointment; he had already left when you called.

I was beginning to feel like i had done something wrong. I had started to lie, as i always did when grown-ups didn't seem to want to accept the truth; i would tell them what would make them feel better, but they often caught me at it. Now it was happening and i was feeling in the wrong.

—I'll make you a deal— my father said gently. —You tell me everything that happened and it will stay between us. I won't tell mother, she is ill and we don't want to upset her. Is that a pact?

—Yes.

We shook hands. Then i told my father about the conversation Sergei and i had. I censored it a little, de-emphasizing the romantic content, but generally i told him the truth, that we talked about our friends at school.

—You just talked the whole afternoon?

—Yes.

—Are you sure?

—Yes! What do you think we did?— I was beginning to feel upset. *Did* something bad happen? I tried to remember.

—Well, you know, Sergei is a young man and you are a young lady now and things happen when a young man and a young lady are together alone . . .

—Oh, Tata!— i said with exasperation. —You are always thinking things like that. NOTHING HAPPENED!

We were a few houses away from home.

—All right— my father said. —If you think of anything else, come and tell me.

—Yes, and don't forget, don't tell mother about it!

—I promise.

As we walked into the apartment i recognized the familiar quiet of days when my mother was ill. There weren't the usual bustle and dinner preparations that made things feel normal.

—Is mother bleeding again?

—Yes— my father answered. —Be very quiet, we'll eat without her.

My brother was reading *Time* magazine in the living room. He grunted as i walked in without looking at me. He was sitting in the armchair by the open window, his feet over the arms of the chair. I felt like talking.

—What's new in America?

—Nothing that would interest you.

I put on the radio. "Stormy Weather" was playing, in Italian. That was comforting. The three of us ate our soup in silence. When i went to say goodnight to my mother she looked at me sternly.

—What's the matter, are you in pain?

—You know what's the matter— she answered.

My father hadn't kept his promise; he had told my mother.

I decided at that very instant never to trust him again. Our special bond had been broken.

It wasn't until much later that i realized that there had been no evidence that he had broken his promise to me, but that i had seized this opportunity to separate myself from him. He was no longer my hero. When i told Clea about this incident she commiserated with me:

—Men are lousy at keeping secrets, fathers included.

Cara's reaction was more blasé:

—What a mountain you are making out of nothing; let's go and play our game . . .

We were walking through the pine forest near my house, pretending to be lovers on a desert island. We walked arm in arm and told each other how much we loved one another. We made plans for the future, we talked about the children we would have.

—This is our Garden of Eden— Cara said. We stood for a moment facing each other, holding both our hands. We gently kissed one another from time to time. The passers-by looked at us, perplexed. We laughed.

One day, as i lay in bed with influenza, Baki came to visit me. I asked her to tell me stories about her youth:

—When i was little, if someone got sick like you it wasn't customary to call a doctor right away, they thought they knew how to take care of it. First they gave us a purge, then they would give us sauerkraut juice.

—That sounds terrible!— i said.

—There were also women who knew how to heal and many people believed these women. There was one in particular, they called her 'Tia Merkada,' and this Tia Merkada would come and she would bring lead with her and we would all go into the kitchen where she melted this lead and then threw the molten lead into hot water and this lead would form into different shapes and by looking at these shapes she knew what needed to be done. Then she would give the sick person water to drink, once, twice, and three times.

—Did it work?

—Well, sometimes yes and sometimes no. During Austria the doctors were against this. One doctor said to this aunt Merkada: "Listen, you can do what you want on the outside of the body, but if you give some medicine or something to drink, you'll go to jail!" And so this poor woman didn't dare to do it, she never gave medicines. But there were other women who cooked medicines and brought them to the patients. They believed in teas. We were lucky, i don't remember being sick very much, but others used teas and herbs and roots. There were people who would sell them, not apothecaries, just people who had these medicines.

—Were there people to go to if you had problems . . . with your parents, for instance?

She laughed her full belly laugh.

—You don't know what problems are . . . But there was a man who solved problems. His name was Hodja. People who had a difficult problem and who didn't know how to help themselves, they went to this Moslem, Hodja. He was a little smarter, a little cleverer than the others and they went to him to talk it out and this Moslem, this Hodja, he gave them advice: "If you are quarreling, make peace" and things like that.

—Did Jews go to him also?

—Yes, both Moslems and Jews went to him. When i was young i believed in these things, but as i got older i no longer believed in the gypsies.

—But you still throw beans. How does that work?

—Yes, i still know how to throw beans but i cannot tell how it's done. That is a secret.

—What kinds of questions did you ask the gypsies?

—When i was young all this interested me. I wanted to know whether somebody loved me. I wanted to know what will happen, what luck i will have. I believed in these crazy things. As soon as we heard that the gypsies were coming to town, we all rushed out to see them and they would be out there asking: "Do you want your fortune, come here, do you want me to read your palm?" They knew that young girls are crazy . . .

—Did the people in the town like the gypsies?

—No, people didn't like the gypsies because they were . . . They didn't know how to keep in step with the world. They stole. They were different from other people. They had entirely different customs. Once there was a gypsy feast and we went to it. In the middle of the feast they had fights, the groom on one side and the fathers on the other and they beat each other up, we weren't used to that. With us when there was a celebration, when there were festivities, everyone got along, but they live entirely differently. They say that now there aren't many gypsies left. I heard that they burnt the gypsies also during the war, they persecuted them like us.

I listened to Baki's tales with great interest. I reclined on my pillow, with my eyes closed, and tried to imagine Sarajevo with muddy streets and gypsies everywhere. I saw their gold dukats glistening on their bright clothes. I wanted to have my fortune told.

—Tell me more about how it was when you were young.

Baki was sitting in her chair, holding my hand, smiling.

—When i was little we didn't have running water, instead we had a jug and we heated the water in the laundry kitchen. The washerwomen washed the laundry in a large sink and they scrubbed and they scrubbed. Before we had baths, we had round wooden tubs into which we poured hot water and we bathed everybody in it, the children and the grownups, that is how we bathed.

—Once you told me that you used to go to the public baths.

—Yes, how you remember . . .— she patted me on the cheek.

—Once a month, after my menstruation, i went to the public baths. There were Moslem baths and Austrian baths. I went to the Austrian baths, but the Moslem baths were good also. There were large tubs and there was a woman who knew how to massage and she massaged us. There was also someone to pedicure, to cut foot callouses and they washed your hair and there was a steam bath, of course. There were very large round tubs and all the women sat in them together. Then they would go into cold water.

—Why did you go after your period?

—With the Jews it was customary that the woman, after a period, jump up and down three times in this cold water, up and down, three times, up and down. Even in the winter, when it was cold, she had to jump in and out of this water three times ... And before a young girl got married, of course, she had to go to this bath, to bathe in this water, yes, yes, we *had* to go. There was a woman who showed you how to jump. If she knew that you were getting married, she would come with you in the water and you would jump together. So we did it because it had to be.

—So, you were religious when you were young?

—I still am! But we weren't strict, i didn't cover my head. Very religious women wore wigs. They were completely shaved and they wore a wig because they claimed that hair was flattering. Women were not allowed to be too beautiful, so that another man wouldn't fall in love with them. Ashkenazic women wore wigs, Sephardic women wore a Turkish headpiece. When Sephardic women got married they wore a kind of cap instead of a hat and on this cap she would sew on a chain with real dukats, little ones, and those who didn't have real ones would get false dukats. That was their sign that they were married. My mother wore that, that was a Sephardic custom; but in my time everyone wore a hat, except Moslem women. They covered themselves up in 'feredze' [veils] even after the Austrians came.

She looked at her watch.

—Look at how you make me talk! It's late, i have to run home now or Dida will be calling for his supper and there will be only walls to answer him ... Don't forget to drink your 'kamilica' [chamomile] tonight before you go to sleep. Goodbye, my little Anica!

She kissed me on the forehead and rushed out, leaving a faint smell of powder behind her.

## 12

At the end of the school year we went to the 'distribution des prix,' a formal compensation for our scholastic efforts, at the French consulate in the elegant Farnesi Palace. We went with the Pregers, in our best clothes, to watch a play put on by the students and to listen to the speeches; first the consul spoke of the mission of French education abroad—"our poets are our best ambassadors," he said eloquently—and then the director of the school praised the French government for its progressive ideas in setting up French schools all over the continent—"or should i say continents, to be more precise?" —followed by the speech of honor given by a guest philosopher on "French Thought Throughout the World." At the end prizes were distributed. The consul went up to the microphone and announced the best student in the school:

—I have the honor to present the best student award to . . .

There was applause, my parents looked at each other smiling, Braco walked down the aisle and up to the podium, in his new navy blue suit, his tie slightly askew, a fixed smile on his face, to be handed four bound volumes of Chateaubriand's collected works. The consul shook hands with him, both facing the audience and the camerawoman in front of them. His intellectual performance was being eulogized. He looked very embarrassed.

Sergei, Alex and i each only got one or two prizes, but none of us seemed to care too much; Braco was clearly the intellectual luminary amongst us. We all went to a restaurant up in the hills outside of the city at Castel di Roma famous for its wines, and had a splendid feast of 'linguini' and 'abbacchio' (young lamb) under a large oak tree. This meal was also a farewell to the Pregers; they had obtained their visas for Brazil and had decided to go there. Brazil, being a lumbering country, would offer Mr. Preger an opportunity to resume his trade, they reasoned.

On the day of their departure, we went to the train station to see them off. I was filled with a sense of loss at their departure; i knew that Sergei and i would never be reunited again. My eyes filled with tears. Somehow i knew that we would not go to Brazil, that our future was in another direction. An important part of my life was coming to an end. I ran along the train as it pulled out of the station as far as i could, waving my handkerchief to them. I thought of our other departures from each other, on Korčula, in Split, but this one felt more definitive; they were going across the ocean, to another continent. As i walked slowly back on the station platform, the smell of engine smoke in my nostrils, i thought of Anna Karenina, or rather of Vivien Leigh.

That summer i was invited often to Fregene where Clea's family had a villa on the beach. Later, when i saw *La Dolce Vita,* i recognized the locale as being the same as the one where we played that summer in the 'pineta,' seeking the shade of pine trees in the middle of the day. Clea and i shared a room, talking late into the night:

—Vincenzo still has a crush on you— she said.

He was the medical student who followed me around after school. He was Sicilian and therefore very passionate. He was nineteen, but he was a little too short for girls his own age. I liked his beautiful deep green eyes, like a cat's, and i liked the letters he wrote me. I showed them to Clea and together we dissected his passion:

—He seems sincere— she said after reading the latest epistle.

—Yes, but tomorrow he will be sincere again . . .

—So what? You wouldn't want to get too serious with him anyway . . .

The word 'serious' made us feel grown up.

—He says he likes my Slavic soul. Do you think he means that or is it something he read in a book?

—He probably means it *and* read it in a book.

I thought that was brilliant. She had a way of expressing the most profound ideas in simple terms. We put on our bathing suits and stood in front of the mirror:

—Do you think my breasts are going to get much bigger?— Clea cupped her breast in her hand; it fitted perfectly. She was very direct in these matters; i liked that about her, i always felt a little embarrassed to ask questions like that, but she made it possible.

—They will be small, not much bigger than now i think. I read in a magazine that by the time you are sixteen most of the breast development has already taken place. That is good. Small breasts are more chic, don't you think?

—Yes!!! But i don't understand why in American movies they always stand there with their breasts in profile like bullets. I don't think they look pretty, do you?

—They call that sexy in America.

—I don't think it is; to me sexy means sensual and they don't look sensual, not even Rita Hayworth even though she has a nice smile.

In this way we often got onto the subject of movie stars, one of our favorite topics of conversation. Clea showed me the latest additions to her Elizabeth Taylor album of photographs and clippings.

—I still think you look more like Jennifer Jones— i said.

—Do you really? I think Elizabeth Taylor has a more classic face . . .

We were standing in front of the mirror.

—Your waist is getting smaller, Micetta— Clea said using her nickname for me, Kitten.

—My hips are too big, though, look!— I ran my hand over my hips and made a face.

—No, they are perfect! Hips are supposed to curve out, now look!

She turned me around, in profile, and ran her hand over my side. Her touch, going down my waist and my hips, felt reassuring. I felt beautiful.

—Do you really think i will be beautiful?

—But, Micetta, you are beautiful!

We looked at each other, face to face, and agreed that we were both pretty.

—Anyway, i could never be friends with someone who wasn't beautiful, could you?

—No, i actually couldn't. My best friend, especially, i feel, needs to be attractive to me. I want to feel like touching her and i have to like her skin and her eyes . . .

—Yes, those are the main things for me, too, the eyes, the skin, the mouth too. And intelligence.

—And humor, yes, and we have it all and we are perfect, *n'est-ce-pas?*

We hugged each other with laughter.

There was less and less talk about the war. It was beginning to recede in our minds. The center of Rome assumed, with ease, its air of luxury, like an old habit. The shop windows filled with delicacies: candied fruits in beautiful baskets, lovely sculptured marzipans and little squares of layered chocolates . . . In the bars people were once again consuming endless cups of 'espresso' and picking up a miniature prosciutto sandwich or a 'baba al rum,' on the run between appointments. Perfumed ladies would walk by in fur coats looking at the new hats, adorned with exotic feathers, on display in shop windows. It all happened gradually, imperceptibly. My mother would say:

—If only they knew how to make good bread!— By that she meant dark bread, with kimmel. But i liked the fresh, crusty bread we bought from the bakery, twice a day, freshly baked morning and afternoon. When i went to get it before each meal i would break off the heel as my reward and eat it on my way home, still warm.

It was 1948, the year of the national elections when the people of Italy were going to decide whether their country was going to go back to being a monarchy, as before the war, or a republic, in step with the times. The Allies were withdrawing their troups gradually, Italy was to be an autonomous member of the western alliance. The republican symbol, a three-cornered ivy leaf, started to appear on the walls of Rome. There were also large painted words: "W il Baffone" (Long live the moustached one) as the communists affectionately called Stalin, in red paint. Others would paint over the W the opposite "down with" sign, M, in black paint. The debate raged on the streets: "W il re" (long live the king), "M il re!" (down with the king). But mainly people were for the republic. There was much talk about centralized power, democracy and political parties. The people voted for the republicans and the Christian Democrats came into power.

—That is good— my father said.

—Yes, i suppose, but we'll still have the church over us— my mother responded.

—Under a democratic system. And besides all the political parties are re-established, dozens of them . . . That is progress— Braco said with finality.

Shortly after the elections we obtained our visas for the United States. My parents were very happy:

—It took six years, but now we have it. That is the best country for the children's future— they proclaimed in unison.

—But i like it here— i said, —why can't we stay here?

—You know why, we are aliens here, we could never normalize our situation.

—But others are buying citizenship papers— i would argue.

With influence and 'good connections' some aliens were obtaining papers.

—Who knows if they'll be valid . . . And anyway Italian citizenship isn't worth much— they would answer.

It was difficult to understand how one passport could be

worth more than another, but it seemed clear to grown-ups: a Swiss passport was good, an English passport was also good, but a U. S. passport was best of all.

We had to go to Naples for medical examinations. The Americans wanted only healthy immigrants. We spent many hours in the army hospital being x-rayed and checked. The doctors seemed young and very efficient. They spoke Italian with a heavy American accent. They gave me a lollipop everytime they stuck a needle in me or shoved an instrument down my throat. We had to prove we didn't have T. B. or V. D. or malaria or typhoid fever . . .

—What is V. D.?

—It's a terrible disease.

—What kind?

—Don't worry about it, we don't have it.

I had heard of it in connection with several poets and writers, but its nature was never specified; it was generally referred to as a 'social disease.'

From then on my life in Rome seemed to acquire intensity. Now that i knew that i was leaving, every corner of that beloved city seemed to sparkle like a precious jewel. On my walks with Cara i would say:

—What other city has a wild pine forest right in the middle of it?

—With a marble staircase leading up to it— she added.

I felt that i was leaving a lover, my first. When i thought of it my throat tightened.

Shortly after we obtained our visas an incident happened at school which reaffirmed my bond with Clea. In English class our teacher called on me, one day, to come to the board. He asked me to write the word 'strawberry' and 'thoughtful' and 'pear' and 'fear' and i wrote 'strauberi,' 'soutful,' 'per,' 'fiar,' and he laughed his nasty laugh, full of ridicule. He walked over to me and stood next to me, tall, for a minute, looking menacing, and then he slapped me full in the face. The class was totally quiet. I stood there, next to the blackboard, humiliated and furious. Clea got up—she was the best student in English and his pet—and said:

—M. Brillaume, Anica will speak English better than you in a few months. She is going to America. I think your treatment of her is unpardonable."

Then she sat down with great dignity. He flushed, and sent me back to my seat. I thought that was so brave, so loyal, so best-friend-like of Clea. At that moment i knew i would always love her.

I started looking at American movies differently now that i knew i was going there. I started seeking out first run films because they were usually subtitled instead of dubbed. I was listening to the sounds, to the inflections of American speech, for clues. "Ai loooov iu" i would say to myself in front of the mirror, imitating Tyrone Power, the most beautiful man of them all, in my opinion. Lana Turner, Greer Garson, June Allyson, Hedy Lamarr, Veronica Lake, Ingrid Bergman all passed my close scrutiny as to the character of the American woman, unable as i was to detect foreign accents. There was something fresh in all their faces, fresh and 'healthy'; Clea thought 'healthy' was a particularly important component for beauty. Cara thought showing one's life in one's face was more important. I decided i liked the combination of the two: Ingrid Bergman was perfect; she looked both healthy and experienced, and besides, people kept saying that i looked like her. Life in America looked quite simple, with nice shiny kitchens and cars for everyone to drive.

There were some positive aspects to our prospective move and i enumerated them to myself often: i would be leaving all my problems at school behind to start afresh. People were always talking about a 'second chance' in life and here it was, being offered to me. I was looking forward to going to school in a place where nobody knew that i had been expelled for cheating on an exam. Of course my reputation as a daredevil individualist would suffer from the translocation. But i would learn about the 'new continent,' i would learn a new language, i would see other landscapes. Large vistas of cowboys riding through the plains and mountains appeared in front of my eyes every time i thought of the American landscape . . .

That year, on New Year's Eve, Vincenzo, my admirer, said he would call me at midnight on the telephone. That was almost like going out, to dance. I thought about it all afternoon and when evening came, after dinner, i sat down in the living room with a book and settled into a pleasant anticipatory state of mind. Unfortunately when my parents decided to go to bed, well before midnight, they unplugged the telephone, ignorant as they were of my appointment.

—There are always a great many prank calls on New Year's Eve, this way they won't bother us— my mother said.

I sat there hearing this sentence, thinking of my precious phone call, but didn't say anything. I watched her unplug the cord with a profound sense of tragedy. I was beginning to learn about the pain of love.

That spring, my last Roman spring, i remember walking in the streets of Rome on the first warm days, my legs and arms exposed to the wind, closing my eyes and feeling the air enveloping my body like a caress from a lover. I was looking at every building, every street, with new eyes. I would walk down Via Condotti, the main shopping street in the center of Rome, and i would look into the boutiques and try to imprint every silk design displayed in a given window. They seemed exquisitely complicated so that as soon as i went on, they disappeared from my vision. Then i would walk back a few steps and look at them again. I stood in front of snack bars admiring the supplì ,calzoni, arancini, pizzette, saltimbocca, imprinting the smells, colors, textures. I walked around and let sounds like "Cinzano," "mozarrella," "viale" float through my mind. I planned to take them all with me to repeat abroad when i felt nostalgic.

The day before we left i went to spend the afternoon with Clea: we sat in her room and talked quietly about the letters we would write one another, once a week at least, in which we would tell each other everything.

—Details are very important— she admonished me, —Micetta, don't forget, don't be too much in a hurry when you write, describe everything so i can *see* it; i have never been to the States, you know . . . Start by writing to me on the boat, telling me about the cabin and what you do to pass the time and then New York, of course, i want to know how people dress, what the buildings look like, the quality of the air. You'll have to help me imagine it!

Clea was very interested in America. She thought it was a modern and efficient country, more like Switzerland, not so disorganized or confused as Italy. She thought it was a good place to go to, she wished she were going too.

—You will come to visit— i said disconsolately.

—Of course i will. Come now, this is a great adventure for you, no reason to be sad. And anyway, look at what i have for you!

And with those words she got up, went to her night-table and brought out a little jewelry box which she presented to me ceremoniously:

—To my best friend in the whole world, with eternal devotion— she sat down next to me and put her arm around my shoulders. —Open it!

It was a bracelet, a silver Florentine lace-work chain with two oval moonstones hanging from it set in two tears of the same sculptured metal.

—I had a choice between this one and another one with square stones, but i thought this one fitted you, Micetta, you are sort of oval . . .

I didn't ask her what she meant by that; it seemed profound and important about how she perceived me, i didn't want to dilute it with an explanation. I put on the bracelet; Clea helped me to fasten it, and i wore it for the next ten years, without ever taking it off.

Baki and Dida looked very grave when they saw us off at the train station. They were staying on in Rome to wait for their visas and to be reunited with their son.

180

You are going now, Ani— Baki said to me, —be a friend to your mother. She will need one.

The five of us, my parents, my brother and Omama started our journey of immigration to the United States of America.

# U.S.A.

# 1

The port of Naples, resounding with songs and curses, became the door to my new life. While waiting to board our ship i thought of great literary men in similar situations: Chateaubriand leaving behind the corruption of civilized society to explore nature in the New Land, with religious fervor; Gide attempting to escape the constrictions of his puritanical background by exploring the life of the senses in North Africa; Rimbaud, giving up poetry to become a merchant in Africa . . . I walked around the port and tried to identify with these men in an attempt to make my own journey more palatable to myself, but i failed. Looking through the racks of used books of a sidewalk vendor i found a battered copy of *War and Peace* in French and bought it in the hope that it would last me through the eleven-day voyage across the Atlantic.

We stopped in Barcelona and took a tour of the city. I liked the faces of the silent women in black.

—You can really *feel* Catholicism in this country— said my mother.

—You can also feel Franco— added my father.

In Gibraltar our ship was quickly surrounded by small boats selling their wares to the foreigners. Young boys shouted prices and the people on deck bartered with them until they reached an agreement. Their goods were hoisted up in baskets and the coins counted when they came down. I

**185**

could smell the scent of oleander trees in the distance. I thought of Sicily. As the ship sailed through the Straits of Gibraltar i said goodbye to the Mediterranean. I stood on deck for as long as land was in sight, humming the farewell aria from *Madame Butterfly.*

—The Atlantic is greener than the Mediterranean, did you notice?— my mother said from behind me. She was comforting me, and herself at the same time. She too was sad to leave Italy. This was our definitive move. We were never going to go home again. Our life in Sarajevo, with its silverware and its servants was definitely behind us. "It is impossible to get domestic help in the U. S.," we had been warned before leaving Italy. My mother was preparing herself, but she was not given to sentimentality. She had made up her mind to make this move and now she was looking at the Atlantic. She was not one to look behind.

—Yes, and it is saltier too, or so they say . . .— i said, trying to be matter-of-fact, like her.

The transatlantic voyage was stormy and filled with stress: Omama became very disoriented on board, unable to remember her way around the maze of corridors and decks; she seemed to forget that she was on a boat in the middle of the ocean and asked, instead, for us to direct her to familiar Roman streets. Braco and i guided her as well as we could through the labyrinth, but her eyes were wide open, shiny, scared . . . When i was 'off duty' i read; lying on a chaise longue on deck, wrapped in blankets, i devoured *War and Peace,* its words as piercing as the sea air. The book engaged me in a very special way: the detailed descriptions of soldiers moving about the vast Russian landscape peculiarly suited my mood, especially late at night, as i lay reading on the upper bunk of our small cabin for four. Tolstoi put me in touch with the psychology of the peasant, directly, immediately, sensorially. Moreover, i considered this journey of ours, the journey across the Atlantic, as our own journey from war to peace: we were leaving war and Europe behind, going toward America, toward peace . . .

Braco and i went to all the meals, no matter what the
condition of our stomachs. It became a contest. At times we
would be the only ones in the large wood-paneled dining
room. Waiters would serve us, balancing their trays, laughing,
and the glasses would glide back and forth on the empty
tables, held in by the edges. Course after course of wonderful
Italian delicacies were placed in front of us. We would
periodically rush to the rest-rooms, vomit and come back for
more. It was a veritable Roman orgy. The waiters were
friendly and seemed to like stormy days — they didn't have
to work very hard. Instead they engaged us in conversations:

—Don't worry, signorina, you will like America, it is a
wonderful place for young people! Learn this word, it is very
important: *fun*. It means something between pleasure and
play, but it is untranslatable, we don't have a word like it in
Italian. Try to say it . . .

—FAN— i said and the waiter laughed.

—Not fan, *fun*.

I wrote many letters to Clea during that journey and i
wrote one to Vincenzo: we had agreed to correspond. I
didn't quite know what tone to assume in writing to a boy,
how affectionate to be, but i wanted to encourage him to
write me passionate love letters in America. I decided to tell
him how much he was in my thoughts, how certain smells
reminded me of him, how for a moment i had thought it was
him when a young man came over to invite me to dance the
night before. In the evenings, in fact, we would go to the
ballroom, my parents, Braco and i, and a young man, taller
and older than Vincenzo, started inviting me to dance. My
parents became nervous, but i kept accepting. What could go
wrong, right under their eyes in the middle of the third class
dance floor? He had a pockmarked face and he smiled very
rarely. I found that attractive; he looked like he was in pain
most of the time. When i succeeded in making him smile in
the course of one of our dances, i felt rewarded.

The evening before our arrival the captain regaled us with
the traditional farewell dinner and we danced, wearing silly

little paper hats. We drank 'spumante,' pretending to be cheerful. The next morning we were wakened by the captain's voice announcing over the loudspeaker, first in Italian, then in English, our arrival in the port of New York:

—Ladies and gentlemen, while you were sleeping pleasantly, i hope, at four o'clock to be precise, we anchored outside of New York awaiting the port to open its operations. We are now ready to proceed. It is now seven o'clock, New York time. On behalf of my crew i wish you a fruitful stay in America!

I got dressed and rushed out on the deck. The Statue of Liberty was standing near us in the grey, sooty morning air; she looked like a Roman statue, large, friendly, with blank eyes.

—Liberty is a woman, you see— i said to Braco, standing next to me.

—Yes, of course, like all abstract words: 'la liberté,' 'la verité,' 'la justice,' 'la démocratie,' 'la joie,'— he said mimicking our familiar grammar lessons from the lycée.—Now we'll see if it means anything.

We were looking at the Manhattan skyline sliding by us, sharply edged, its skyscrapers casting a grey glow in the rising sun. It all looked familiar from the movies: there were bright red and yellow dots darting along the highway which i later discovered were taxicabs.

The immigration formalities took many hours. We finally got out, through the heavy iron gates in mid-afternoon, perspiring profusely in the heavy air. Some Yugoslav friends greeted us; they looked healthy and well-dressed. They reassured us that we had made the right choice:

—It's a shock when you first arrive, but you'll get used to it very quickly. You'll learn English in no time— said one man, taking my hand, leading us to the reception area. Here we were met by our sponsor, a distant cousin, a professor at New York University, who looked very uneasy. He had signed our affidavit, guaranteeing that he would be responsible for us, that we wouldn't become a burden to the government. There were long tables set up, with little American flags for us to take, tended by charity ladies. They were sitting there, with fixed smiles on their faces, their hair dyed in bright colors, red, yellow, blue-grey. They said words in Yiddish which none of us could understand. When they spoke English they shouted, the volume making up for linguistic differences . . . They wore blue and white buttons on their clothes with the word 'Haddassah' printed on it.

We were assigned to a hotel. Our cousin looked relieved. He said we'd have to come for coffee to his house soon. One of the Haddassah ladies offered to drive us to our hotel. We put our luggage into her immense trunk and piled into her Lincoln Continental. She chatted loudly all the way to the hotel, pointing out sights:

—This is Riverside Drive and over here we are coming to Broadway, you've heard of it, am i right?

Braco was our official translator. He explained that we were going to be near the theater section:

—How convenient!— said my mother, —first things first.

—This over here, see that blue light over there, that's the subway, tell them, they're gonna need to use it!— she said to Braco.

The streets were filled with people; while the city looked dirty, there was something lively and interesting in the inhabitants' faces.

Our hotel was on 87th Street, off Broadway. It was an old, narrow brick building with a faded H-O-T-E-L sign affixed over the entrance. We walked through the corridors, passing the other clientele, Orthodox Jews, dressed in black wool in the middle of the summer heat, the men wearing hats, their hairlocks stuck behind their ears. The elevator was used for the luggage and Omama; the rest of us walked to the fourth floor up the stairs covered by a dirty green carpet with large floral designs on it. When we got to our two rooms, one for my mother and father, the other for Braco, Omama and me, i cried.

—Just start unpacking— my mother said, on the verge of

tears herself, —that will keep you from thinking about it.

—Did you see how they treated us— i heard her say to my father as she walked into their room.

—They treated us like immigrants— he answered, —which we are . . .

—They were immigrants themselves not so long ago, and anyway they are Jews, they should know better!

—American Jews are a different breed, everyone says so, they haven't been through the war, they don't know who we are, to them immigrants are immigrants, all the same.

—And they wish we had stayed where we came from . . .

—Anyway they are being kind to us, they are doing the best they can— my father admonished, —they are not especially educated people, you know, even if they have money now!


We spent the next few weeks, my mother and i, exploring all the public establishments that had air-conditioning. We were overwhelmed by the heat. It had an entirely different quality than Roman summer heat, it was stifling and wet. People said:

—This is very unusual, we rarely have *such* humidity; we always have humid summers, but not like this! You hit a bad one . . .

One of our favorite oases was the automat. There we could go and sit as long as we wanted to cool off without having to speak English and thereby incur the usual "WHAT? WHAT ARE YOU SAYING? I CAN'T UNDERSTAND YOU . . . SPEAK UP!" delivered in proper New Yorkese by most shopkeepers. I liked putting the coins into the slots and watching the dishes go around the turnstile to the little door which opened automatically as it arrived in position. We tried all the different foods, often not knowing what they were.

—These hamburgers are good, a little dry, but tasty— my mother said.

—Careful, don't put the mustard on, it's inedible!

—Did you try this?— i asked her pointing to the relish, —it's sweet . . . Ugh!

—I want to try their famous catsup— my mother said putting some on her finger, —it's just tomato sauce, i don't understand what is so special about it!

—They call fried potatoes "French fries" isn't that strange?

—Yes, they seem to have a lot of French foods which the French would not recognize . . .

—I think the word 'catsup' comes from 'cat-soup' .. .

We were constantly trying to guess the etymology of American expressions.

—Some of their phrases are very colorful, like 'hot-dog' . . . I still can't imagine why they call sausages hot dogs . .

—Perhaps they were made from dog meat, they taste as if they were . . .

—Don't be so negative!— my mother said with irritation. She found me very difficult since our arrival in New York. —Let's have a dessert instead of criticizing everything!

I had bright green jello. I watched it wobble in the dish. When i tasted it i wanted to cry.

Finding our way around Manhattan was easy, with the streets and avenues laid out conveniently on a grid pattern in numerical order. Broadway, askew across all this symmetry, began to look like an old friend.

—This city really is like Bari— i said to my mother one day as we were going to our favorite automat, the one with beautiful mosaic tiles.

—Yes, it is. Do you still remember?

—Of course i remember! But still i wish they had names for their streets, numbers are so cold . . .

—They are more practical, you have to admit.

—Well, yes and no. You know what happened to Mr. X.— we both laughed.

That was a reference to a joke which was circulating among the immigrants. Mr. X leaves his hotel to go out and look around Manhattan for the first time. He says to himself:

"I'll write down the name of the street and the number, just in case i forget" and off he goes, his note safely tucked away in his pocket. When he is ready to go back he stops a police officer and shows him the note asking for directions. The policeman says, "Sorry pal, i can't help you." Mr. X looks perplexed. The note read: "375 One Way Street."

We went to the movies several afternoons a week to stay cool and to study English. With the help of visual images i could usually infer what was being said. I saw *The Third Man* and hummed its theme for days afterwards; watching Alida Valli in an international intrigue with Joseph Cotten helped link the continents. We saw Rita Hayworth and Orson Welles in *The Lady from Shanghai* and Humphrey Bogart in *The Treasure of the Sierra Madre.* Their voices surprised me; they were less melodious than their dubbed Italian versions, more direct. When we went to see 'light' films we took Omama along. She came to see Gene Kelly and Frank Sinatra, Fred Astaire and Ginger Rogers, but i preferred the others. When we saw *Kind Hearts and Coronets,* Braco whispered translations into my ear. He was treating me with kindness since our arrival in the States, marking a new era of maturity for both of us.

My father was looking for a job. He came home, to the hotel, exhausted from the heat, discouraged:

—There is nothing, just manual labor, and we all know i can't do anything with my hands— he looked at his fine, well-manicured hands.

—Yes, yes, we know, you can't even drive a nail straight ... But the question is what shall we do?— my mother said. We were running out of money and there seemed to be no prospects.

—Something will come along, don't worry— my father said unconvincingly, —with all our connections, i will find something.

He spent much of his time running around the city, up and down the subway stairs, with temperatures in the nineties, looking up old friends who had immigrated to the United

192

States earlier and distant relatives who were already established. His pockets were filled with bits of paper with names of firms and addresses scribbled on them:

—They like young people in America— one would say.

—Yes, youth is everything here. Besides, we are entering a bad economic period, it seems. You should have been here a few years ago, there was gold on the streets . . .— another said.

—Wonderful!— my mother said. —Unusual weather, unusual economy, special for us . . .

**2**

When i was young we didn't know much about vitamins, your mother
knew, she taught me and then i paid attention, but before that no. We
used to bake our own bread, we kneaded it and baked it ourselves, we
didn't have much ready-made bread, mostly it was baked at home. And
then we ate . . . We didn't watch our diets, we ate as much as we could
and got quite fat and of course we all had some illness from that. We
were so fat we couldn't move! Everybody was fat, the rich and the
poor, because the poor ate a lot of bread, a lot of potatoes, a lot of
'procha' [cornmush]. I didn't know much about nutrition. We ate
everything. We even ate fat: there was goose fat—the geese came from
Hungary, Hungarian women forcefed them. They also plucked the
feathers from live geese for pillows, the best feathers came from live
geese.

Goose fat was very rich and the meat was fat, very tasty to us. We
used to dry the goose meat ourselves and we made our own sausages
which we dried over wood, over smoke. We had a stove in the attic
which we heated with wood and on top, where the smoke goes out, we
hung this meat and that is how it dried. It was a delicacy! We used
meters and meters of sausage lining and we filled it ourselves; we
ground the meat, put salt and pepper and oil into this meat and then we
filled them. We used geese instead of pork because we don't eat pork.
The lining was the intestines and then we put air holes in them and
hung them. When they were dry it was customary, in the evening, when
the 'chief' came home, to offer him a little sausage and he would wash

it down with rakija [plum brandy]. In our house, since we were always pretty well off, we burnt our own rakija.

We bought plums by the barrel from the peasants, five or six of them, we put the plums in a big vat and it stood there until it started to ferment and then they put it in another large vat and they burnt rakija from these plums. My late father always did it, so that we always had home-made rakija. We also made 'lekvar' [plum butter]. We bought the plums, we opened them and we made the marmalade from the plums ourselves. Plums grow in Bosnia. At my late mother's house there were twelve of us, eight children and the maids, so we had a big vat and we made this 'lekvar' and we put it in large earthenware pots and in the morning we ate 'lekvar' on bread, with milk, we used it instead of butter. We hired a man to come and mix it. The vat held about 100 kilograms of plums. We washed the plums, pitted them, put them in the vat, lit a fire under it with wood and this man mixed it all day long; toward the end we put in some dried orange peels, we always dried the peels of oranges after we ate them, that was very good. We put a little sugar in at the end, not before, otherwise it would burn. When the man saw that it was mixed, that you could see the bottom—that was the sign that it was almost finished—he called us, the children, to lick all around the vat with little wooden spoons. When it was all done they poured it into air-tight earthenware; pottery is very good for such things.

We made everything in the house: we cooked tomatoes to preserve them, we made marmalades from peaches, from oranges, which were wonderful. We didn't have prepared foods. Toward the end. it came: a delicatessen opened, it had everything, but i didn't use it, i still made everything at home. We bought eggs in the summer and put them in water with some liquid to preserve them for the winter. In winter everything was more expensive, we were very careful about spending less, about saving the most. In the summer, when eggs were cheap we made 'tarana' [egg barley] at home: we called in a woman, we who could, and those who couldn't did it themselves, and this woman would knead the dough; about fifty eggs in one day, without water, she kneaded it fairly hard and then she made 'tarana,' with a small axe in a wooden trough and she chopped the tarana. The other kind she made was something like macaroni, with something like a long needle: she spread the dough out, cut it in small pieces and curled it with this needle, the dough wouldn't stick because it was coated with oil. That was the greatest of delicacies. When it was half dry, it was cut into very small pieces, for soup. We had sacks with air holes in them and all of this went into the little sacks, each kind separately and then we hung it in the pantry so that there was air and it wouldn't spoil.

We also roasted our own coffee at home, for Turkish coffee. The best coffee was when it didn't burn, we watched over it very carefully, the coffee would let out some oil and we ground the coffee at home, that was the best coffee. We also made our own sauerkraut. We bought cabbage wholesale and then we made it so we would have some for sarma, whole pieces, and some shredded. We took a barrel which was quite dry and this barrel had a cork. We shredded a lot of cabbage and for the whole heads we took out the inside and put salt in the opening and the part that wasn't meant for sarma we shredded and salted it to let it stand, always in wooden receptacles so it wouldn't rust. After three or four hours, we stacked the cabbage in the bottom, then came the heads, five or six little heads, as many as would fit, then cabbage again, then we had this stone and we would beat the cabbage until it was covered with its own water; then we would cover it nicely with a clean cloth, a heavy board, the stone on top and in this way this cabbage was always under juice for fifteen or twenty days, it would form a kind of foam; then we went downstairs and we washed the stone with cold water, the wood, the rag, we wiped the cabbage nicely, we had to keep it very clean and it was very good cabbage. We put quince in it for flavor, cut in pieces, that gave it a *very* good taste. When this cabbage was about three or four weeks old, if there wasn't enough juice we added a little lukewarm water, we always made sure it had enough juice. Then we cooked with this cabbage, we cooked it with dried meat, and with the cabbage heads we made nice sarma, wonderful sarma. We kept it three or four months, the whole winter, until we used it all up. It was believed that the juice from this cabbage was very healthy, so we often drank it with a little oil.

We also pickled cucumbers, wonderful cucumbers. We used empty oil cans, ordered cucumbers from the gardener, medium size, not too big, not too small, and we used freshly picked cucumbers. We washed them and then we stacked them in this can tightly with dill, garlic, pepper and then we boiled some water with salt, let it cool and when it was lukewarm we poured it over the cucumbers until they were covered and on top we put some more dill. Then we soldered the cover on so that no air could come in and left it in the sun for about three weeks and then it was ready. We opened the can, these cucumbers were a delicacy because it was all fresh and good. If we wanted them to ferment faster, instead of closing the can we put some bread on top. We also made yogurt with goat milk which we left to sour by itself, in earthenware, not metal. The cream was so thick we delighted in it, wonderful sour cream which we ate on bread and the left-over yogurt was delicious. We also made sour milk by putting it in cups on top of the stove and they would sit for two or three days. Other people made cheese, from goat milk, and we bought it from them, *very* good cheeses. Many Greeks in New York know how to make this cheese and this yogurt and sauerkraut, but not as good as in Yugoslavia . . .

We also preserved tomatoes; we were very careful that they were healthy and only used that part, we washed them, cleaned them, cut them, cooked them, strained them and then we put them in jars. At first there weren't such good jars so we had to seal them with lacquer so that no air would get in, but toward the end there were better and better jars, so we used to buy 'Rex' jars and we filled them, put a little oil on top and just closed them and then cooked them in steam. That was a lot of work. For the steam we had a big pot into which we put rags, on the bottom, then the jars and rags between the jars also, covered it with rags and this cooked on the stove this way. When it started boiling, it boiled for about an hour, an hour and a half, then we shut the flame off leaving the jars until the next morning to cool off by themselves, then we took them out and put them in the pantry; of course the pantry was always full, for the winter things.

Women never drank rakija, just men, i don't know that i ever drank rakija; with us it wasn't even customary for women to smoke, if a woman smoked it was considered . . . tactless, but among the Moslems women also smoked, that was customary. Later in your mother's time women also started smoking, it wasn't any longer so tragic, it was already modern. The Moslems, they smoked 'nergila' and they somehow smoked it in water, i don't know how. And there was some tobacco, for smoking, from Mostar, which was a little stronger, and this tobacco wasn't legal, so they smoked it secretly, it was sold on the black market. They sat on this 'minder' [pillows] and they had some kind of a bottle and some kind of a tube and that was the greatest pleasure for them when they smoked this. Just men smoked this, not women.

In my mother's time it was customary to take blood out of their veins, after they stopped menstruating; they used leeches. I remember my mother used to buy them and put them on her veins and these leeches would drink so much blood that they couldn't any more and then they would fall off. In this way their blood would be cleansed, this way they were healthier.

3

The Jewish refugee association offered to send me to summer
camp, in the mountains. It was decided that i would go. In
this way, at least one member of the family would not be
suffering from the heat and besides, it would be a good
opportunity for me to learn English—through the total immersion method. I had never heard of summer camps. In
some ways the United States felt very familiar and in others i
was constantly surprised. In Italy children spent their summer vacations with their parents, with their grandparents;
here they went off in groups to the country. There had been
no mention of that in the American films i had seen . . .

On the day of departure we arrived at the office where we
were to register and load onto the bus. We had put name tags
on my clothes and checked off all the items on the camp list:

—This is American efficiency— my mother had said when
we were packing, —they leave nothing to your imagination,
they even tell you how many pairs of underpants to bring . . .

My parents were filling out some forms, releasing the camp
of responsibility for certain kinds of injuries, listing names of
relatives for emergencies and all my childhood diseases.

—She is fifteen years old, you know— my mother reminded the receptionist, —she can take care of herself.

—Just fill out the form, lady, i don't make the rules around
here— said the woman behind the desk, cracking her gum.

I looked around at the other girls. Most of them were

younger than i, many had pimples on their faces. They weren't very pretty, their clothes didn't fit, they wore their shirts outside their cotton pants, they didn't seem to care what colors they put together. All of them had similar hairdos, with bangs on the side and loose, regular curls at the base of their necks. They wore thick make-up over their blemished skins and bright pink lipstick. In Italy the secret of looking good was to wear make-up so nobody could tell, to fix your hair so that it looked 'natural,' to wear dresses out of 'good' materials. Here it seemed all the other way around, the more it showed the better. There was one girl, however, who was different from the others: she was taller than i and looked rather miserable, shy, ill at ease. She was black. As i looked at her i thought to myself: "That's a triple tragedy: not only is she female, and Jewish, but she is Negro besides . . ." And then it was time to get on the bus and off we went to New Jersey.

The first few days at camp were perplexing to me. I understood little of what was being said and spoke even less: i was having difficulties pronouncing English sentences. The individual words were not as much of a problem for me as catching the rhythm and the tonality of the speech patterns. "Sure thing! I'll catch ya later . . ."—in hearing that i wouldn't know where one word stopped and another started. The other girls and counsellors were being friendly to me, not at all malicious, as they might have been in Italy in a similar situation, but we just didn't connect. They all seemed to know just what to say and do, as though they had all taken lessons, while for me every detail of the day was baffling.

On the first morning, we went to the cafeteria for breakfast. There were eight or ten of us, sitting around a large plastic table. Some boxes were passed around and everyone poured some of the contents into their bowls. I did the same. It was a flaky light brown substance. Then they poured some milk over the dry food.

—No sank you— i said refusing the milk.

—Put on cereal!— one girl shouted.

I didn't want to be impolite; milk was obviously a necessary part of this meal. I took it and carefully poured some into my bowl, watching the flakes come up to the surface. I tasted the mixture. It was horrible. I ate it all, still being polite, while others left various amounts in the bottom of *their* bowls. I looked around for coffee. Nothing but milk in sight. I consoled myself by drinking the cool orange juice that was in front of me, all in one gulp. That was delicious.

After the preliminary confusion i settled into quite a pleasant life at camp. The surroundings were beautiful, with paths running through thick gentle forests; the swimming pool was large and one could see the mountains while swimming in it. In a clearing in the forest there was a theater where some of the campers staged a play. We sat on benches and listened to woodpeckers working while our actors performed. At night they built fires and sang songs: "Goodnight Irene," "I've Got T'pence," "She'll Be Comin' Round the Mountain," "Working on the Railroad." These were all new to me and i didn't understand all the words, but i loved the melodies, their distinctive *American* sound. They made me think of cowboys and open plains and they made me sad and that felt good.

And there was Jeannie. She was a counsellor, not much older than i, maybe eighteen or nineteen. She was tall and thin, with short black hair. When she looked at me across the fire i felt recognized. She said she was Italian, which meant that her family was, but she was born in New York. She spoke a funny mixture of Neapolitan and English which made us both laugh. I started seeking her out. One day i met her in the middle of the woods.

—What are you reading?— she asked, looking at the book under my arm.

—*Le rouge et le noir*— i said, showing her the volume.

—Ah, it's in French! That's not one of my languages— she said with a self-deprecatory gesture that moved me.

—I can teach it to you.

—Okay, that's a deal. See you later!

I waited for her all afternoon. I figured out eventually that 'see you later' meant 'good-bye.'

One Sunday my parents came to visit me and i showed them around. We first went to my cot in the dorm:

—You even have your own reading lamp!— my mother said. —It looks very comfortable.

—Yes, except they complain if i leave the light on at night, nobody reads here . . .

—Well, you need to get your sleep at night, being outdoors all day.

We walked all around the camp, i showed them the archery field, the amphitheater, the cafeteria and even the showers.

—It's very clean— said my mother, —isn't it amazing what they can do! Here you are in the middle of the wilderness with all the modern comforts!

She stopped and turned to look at me. She lifted my head with her hand, toward hers:

—What happened, Anči, you forgot how to talk!— She turned to my father:

—Our Anči is so quiet all of a sudden . . . did you notice?

—Yes, it's the language problem. But soon she will be talking as usual, in English, like a real American!

I felt tears well up in my eyes. I realized at that moment that i had been feeling very lonely. I was relieved to speak Serbo-Croatian.

—I never thought English would be so hard! I can't seem to get used to the sounds. I don't understand them most of the time and *they* don't understand me!

—Be patient, my little girl— said my father —you remember, it was the same with French. It looks impossible for a long time and then, *puff!* it all starts being clear and easy.

I knew he was right. The brain assimilates words in a foreign language unconsciously, like a baby's in her first year of life, and then they start flowing out of our mouths, as if it all happened overnight.

I introduced Jeannie to my parents. She was friendly but not too interested.

—Who is she?— my mother asked.

—Oh, she is one of the counsellors.

—She looks a little strange, with those pants hanging on her like that.

—She is very nice— i defended her.

My mother was right, as usual. As i looked at Jeannie walk away i had to admit that she wasn't pretty and that i didn't really know why i liked her. After my parents left that evening, i wrote a long letter to Clea, describing their visit, their remark about how i had forgotten to speak, everything. Except i didn't mention Jeannie.

When i returned to Manhattan my parents told me that they had inquired about schools for me and that they were told the Julia Richmond High School was good, that it had special classes for foreigners. We went to visit. It was situated in a large, solid, brick building. I thought of my pretty white villa in Rome as we walked up the stairs to the office. It was awkward to be going to school with my mother at fifteen, but i was glad she was with me. The women in the office looked busy, distracted, typing, talking on the telephone. They did not look particularly strict, however. One of them motioned to us to sit down. There was another girl waiting, with earrings and lipstick. I looked at her and turned to my mother:

—Do you think i should start wearing lipstick?— i asked her in Yugoslav.

—Lipstick, at your age?

—Well, here it seems to be the custom . . .

—Yes, and they look like monkeys!

I enrolled. On the form i put down 'Anita' as my first name, so that Americans could pronounce it; while not my name, at least it carried with it an echo of Italy . . .

I spent the next few weeks waiting for school to start, disoriented, with no one to talk with. I missed Rome terribly. As i walked through the streets of Manhattan i felt the same hot air as in Rome, on my arms and on my legs, but here it felt like an intrusion, like the caress of a child with sticky fingers.

—It's the humidity, they all say— my mother reminded me.

—Yes, and the dirt.

The people of Manhattan didn't seem to like their city. They threw their hot-dog wrappers on the streets, leaving trails of yellow mustard on the pavements. There were little neighborhood parks here and there, islands in the middle of Broadway, where people sat on benches, facing the traffic, their backs to the greenery, except for women with babies; they usually sought out the most protected spot, in the sun . . .

I watched the brick structures with iron staircases on the facades with bewilderment, not understanding why these stairs were exposed like that. Someone finally explained to me that those were fire escapes. Of course, New York is not America, i reminded myself, and New Yorkers are certainly not Americans—they mostly had foreign accents! But certain traits, as they revealed the American character to me, continued to shock me: while people didn't seem to care about their city and its components, they certainly seemed to care about their dogs! I was used to seeing dogs kicked or ignored in Italy, in Yugoslavia. Here people stopped in the middle of the street, smiling complacently at each other's dog, holding the leash proudly, to discuss the animal's health, character, habits. Then they would pet them and give them special little biscuits from their purses or pockets.

When i started school i was classified a 'junior' and placed in a special class for foreigners, to study English. This was my worst hour every day. The teacher would call on us, one by one, to stand in front of the class pronouncing words after her: "BOW," "COUGH," "LEAF," "THINK," "THOUGHT," "THROUGH." These were some of her favorites. She would pronounce the word very loudly, grimacing to exaggerate the sound, and then we were supposed to imitate her. She sounded like a cow. She corrected us by shouting:

—Not, "SROO," "*TH*ROUGH!"

"If i could say it, i would," i thought to myself with irritation. Most of the other students were from Puerto Rico, some from the Philippines, China and various European countries: our speech patterns covered a wide range but we all had trouble with the 'th' sound . . .

Schoolwork in other subjects seemed very easy by comparison with the lycée. That reassured me. I decided that once i learned English i could get through high school very fast; i would try to graduate as soon as possible. I didn't feel in harmony with the other girls: they were too loud, too big, they wore too much make-up, they were 'boy-crazy,' as they called it. They talked about getting dates, especially for Saturday night, and the strategy involved in accomplishing that. I thought with nostalgia of my talks with Clea. We too talked about boys, but never about how to 'catch' one. We mainly talked about how to keep them at a distance, we assumed that they were 'caught' . . . In Italy boys followed you on the street, sent you love poems, courted you. And they were usually older. Here the boys were the same age as the girls, too young for my taste. Their 'courting' was limited to a phone call: "Do you want to go out with me?" or "I thought we'd take in a movie Thursday night, how about it?"

The girls reported verbatim their phone calls to each other. Some even invented them:

—And what did you say about Thursday night?

—I said i am sorry but *i* am busy Thursday night.

—And what did he say then?

—He said: "Oh, what about another night, then?"

—And you?

—I said, taking my courage in two hands, but real casual-like: "What about Friday?" I didn't want him to know that i was free on Saturday, and you know what he said? He said "O. K." Not bad, huh?

I was fascinated and repelled at the same time at this way of handling romance.

One day my father came home, to our miserable little

rooms in the immigrants' hotel, and announced:

—I was offered a job in California.

—In California?— my mother said, surprised.

—Yes, it's a professional job. Teaching Serbo-Croatian.

—Who would want to learn Serbo-Croatian?— she asked with suspicion, preparing herself for a disappointment.

—The American army!— my father answered triumphantly. —They have a large language school there, in a town called Monterey. It seems that the Americans were caught unprepared when the war started, with no competent personnel to speak Japanese, German or any of the other languages. And so they established this school where they teach twenty-nine languages so that the same thing wouldn't happen again! And they need native speakers to teach the soldiers.

At the mention of the word 'California' images of Hollywood started moving through my mind. Perhaps now i could fulfill my secret dream of becoming a movie star. I went to the bathroom and looked at myself in the mirror: my face was finally getting thinner, less childish, it was gaining character. If i can't start my movie career at least i will be able to ride horses through the vast California landscape. I imagined a beautiful, unpopulated countryside with cowboys roaming about freely.

After some discussion it was decided we would go. We had no other options, in any event. Braco was to stay in New York, having just obtained a scholarship from N. Y. U. We were to take the train across country, to San Francisco.

On the map, San Francisco was on the other side of the United States, right on the sea. Next to it, in smaller letters, was Monterey, situated on what looked like a bay. My mother was very sad at leaving Braco.

—He is only seventeen!— she said.

—Yes, but his education is at stake; his future, his career depend on what he does now and N. Y. U. is an excellent university!

My father's argument was irrefutable.

**4**

My father left almost immediately. We stayed behind, waiting for word that he had found an apartment. Braco rented a furnished room near the university. My mother inspected it to make sure he had all he needed, a hot plate, cups, soap, toothpaste. She was uneasy about leaving him in New York, all alone. He was quite stoical about it, perhaps even looking forward to it.

—It looks like Baki and Dida will be here pretty soon— he reminded her.

They were going through the last formalities in obtaining their visas; Vito had joined them in Rome, via Israel.

—Soon is not the same as now— my mother said —i don't like leaving you behind without any family.

As for me, i was looking forward to being the only child, or to be exact, i was looking forward to being one of the adults.

The three of us, Omama, my mother and i, started the last stage of our journey, a three-day train ride.

—This will be like crossing Russia; did you know that America is as large as Russia?— i said to my mother.

—That is all they have in common, believe me— she answered curtly.

The countryside was bleak outside of New York, with small, barren trees sticking out of icy fields. The light was grey. It was December. Nothing much was growing.

I settled down in my seat and began reading. Omama was sitting next to me; i was to look after her, make sure she didn't get lost. These last few months had taken their toll on her. She had lost some of her vitality, her eyes were less shiny. In the absence of my father she had nobody to talk to. She talked to me, but my German was rusty; i listened, uneasily. I felt sorry for her, a strong-willed old woman, disoriented, anxious; but i wouldn't let her complain to me about my mother, toward whom my basic loyalty flowed. I didn't like having to choose between them. With my father gone the relationship between the two women had shifted and now it was clearly established that my mother was boss. The long struggle for control was coming to an end: the old woman had had to step aside and let the younger woman take over. She had no daughter and therefore she had to accept the daughter-in-law. This was a bitter pill to swallow, but such was the unspoken matriarchal law. She still drew her son aside, when she could, to whisper directions:

—She isn't buying kosher meat . . . The children's Hebrew education is being neglected . . .

But mainly she shrugged powerlessly and he whispered words of reassurance:

—Don't worry, *mamili*, we'll take care of everything once we are settled in our new home in California!

—California? Is that where we are going?

—Yes— he replied impatiently —i told you a dozen times!

—Are there any Jews there?

—There are Jews everywhere!— my mother interjected as she walked into the room, ending the conversation.

On the third day of our journey we awoke to the sight of dramatic mountains rising into a dark blue sky. We were in Colorado. The trees were thick, tall, full. The train was working its way up a narrow edge overlooking a white abyss below. I imagined we were in Switzerland, crossing the Alps, safe, away from the Germans. I was strangely moved by this landscape; i couldn't read, i kept looking at it. There was a silence, a vastness, a virgin quality to it that inspired awe. I thought i would take up painting in California.

When we arrived in Oakland, my father met us and we took a ferry to San Francisco. The bay was beautiful, punctuated by sailboats. I thought of Sicily. We took another train to Monterey, three hours away. A Yugoslav man from the Army Language School met us there. He was burly, but it was comforting to all of us to hear some Serbo-Croatian spoken. His movements were familiar, jagged, physical, he smiled broadly and said something about the daughter being quite a young lady already. In his blue Pontiac he drove us to our apartment, a duplex in the army's family village. As we drove in i noticed that all the buildings looked the same: wooden barracks, painted yellow, with green roofs, and each unit had a patch of lawn in front; the streets were evenly paved and curved in semicircles around each other. Children were riding bicycles and tricycles, oblivious of cars. It all felt very safe, protected, quiet.

—This is Ord Village— said our guide —the home for Fort Ord which is one of the largest basic training camps in the United States.

—What are they training them for?— my mother asked uneasily.

—Oh, they can't afford to be caught unprepared this time. There is trouble brewing in Korea, it looks like the civil war will erupt any day now. We must be prepared.

My father had bought some beds, there were towels in the bathroom, a few dishes in the kitchen. He had stocked the refrigerator with eggs and orange juice and bread. He had put a vase of fresh flowers in the middle of the empty living room floor. I had never lived in a two-story house before; it felt very luxurious. The other Yugoslav instructors and their families lived around us and the women came over with offerings of food and rides to town.

We went across the street to visit one of the families. They passed around some cheese and spinach pie and drank a toast to us. An old grandmother called 'Baba' lived with them. She had come to the United States as a young woman but had always lived among Yugoslavs and had never learned English; she had also forgotten much of her original tongue. She had her own vocabulary that her family understood; she said 'peda' and it meant 'payday.' She loved bananas and didn't seem to remember that there were no bananas in Yugoslavia. They were among the few foods she could still chew with her toothless gums.

The next day i went to enroll at Monterey High School. It was located on top of a hill, the buildings were new, vaguely Spanish in flavor, and it had a large football field.

—What grade are you in?— the woman in the office asked me.

—I am a senior.

—Were you a senior in New York, at this here Julia Richmond High School?

—No, i was a junior but they said that as soon as i learned English i could be reclassified to senior. Now i have learned English.

My accent was quite pronounced but i was able to speak freely.

—You're doing good— she replied. —Okay, we'll put you down as a junior-senior, how is that? You need to take American history, civics and senior English before we can graduate you.

—Okay. Thank you very much— i said. "What is 'civics'?" i asked myself as i walked away; i had decided not to share my ignorance for fear that it might impair my chances for graduation.

When i went to my 'home room' i was shocked at the noise level. The boys were all very big, wore jeans and never sat still. They draped their legs over chairs as if they were rolled-up rugs. The girls wore pleated skirts and sweaters; their shoes were thick-soled, white and brown or white and navy, with their socks rolled in a peculiar way low on the ankle. They all looked alike. Their hair was curled—they set it every night, they later revealed—their bosoms prominent. I

210

wondered what kinds of bras they wore; they all had the same outline, some larger, some smaller, but basically their breasts looked like symmetrical cones, propped up high on their chests. Their blouses were white and starched, their skins oily, they ate frequent candy bars and chewed gum constantly. They laughed a great deal, loud, raucous laughs. They seemed to enjoy themselves at school. In fact, it didn't feel like school at all.

The teacher was a thin, bespectacled man who would occasionally say meekly:

—Let's try to keep it quiet, boys and girls, *please*.

Nobody seemed to pay any attention to him. I thought of the lycée, of how those of us who sent a paper airplane flying across the room had risked the dreaded 'conseil de discipline.' I felt like asking them to be quiet, i wanted to learn. This noisy classroom gave me a headache after a while and i was bored. Mostly, however, i was repelled by the boys. They all walked like gorillas, legs wide apart, arms dangling at their sides, their hair cut short and flat on top of their heads. Their necks were thick and they still looked like babies, big noisy, awkward babies. When any of them tried to talk to me i acted very proper, ladylike, dignified.

One day my home-room teacher, who was also our English teacher, asked me to stay for a while after school. He had noticed that i wasn't happy.

—What would you like to be doing?— he asked.

That was a strange question for a teacher to ask a student, i thought, but i was grateful for his interest.

—I . . . i don't know. I would like to learn something about American literature.

—Here, take this home to read and tell me what you think of it. It's a great novel by my very favorite author.

I looked at the brown book he was handing me and read *Look Homeward Angel* in gold letters on the binding. Thomas Wolfe. I had never heard of him.

—Sank you— i said, taking the book.

—And don't worry, you're doing fine. These kids are a bit

rowdy, they are used to being outdoors; they mostly come
from fishermen's families, they aren't too interested in literature, but they're good kids, you'll get to like them after a
while.

I had a hard time reading that book, i wasn't sure i
understood it. The language was still difficult for me and i
wasn't too interested in this kind of psychological self-
analysis. I preferred reading in French and was a frequent
visitor to the Monterey library's French section. I had just
checked out several volumes by Jean-Paul Sartre and *L'Invité*
by Simone de Beauvoir. These were much more inviting at
night, when i went to bed.

My worst problem in high school was P.E. At the lycée in
Rome that was not one of the school subjects; some girls
took ballet lessons, others went to gymnastics, i played tennis
and took fencing lessons, but that was done outside. In
school we dealt with knowledge . ... Here P.E. was required.

—You can pick out the activity you like— a girl told me
—just go down and sign up.

I decided to try baseball, since that was the most American
sport. It was a dreadful experience. On the first day the
teacher, a muscular short-haired woman, told me to go bat a
few balls with another girl, to stand there and hit the ball
with this long stick.

—This is a softball, not a baseball— she explained to me.

As she threw the ball at me, i ducked instinctively and the
ball hit me right in the eye like a hard slap in the face. I
started to cry from the shock. I was taken to the infirmary
where they put some ice on my eye. They said it was closing
up fast and that it would probably get purple, but that i
would be okay in a few days. I took up archery instead.

Across the street from us, in Ord Village, lived a
Japanese family. They had two daughters. The eldest, Joy,
was a slight, smiling, gentle girl who helped me understand
the system at Monterey High. We often went home together
and, after a while, we started visiting each other. She didn't
like to talk about herself, but she was sweet and warm to me.

Her father, too, was an instructor at the Army Language School, a colleague of my father's. He was a short, stern man who seemed to frighten her. Her mother was also small, even quieter than Joy. Her little sister, Amy, was the liveliest of the family; she would burst into Joy's room and demand:

—Let me have your pink sweater, i *have* to wear it tonight!

Joy always agreed; there seemed to be no fighting between the sisters. I was awed.

I tried to tell Joy about my life in Rome. She listened with interest, but i could see that it was hard for her to imagine it. Her big dream was to go to Hawaii. She played Hawaiian music on her record player, hour after hour, swaying back and forth, making lovely ritualistic gestures with her fingers. She told me what some of them meant in an attempt to help me appreciate the music which to me sounded monotonous. But i liked watching her face as she listened to it, her eyes half closed, her body like the stem of a flower, swift and graceful in the wind.

—One day i am going to go there, for sure!— she would say.

—On your honeymoon?— i would tease her.

—Maybe.

—How do you know you'll have one?— i said. —I am not sure that i want to get married at all . . .

—Oh, i am! I want to get married and i'll ask my husband to take me to Hawaii, unless, of course, i can save up enough money to go there before that.

One day we were talking about the war when much to my surprise she said:

—I was in a concentration camp, you know.

I thought she didn't know what she was saying.

—What do you mean, how could you have been in a concentration camp? You weren't even in Europe during the war!

—I was in a concentration camp here, in the U. S.

—What? Where? How come?

She was sitting on her bed, her hands in her lap. She

looked very calm. Her black hair was parted on one side. She, too, set her hair every night, she had told me.

—Right after Pearl Harbor when the war was declared between the U. S. and Japan, the American government decided that all Japanese should be put in camps so they wouldn't help the enemy.

—But you are an American. You told me that you were born here!

—Yes. I have never been to Japan. I am a Nisci, a Japanese-American. My father was born in Japan and so they locked up our whole family. We owned a house and some land in the country. They took it all away from us and sent us to Illinois. I spent three years in camp there.

—How old were you?

—I was eight when i went and eleven when i came out.

—How was it there for you, did they torture you?

—No— she smiled. I knew she was thinking that i couldn't imagine her experience. —I went to school in the camp with the other Nisei children. We lived in barracks, we had enough to eat. But i still feel ashamed of it, i don't like to talk too much about it.

—Did you get your home back after the war?— i asked.

—What do you think?— she said with the first tone of bitterness i had ever heard in her voice. She pointed to her rented army quarters. —None of us got anything back.

I went home that night, thinking about what i had learned. We hadn't known much about such things happening in America. Suddenly the horror of Hiroshima and the devastation of Nagasaki had some tangible background. I went to bed early and plunged into Sartre. He seemed to address himself to these issucs; he presented a philosophical base upon which to form my opinions. What happens in Normandy affects the people of Texas, and vice versa. That idea seemed to literally apply to Joy and me. I read on, late into the night.

Boys started calling me for 'dates.' I didn't like the idea of going out with a boy my own age at night, but when my parents raised their objections to it i began to want to go on principle. Being picked up by a sixteen-year-old boy in his father's car was not my idea of glamour and passion. But i didn't like to say no, i can't go with you, my mother and father won't allow me to go out at night. That would have been humiliating.

—I think this is a ridiculous custom— my mother said —to let children go out driving at night, going wherever they please!

—It may be ridiculous but it is even more ridiculous to put me in a position to say "Mommy won't let me!"; how do you think i would look? And anyway you are always telling me to accept the 'American way of life' and when i do, you object!

—There are other, more interesting aspects to the American way of life— she would retort. I could never quite pin her down to what these were. Occasionally she would say:

—Like sports, for example . . .

So i went on very few dates. Occasionally i was allowed to double-date with Joy—she was going 'steady' and my parents trusted her boy-friend's driving. We went to the movies, and afterwards we went to a drive-in. That was the American date. I thought it was boring. The boys always paid. I was never hungry enough to eat cheeseburgers and milkshakes at ten o'clock at night, they didn't even go together. I liked the french fries, though.

School was easy and i was catching up in English and American history. Now i was officially a senior and i was going to be allowed to graduate. I wanted to go to college and learn something. My grandparents had arrived in New York that spring with Vito and were greeted by my brother. My mother was relieved. When i graduated that year, i went home with my parents and they toasted me and the new decade:

—This is a new phase of your life, Anči— my father said —and for all of us. Here is to the fifties!

5

That summer, when i decided to get a job, my mother said:

—That's a wonderful thing about America; young people can go to school and work at the same time, be independent. Such opportunities are unheard of in Europe!

I asked Joy how to go about getting a job.

—Just go downtown, to Woolworth's and J. C. Penney's, and apply. They all have personnel departments. And don't forget to say you have some experience!

Experience was the magic word in America, youth and experience, a contradiction.

My first interview was quite humiliating. A young man sat behind a steel desk, his legs propped up, asking me questions:

—How long have you been in this country? It says over here that you worked at Macy's in New York. Were you a salesgirl?

—Yes.

—Did the customers understand you, were you able to talk to them?

I was nervous about having lied concerning my work experience, but i was also getting angry at his lack of manners. He obviously found my accent disturbing. A serious impediment in business affairs. He hired me but decided not to put me 'on the floor'; instead he assigned me to 'the cage,' the area on the second floor where i was to make change for the salespeople who sent their money up to me in little containers, on a funicular. My wage was to be $.50 an hour.

Braco came home for the summer. He hitchhiked across country, which was an education in itself, he said. In the middle, between the two coasts, America is altogether different. There are people roaming around the country looking for jobs; towns are quiet and sleepy, people seem to have already forgotten the war. They were cordial, easy-going, helpful to strangers. We sat around the dinner table listening to his adventures.

—So here we are, all together— my mother said.

Everyone was smiling, happy for the family reunion. My mother had cooked Braco's favorite dishes: Wienerschnitzel, sacher torte . . .

—You are looking thin and pale, but now we'll take care of you!

He looked pleased, relieved at being able to become a little boy for a while again. He brought news of Baki and Dida. My mother pressed him for details:

—How did they look when they got off the boat? What were they wearing?

—They looked fine, a little tired, a little thinner perhaps, but all in all they looked fine. What difference does it make what they were wearing, i don't remember!

—It makes a difference, it tells me if they need something, if they have enough, and so on.

—They have enough to eat, they are all right, don't worry!

On weekends we went to the Naval Postgraduate School to swim in a large swimming pool surrounded by trees to which we were entitled as civil servant family members. Braco and i played ping-pong with each other, furiously, intent on winning. The rest of the time i lay in the sun and read. I bought myself a white swimming suit, with stays, which made me look like a soldier in armor. I wanted to get very tan in the golden, caressing California sun. My hair would bleach out and i would look like a Californian. I had bought myself a razor and started shaving my legs. I cut myself constantly and had to borrow my father's styptic pencil to arrest the bleeding. I also shaved the hair under my arms even though i couldn't get the Italian belief out of my head that "only whores shave under their arms"; here the girls were shocked to see me unshaven in gym.

—How do you apply your deodorant, with all that hair there?— one girl had asked me.

—Oh, it's the same, it doesn't matter— i lied in response. I didn't want to say that i didn't use deodorant.


Tension between my mother and me increased. Since my graduation from high school, i was working, saving money, talking about going to the university.

—I want to go to the University of California— i announced one night at dinner.

—But that is three hours away. You can't leave home at the age of fifteen! That's unheard of!

—I can live in the dormitory, that way i would be under supervision, you wouldn't have to worry!— i argued back.

—What's wrong with our Monterey Peninsula College, you can go there and still live at home. In two years, you can go to Berkeley. It's too expensive if you don't live at home, anyway.

—I'll save my money and anyway why does Braco go to a university and not i?

—He is older. He is a boy . . .

That kind of remark usually unleashed violent, screaming fights between us during which we said hurtful words to one another which we both regretted two hours later. My father would look at us, pained. Braco hid behind his newspaper, sitting in the living room, in an armchair, as if nothing were happening.

—One day, as i was sitting on the edge of the swimming pool, attempting to release my head from the entrapment of a bathing cap, i heard a voice rising from the water:

—Hi.

A man pulled himself out of the water. He had nice smooth skin, blue eyes and an intimate smile. He sat down next to me.

—I've watched you playing ping-pong, you're a good player. Permit me to introduce myself.

He stood up and bowed as water dripped off his nylon shorts. "He would look better in a bikini," i thought to myself.

—My name is Sandy Patterson— he continued.

—How do you do— i said.

—And what is your name?

—My name is Anica, but here they call me Anita.

—Anni-tsa— he said. —How is that?

—Pretty good.

I appreciated his trying to pronounce my real name. We talked for a while. He told me he was studying Japanese at the language school, that he was a captain in the army, just back from a tour of duty in Japan.

—The army does things backwards, you know, they first send you to Japan and then they teach you the language . . .

He had a nice, easy manner about him. We talked about the new language-teaching method used at the school, total immersion: six hours of instruction every day followed by three hours of homework. It worked, he said, he was really learning the language. I told him that my father was an instructor there. He asked me where i was from and he said he liked my accent, that it was 'charming.'

—Actually, to tell you the truth i had something in mind when i came to talk to you.

—Really?— I was beginning to like him.

—Yes. I told you that i am in the army. That is true. But underneath my uniform— he pointed to his body, glistening in the sun, and smiled —i am an artist. When i saw you i knew immediately that i wanted to paint your portrait. You have a classic face, mobile and lovely.

I looked at him. Was he serious? Was he fooling me? I

wasn't sure, but i was enjoying this conversation.

—So, the question i came to ask you is: would you like to sit for me sometimes?— he continued.

—Sit?

—Yes. Pose for a portrait.

"How full of surprises life really is!" i thought to myself. Unexpectedly, right here next to a California swimming pool, the perfect nineteenth century novel situation presented itself to me. "Flaubert? Stendhal? Balzac?" i thought rapidly, but i needed to concentrate on my response.

—Perhaps— i replied nonchalantly.

—When would you like to start?— he continued unabashed.

—Oh, i don't know, i'll have to ask my mother.

—Of course!— he said. —Is she here? Let's go ask her right now!

—No, she is at home. I am here with my brother.

—Let's go meet him, then. You can introduce me.

Braco and Sandy shook hands, with Sandy doing all the talking, joking about ping-pong, asking Braco if he ever played tennis. He seemed totally comfortable with the situation. When it was time to go home he said:

—I'll tell you what, 'Annitsa,' write down your telephone number on this piece of paper and i'll invite myself over to meet your mother. Okay?

—Okay.

He said he would call the next day.

I went home that afternoon, elated. I thought of Sandy, his joviality, his gentleness. My life seemed fuller all of a sudden, more interesting. An artist wanted me to be his model . . . That was more what i had in mind, instead of all those little boys from high school with their football and their hamburgers! Sandy had been to exotic lands, he had 'savoir faire' . . . I told my mother about him with some trepidation.

—But what do you know about him?

I told her all i knew.

—He sounds too old for you.

—He is not *for* me, he just wants to paint my portrait, that's all!

—We shall see— she said.

When he called the next day he asked to speak to my mother. He was very polite. She invited him over for a cup of tea. The three of us sat around the kitchen table, drinking Lipton tea. I watched him from the corner of my eye being charming to my mother, complimenting her on her English, being helpful, offering to take her in his car to the P. X., answering questions about himself and his family. He was from New York where his mother lived and his three sisters. His father was dead. He was getting out of the army in a year. He had thought of making it his career, but he really didn't like the regimentation, although he agreed with her that some discipline is good, especially for artists. He was having a show in a gallery in Carmel, he would invite our whole family to the opening. Would we like to come? Yes, we would have to come, then we would decide if he was a good enough painter to do my portrait! He was a good listener, he made us laugh. "The most important thing about a man is whether he makes you laugh," Clea had once said to me. By the time he left, my mother had to admit that he was a pleasant man. He had arranged to come back to visit in a few days.

This is how i fell in love with a man, the first time; i didn't know i was in love, i didn't want to admit it, for fear that it might denote weakness. My life was transformed: i couldn't imagine how i had filled my time, my thoughts before meeting Sandy. I thought of him constantly. I would go to my room, after dinner, just to have time to think about him. It wasn't exactly thinking, it was dreaming, envisioning him. I tried to 'see' his face in every detail, but i never could; i captured his smile, his skin, a nice smooth, tanned color. I lay in bed and swayed my body to the rhythms of my fantasies. I imagined us on a train together, going to a hidden cottage in the woods where we would live together, all alone, surrounded by trees; we would build a fire, embrace gently and languidly. I embraced my pillow. It seemed to respond.

Working at Woolworth's suddenly seemed more meaningful. I thought of presents to buy him. It was early, of course, i didn't know him well enough yet, but later i would buy him some cologne. I liked men who wore cologne, it was an invitation on their part . . . Sandy was light and solid at the same time. He knew about suffering, about war, but he talked about these things in a reassuring way as if to say: "It's all over now and we have all learned a lesson from it." I told him about the bombings in Sarajevo, in Split, in Bari, about concentration camps, of how i couldn't get the images of people dying out of my mind. He didn't know many of the things i told him, but he told me about what he had seen in Japan, of how he had gone to Hiroshima, to the museum, and seen the mounted photographs of children with their flesh aflame . . .

—We Americans have never fought a war on our soil, not since the Civil War; we like to fight our wars on other people's soil . . . That is why we seem childish to the Europeans. We are childish.— he said, popping his gum to prove it. —You are older than i, did you know that?

I knew what he meant; since my arrival in the United States, i often felt older than i was.

—There is one thing i don't understand, it's about Korea. There is a war there, right?

—Right.

—And America has gone to fight against the communists, on the side of the South Koreans, right?

—Right.

—So that means that we are at war with North Korea. Right?

—Wrong. We are not at war, we are 'performing a police action' . . . You still don't understand America!

He took my hand and caressed it, pressing it down on the nylon fabric of his car seat. We were driving in his new Ford, a green convertible that looked like a fish.

The trees, the sea, the rocks along the California coastline, everything around me that summer looked brighter, more alive. Even the seals, barely perceptible through the thick fog, seemed to be in a good mood. It was like seeing all of life through special 3-D glasses which make the film acquire depth.

I tried to tell Joy about my new focus, but she seemed uneasy about it. I felt she didn't approve of my going around with 'older men.' I missed Clea; she would really be interested. I wrote her long letters describing all the obstacles. She had also fallen in love and her parents were opposed to her romance as well: her lover was a Sicilian, which was worse than an Italian, which would be bad enough from her family's Swiss perspective . . . As for Sandy, he was too old for me:

—He is eleven years older than i— i would say to my mother when she raised objections —father is nine years older than you, so what's the difference?

—The difference is that you are fifteen and at that age it's a big difference, you are a child and he is a grown man!— she would say with finality.

On weekends if we wanted to go dancing we had to go with my parents, they wouldn't let me go out with him alone. The four of us would go dancing together at the navy school's Saturday night dance; we sat around a small table in the dim light sipping cocktails. We tried them all: brandy Alexanders, whiskey sours, grasshoppers . . . I was offered sips from the adults' drinks, and had to content myself with pink lemonade. It was difficult to carry on a romance under such circumstances; but as soon as Sandy and i got on the dance floor, and he put his arm around my waist, his cheek touching mine lightly, to the sound of "Oh! My Pa-Pa," "Angel Eyes," "Music! Music! Music!," whispering "Don't worry, we won't let your mother see us, we'll go over here to the other end of the floor," i felt better. My breasts tingled as i felt his sex hardening.

He painted my portrait that fall. It came out looking like a Rembrandt, a dark canvas with the light focused on my forehead. It didn't look like me, but i was pleased with his interpretation of my soul. At the junior college where i had enrolled, postponing my real education for a couple of years in compliance with my parents' wishes, life was a vast improvement over high school. The campus was on a hill overlooking Monterey Bay, with large, carefully clipped lawns. I took photography and French. The teachers were uncritical, encouraging. I started getting A's. After school i worked with Joy in a ceramics studio, molding clay jewelry in the shape of sea horses and shells. Everything was falling into place: my interest in art blossomed, coinciding with my interest in Sandy . . .

Sometimes i cut classes to see him secretly in the afternoons. We took long walks in the Big Sur mountains, on the Pacific Grove beaches. He carried an army blanket in the trunk of his car which he would lay down for us; we would talk and then slowly we started kissing, like insects reaching out to one another. He knew how to explore my soul with his tongue. I ventured into his with mine. I asked him about the tall young woman with curly hair i had seen him with at the pool. He made light of it, but i knew that he saw her at night and that, with her, he probably went 'all the way' . . . I was both flattered and jealous: she was beautiful and sophisticated and he was interested in both of us. I put to practice my theory about jealousy, learned from years of experience with my brother: there is room for both of us. It worked some of the time.

My romance with Sandy lasted a year. One spring day, he told me that he would be going home, to New York, as soon as he was released from the army, for a visit. But that he would come back and that he would write to me.

—Every day?— i asked.

—Almost, i promise.— he said.

"Cry," that year's hit, was playing on the radio:

"If your sweetheart sends a letter of good-bye,

It's no secret, you'll feel better if you cry."

He did write me, many beautiful love letters, but he never

came back. I missed him terribly for a while. I felt that i had reached a new plateau in the adult sphere where pain and pleasure mixed inextricably. While i didn't consider this mixture salubrious, that summer i acquired a taste for it. I savored it for the next twenty years, before giving it up.

**6**

In the course of our sessions in front of the fire in his little house in Carmel on rainy afternoons, Sandy had played Mozart for me and i had acquired a taste for his tingling piano, caressing flute. ("Mozart is like chocolate cake," my brother once said; "just the right amount is ecstasy, too much gives you indigestion!") I signed up for a music appreciation course at the college.

The teacher played pieces with stories attached to them, *The Sorcerer's Apprentice, The 1812 Overture, Death and Transfiguration.* I was bored and insulted by this approach.

—Americans are realistic, concrete, they deal with the material world, they don't sit around and dream— said my mother when i told her about the music course.

My parents' analysis of American traits always focused on their positive aspects. We were all trying to understand these people by observing their customs, their manners, their family relationships. They were definitely quite different from Europeans.

—Americans are superficial, ignorant and arrogant. That is why they examine the concrete world; they don't know anything about other worlds, they are not philosophers.

—Like you— my mother said mockingly.

"Yes, like me," i thought to myself in reply. I was reading Dostoievski: "The only truly interesting part of human nature is in the lower depths," i said to myself. I was fond that year of making definitive statements about the human condition.

While my music class was disappointing, others weren't. In English we were told to select a book by Virginia Woolf for a report. I read them all. She opened my eyes. "She writes with the same pen as Proust," i wrote in my paper, "but her ink is of a different color." The teacher put a question mark in the margin.

That year i became 'popular': boys were after me for dates. I rarely accepted; they seemed too young, uninteresting. I was asked to model for the photography class; i was given three units for sitting in front of the camera while the students practiced their 'angles.' This gave me an opportunity to try all the poses i had invented in front of the mirror over the years: the serious Ingrid Bergman look, my head propped on my chin, looking directly into the camera; the Rita Hayworth look, standing, my head tilted up, evading the camera provocatively. I tried the lady-like Grace Kelly look without much conviction and of course the devastating Greta Garbo look; i felt i definitely did not succeed in that one.

I got a part-time job at the college coffee-shop. As a 'soda jerk' i learned to make milk shakes and tuna sandwiches on an assembly-line model. Mrs. Stanley, the cook, showed me how: you take a loaf of the spongy white bread and line up an even amount of square pieces facing each other. Then you take the big jar of mayonnaise that looks like sour cream but tastes like nothing else, and with a spatula you splash a little of the goo on each row, then you splash the tuna mixture, itself dripping with mayonnaise, then you put a stiff piece of lettuce on top of each, close them, and wrap them in wax paper. The entire operation took twenty minutes: one hundred sandwiches, our daily quota. The hot lunch consisted of chili and grilled-cheese sandwiches which i ordered by shouting to the red-faced Mrs. Stanley standing over the hot grill.

Then i met Frederick. He was tall, dark and handsome. He

looked like Tyrone Power. He had curly brown hair, sparkling dark eyes, a permanent tan and he was six feet tall. He
only drank orange juice, never touched alcohol and could do
fifty push-ups in a row. He was a California god. He was
twenty-two, just graduated from college. He had spent his
youth on the beaches of Southern California. Malibu. Santa
Monica. Santa Catalina. They sounded like islands in the
Pacific.

—Santa Catalina *is* an island in the Pacific, dummy!

—Don't ever call me 'dummy'— i snapped back.

—Oh, relax, will ya? It was just a joke . . .

Americans were always telling me to 'relax'; how can you
relax when you are angry, i wondered.

—I don't like your jokes. I may not know California
geography but *you* don't know where Yugoslavia is!

That was an exaggeration. He was one of the few people i
had met since coming to America who had heard of my
country of origin and even knew something about it. But the
tone of our relationship was set by this original argument. It
seemed important to demand that he take me seriously from
the beginning. He had majored in philosophy in college, read
Sartre and was interested in theater; in fact he was going to
appear in a local production of *No Exit*. He was an actor. I
was pleased. I told him i was reading Simone de Beauvoir,
*The Second Sex*. He had never heard of her.

—She is wonderful! I think Sartre got a lot of his ideas
from her. They are lovers, you know . . .

—No, i didn't. I'll read her.— He was open to my suggestions, i liked that about him.

—She says that women are in a dual position at this
moment in history, that men expect them to be a com-
panion, an equal, and at the same time to be inessential.

—What do you suppose she means by 'inessential'? I think
women are totally essential!— He laughed, pleased with himself.

—Yes, of course, but not in the broader sense of the word;

they are not the essence, they are still expected to play
second fiddle, to be second rate . . .

We often talked like that, with me telling him what i
thought, what i had read, and with him commenting on it. I
told him one day that i had decided having children was
immoral, that the world was in too terrible shape to bring
innocents into it. Images of starving people, burnt people,
little people with enormous eyes, emaciated bodies, torn
flesh, people looking through prison holes haunted me at
night. Concentration camp images fused with nuclear disaster
images. I went to see films of the Hiroshima and Nagasaki
raids. They were being released, shown quietly, privately by
the Quakers. . . . I abhorred my fascination. Frederick was a
ray of sunshine in all this.

—Yes, but look at the birds and the mountains and the
foam on the sea. It's still all there, as beautiful as ever.
Doesn't that give you hope?

And it did, it made me like him. He seemed healthy, in
every sense of the word. His teeth were perfect, like a movie
star's, his mind was not corrupt. When we held each other
and 'petted,' as the girls at my college called it, his body felt
muscular and direct. His penis would make itself known
without shame, it would just be there, between us, jabbing
me gently in the stomach, without making demands. There
was an innocence in our love-making that moved me and
made me irritable at the same time. We never even considered 'going all the way.' I told him that i was planning to
remain a virgin for the man i married. He seemed to expect
to be that man and, therefore, there was no hurry. He too
was a virgin, i later discovered.

Frederick and i made the rounds of teen-age love until we
finally consummated the act three years later and let the
candle go out . . . We petted above the waist and below the
waist, in cars, on mountain tops, on beaches by bonfires, in
beds in the afternoons while his parents were out. We stuck
our tongues in each other's mouths and we sucked. I sucked,

to be more exact; he licked. Holding a penis in my mouth, vibrating, pulsating, was an astonishing sensation. I often had the urge to laugh and sometimes did, with catastrophic results. I learned to read pre-ejaculation signals and to gently take the tip of his penis out of my mouth and cradle it in my hand as if it hadn't changed places. I didn't like the taste of sperm. My feelings for Frederick were a mixture of comfort, health, affection, sexuality. I did not feel erotic, sensual, in love. But i felt free.

One day when i came to work at the soda fountain at school i was informed that the night before the football players had passed a petition around, on the bus coming back from a game, asking that my name be added to the list of contestants for homecoming queen. I had always made their milk-shakes with real ice cream instead of ice milk and they were grateful. Besides, they thought i was 'kinda cute' and that i had a cute accent. My name was added to the list of candidates. The other three contestants had already danced and sung in front of the school assembly; i would be spared such humiliation. They took some pictures of me in my photography class and the art students made up some posters. I was suddenly smiling at the passers-by from the campus trees: "Vote for Anita, our next Homecoming Queen!" I was amused; it had all happened quite un-expectedly.

When i was actually elected—"On a write-in ticket!" my faithful football players pointed out—i began to feel ex-hilarated. Frederick was going to be my escort at the corona-tion ball. The football game was scheduled for Thanksgiving weekend, as usual. Monterey Peninsula College was playing Hartnell College from Salinas. The sons of fishermen against the sons of lettuce growers. It was going to be a close contest. Last year our school had lost. I had never yet attended a football game.

Before the game they rode me around the field in an open car and i waved to my constituency. My parents were sitting in the bleachers, smiling uncertainly. I wore a white wool jacket over a grey plaid dress and was escorted by the president of the student body, a pudgy, bespectacled young fellow who later became the head of a local savings and loan association. Every time i waved my hand, i laughed at the absurdity of the situation i found myself in and hoped that it would be mistaken for jolliness. The game was boring and we lost.

That night Frederick came over and brought me a white orchid corsage. I had never seen a corsage before. I noticed the ingenious way they wired the stem of the orchid into a little vial of water, to keep it fresh. Frederick was wearing his father's tux, looking very handsome, his curly hair, bright teeth and smiling eyes reflected in the satin lapels. My turquoise gown had a tight satin bodice with an appliqué of tulle on the chest, creating the illusion of full-breastedness, and a full, fluffy skirt composed of several layers of net gathered at the waist. I wore a matching satin jacket to cover my shoulders, leaving my not-so-plunging neckline exposed. I pinned the corsage on it and while i was looking in the mirror i noticed that my hair, freshly 'done' that afternoon at a Monterey beauty parlor, was like my gown, fluffy and symmetrical. My parents stood by the door as we left, smiling proudly. Frederick opened the door for me to his family's Chevrolet, helping me with the gown, and i slid over on the plastic toward the driver's seat. He drove with one hand and draped the other arm around my shoulder. *"Non Dimenticar"* was playing on the radio, in Italian and in English alternately: *"Non dimenticar che t'ho voluto tanto bene, t'ho saputo amar, non dimenticar! 'Non dimenticar'* means don't forget you are my darling . . ." I closed my eyes and imagined that i was going to a grand ball in Rome.

When they actually placed the crown on my head i felt nothing. I thought to myself that i might write a short story about this, entitled "Modern Day Cinderella," and send it to *Seventeen.* Frederick and i first danced alone to the tune of "Let Me Call You Sweetheart" played by the college band, followed by a medley during which my attendants and their escorts joined in. Then the lights dimmed and everyone joined in, cheek to cheek. Frederick was too tall for cheek-to-cheek dancing with me and anyway i had indicated to him in the past that i preferred the more dignified European face-to-face position. We left at midnight and went for a long walk in the moonlight, on the Carmel beach.

Later that year Eisenhower was elected President, a familiar figure from the days when he was our friendly general in Europe and now here he was again, a jovial, grandfatherly sort of man who would take care of everything and establish peace. People wore "I Like Ike" buttons and talked about the 'cold war.'

—That's an interesting phrase— my father said, —Americans have a gift for slogans.

I wondered if that was a slogan, i wasn't sure.

—It's double-talk— i replied, trying out *my* newly acquired phrase.

—Don't be so cynical!— my mother interjected with impatience.

She didn't like my criticisms of America. She reminded me that i didn't understand communism; i told her that she didn't understand America.

—America took us in, don't forget. Nowhere in the world are people better fed and freer— she continued.

—There are Negroes in the South who are starving. In the North, too . . .

This discussion went on endlessly. I felt the hard edges of America on my skin, the hypocrisy, the 'better than thou' attitude. My parents noticed the abundance, the generosity, the laughter, the optimism.

Clea wrote me a disconsolate letter: her parents had made her break up with her lover, the Sicilian. She was practically under house arrest. She cried all day—there were tears on the letter—and at night she wrote in her diary. There was one

232

positive aspect to this tragedy: they had offered to send her to the United States for a year, 'to forget him.' Her only consolation was the prospect of spending a year with me, of seeing America. Would i try to get her accepted at the University of California in Berkeley where i was going to go and find her a place to stay, preferably with me? I jumped up and down in my room when i finished reading that letter. My mother, from downstairs in the kitchen, shouted:

—What are those thumps, what do they mean?

—Clea is coming, Clea is coming, for a whole year!— i shouted, running down the stairs.

—Wonderful!— My mother liked Clea and thought she was a good influence on me.

I started making arrangements for the following year, saving money from my job, applying to the university, writing to dorms. At the junior college i was fulfilling all the requirements for a B.A., i was getting all the science courses out of the way, so that i would be free to take only those subjects that interested me once i got to Berkeley. I was looking forward to some intellectual stimulation, but mostly i was looking forward to having my best friend with me to talk and talk. I felt a need to tell her about my newly expanded love life, to explore it with someone. Frederick and i had fallen into a comfortable routine of sexual gymnastics: we rolled and wrestled and rubbed against each other. We kissed with vigor. It wasn't exactly passion, but it was satisfying. I taught him to waltz and he taught me to square dance. We danced under the moonlight at Big Sur, overlooking the Pacific Ocean. He took me to the sulphur baths and we swam naked, unashamed.

When i saw Clea on the train, her leather suitcases and passport in hand, i realized that three years had passed: her beautiful long eyelashes were accentuated by a touch of mascara, she wore a bit of rouge on her cheeks, and dark lipstick. Her wool suit was well tailored, her movements self-confident. We kissed and embraced:

—Micetta! Micetta! I am so happy!

—Yes. We will have a wonderful year together. Welcome to America!

I was aware of my clothes; they were obviously not in step with fashion. But now that Clea was here we would take care of that.

Her reaction to the United States was very positive in most respects, in sharp contrast to mine. She noticed everything, minute details which i had already absorbed and begun to take for granted. It was interesting to take a look at it all over again through her eyes; she admired the kitchens, the orderliness of people standing in line for buses, at banks, in supermarkets, she even liked the buildings:

—You have the best modern architecture here, do you know that?

No, i didn't know that. I missed the gothic, the romanesque, the rococo . . .

—In Switzerland, American architecture is highly regarded. That means something. Le Corbusier is Swiss, after all, in spite of what the French say . . .

Clea smiled as she said that, with the knowledge that i would understand what she meant. We both knew that she much preferred Italy to her native Switzerland but she nonetheless was proud of Swiss accomplishments and America reminded her of her country of origin.

—You call that architecture? Look at these buildings, they have no soul, they are all glass and concrete. They go straight up and down, they are 'phallic' . . .— I said my newly acquired word in English, i didn't know its equivalent in Italian.

—What does that mean?— she asked.

—It means like a penis. My art teacher says that all art forms are based on natural forms, that man hasn't invented anything, that he just copies nature. Americans have chosen the phallic form, i don't like it. I prefer curved, complicated forms, you know that— and i pointed to the bracelet she had given me when i left Rome —give me our Colosseum anytime . . .

She laughed:

—You know, Micetta, you have changed quite a bit since you have been in America, you have become much more critical. But you are still my best friend, and always will be, of course! For life.

It was fun showing Clea around the 'Cal' campus; she liked everything, the trees were greener and bigger than in Italy, the cafeteria food, while not tasty, was more wholesome, more balanced—she especially liked California salads, with all those surprises amongst the lettuce—and the boys:

—They are tall and you know that i like tall men. And their eyes! They are so open, direct, innocent. Moving— she explained.

—Natural. Simple. Back to nature . . .— i teased her.

—No, seriously, don't you think it's important to have an honest relationship with a man instead of playing those games Italian men play; one day they are ready to die for you and the next they are buying roses for someone else. I like the Nordic type— she said with finality.

I didn't share her tastes but we totally accepted our differences, they didn't affect our friendship, they were part of it.

One night, as we were leaving the cafeteria in our dorm, after dinner, Clea took my arm, as usual, on the way back to our room. A girl behind us looked at us and whispered something in another girl's ear. Clea looked at me perplexed.

—What are they saying about us?— she asked in Italian.

—I think they are saying something about our walking around arm in arm. Here it is not done. I heard her say the word 'lesbian' . . .

That was the first time i had ever pronounced that word; i had just heard it recently for the first time. The girls at the dorm would snicker and make faces as they talked about women making love to women. I wasn't sure Clea knew much about it. She looked like she understood, however. Her face became pale. She took her arm away and from that day on we never again walked arm in arm in the United States.

7

That year, 1953, was a rich year for me. Outside events were forcing me to draw some conclusions on such words as 'democracy,' 'freedom,' 'communism.' The 'cold war' was raging, the Rosenbergs were being tried for allegedly spying for the Soviet Union.

An air of repression descended on the country. It was difficult to get any real information. I started going to political meetings, to listen to the listener-sponsored station in Berkeley, KPFA, in an attempt to find out what was going on. Some talked about purges, others about 'containment.' McCarthy was making speeches calling intellectuals 'Commies, Reds.' The whole situation was confusing.

In the meantime Clea had acquired a boy-friend, a tall, blue-eyed, blond, well-mannered young man. One day he suggested that we double-date, he had a friend he wanted me to meet, Theodore. He was a graduate student. Very serious. A scientist. He looked like Mozart. I liked him immediately. I was still seeing Frederick on weekends when i went to visit my parents, but we were drifting apart. I was ready for an intellectual. Theo came along at just the right time. The four of us had a quiet dinner in an Italian restaurant in Oakland. The men talked and Clea and i listened. When they turned to us, Theo addressed himself mainly to Clea, ignoring me. I didn't recognize his shyness, i thought he liked Clea better because she was more adult, more sophisticated, more beautiful.

A few days later, however, Theo called me and invited me to dinner. We first went to his apartment and he played some Mozart for me. He had a 'hi-fi' system, the first i had ever seen. He also had a slide projector and he showed me some slides of his trip to Europe. He had visited the concentration camps; there were the incongruous colored slides of asphalt with weeds growing through the cracks, like in Resnais' *Night and Fog*. And there were many slides of a slim young woman with long curly brown hair.

—Who is that?— i asked.

—That is Elise— he said tragically. (I decided at that point that we were going to be 'just friends.') —We traveled through Europe together. We went to Hungary, to the youth convention— he explained.

Theo had a car and a private income. He took me to concerts, to hear Lili Kraus play Mozart, and to Trotskyite meetings where there was talk of Marx and Lenin and of Trotsky's split from them. We walked through the hills of Berkeley and he told me of neutrons and protons. We agreed that the Rosenbergs were innocent. He talked of sexual repression—he was going to a psychoanalyst—and i talked of political repression. I told him about American arrogance as i had witnessed it in Italy. We talked about colonialism, we read Camus together. He said that the French were the colonialists, not the Americans. I claimed it was a matter of semantics. He recited Baudelaire to me, in French. He had a good accent. After that i let him kiss me, ever so lightly.

Clea and i had moved to another dorm, a smaller, more intimate one, with no meals. We ate a great deal of cottage cheese. When Theo took me to dinner, we went to San Francisco, to Italian or Chinese restaurants; i ate as much as i could, to make up for the rest of the week. One night he took me to the 'international settlement' in the heart of North Beach, to an all-black striptease show. I watched the women moving to the music with grace and sensuality. The white men in the audience drank endless scotches and leered. The 'literati,' in the meantime, back from the Paris cafés, were taking themselves very seriously on Grant Avenue, a few blocks away.

At the dorm, there was much talk about sex. Clea was considered a great expert, highly regarded, because she had actually slept with a man, a man she loved, of course. Most of the girls said they believed in 'preserving themselves' for their husbands, but there was a great deal of leeway, short of going 'all the way'; the discussions were highly technical, lacking in erotic content. When we were alone, speaking Italian, i asked her to describe to me what it felt like to make love. She said it hurt a little the first time, but that if you feel passion it is a pleasurable kind of pain. She used words like 'overwhelmed,' 'tenderness,' 'languor' to describe the experience. I had noticed a subtle kind of difference in her demeanor which i began to attribute to her loss of virginity. She seemed more sure of herself, more poised, i told her.

—I know, i think i can always tell a virgin from a non-virgin. I think some of the girls here are lying, i am pretty sure Linda, for example, has gone all the way ... They just won't admit it.

—How can you tell?

—Oh, you can tell by their eyes— and she gave me her sweet, special-friend smile.

I was interested in these discussions because my own virginity was beginning to weigh on me. Theo had traveled with a woman, Clea had had a passionate, tragic love affair, while i ... There had been Sandy, of course; Clea thought he qualified since he had painted my portrait, and Frederick, whom she thought very handsome, but there was more to life than that and i was ready. I was beginning to think i would have to go back to Europe where romance was still romantic. I decided i would not save myself for my husband and in any event there was not going to be a husband, not for a long time at least. Marriage was a trap. I wanted to travel, to work,

to enjoy myself, to have a career even, and none of those
things seemed possible if i were to get married. I was scared
of sleeping with a man, scared that it would hurt, scared of
getting pregnant, scared of the unknown. But i was preparing.
"Don't be scared, be prepared" was a refrain i had heard at
the "Hungry i" one night, and i adopted it.

—If you have enough information and if you know the
man well enough, there is very little danger— Clea said with
the voice of experience.

—What kind of information do you mean?— i asked.

—Oh, you know, how not to get pregnant . . .

—How did you do it?

—Well, with us, he always pulled out just before . . .

—And how is that, doesn't that spoil it?

—Oh, no, it's just a little messy— and she laughed.

—Did you ever taste it?— i asked, bringing the conversation
to an area i knew something about. —I didn't like it much.

—If you truly love the man, it tastes good, if not, it
doesn't. That's the test of true love. It's natural, after all! I
would never do that for a man just to please him, would
you?— Clea asked.

—No, of course not! I was just curious. It's not too bad,
actually, but i prefer caviar . . .

We both realized we didn't know much about what Americans called birth control. We decided to read up on it. The
rhythm method sounded too unsafe and the diaphragm, well,
we just weren't ready for it. Condoms were the best solution,
we agreed; that way 'they' could worry about it!

—Did you ever do it while menstruating?

—That's the best time, then you needn't worry. Of course i
was lucky, not all men like it when you're bleeding— Clea
answered.

—But does it feel good, all the same?

—Yes! And it's very good for cramps!

That was interesting to me: my menstrual cycles preoccupied me. I would feel my body get fuller, and slowly, as
the blood started flowing, i felt slower, more internal. On

those days i walked around with a feeling of private jubila-
tion. Even the cramps felt rewarding. I would lie down and
close my eyes to better sense the churning inside of me. It
was like a powerful mechanism teaching me something
about myself; it was a feeling of expansion.

—You should really keep a diary. When i am menstruating,
i find it is important for me to write down my thoughts, i
seem to have much to write about on those days. And if you
kept a diary of *your* menstrual thoughts we would truly be
blood sisters— Clea suggested.

And so it was agreed.

I decided to try to graduate that year, by taking language
exams for credit. In Italian and French literature courses i
had an advantage over other students who struggled with the
language while i could concentrate on the form. I read the
*Divine Comedy* and liked the 'Inferno' section especially. The
problem of good and evil seemed basic to the human
dilemma. This dichotomy made me uneasy but i didn't know
why. I didn't believe in hell and paradise, but they seemed to
be useful metaphors; it was freeing to think of them in a
literary sense. Something like that was operating in the
world, after all: the war had been over now for several years,
and evil still reigned; it was part of the human condition, it
seemed. I was eager to start real life, i wanted to finish school
to plunge into it.

We spent our university vacations at home. My parents had
moved into a large Spanish-type old house in Pacific Grove,
surrounded by trees. They treated Clea like a member of the
family and that made me happy. She always said that they
were 'good' people and that i should be more understanding
about their sadness over losing their home and having to
emigrate. My father did seem sad: he was having some difficulties with his colleagues at the Army Language School;
they considered him disloyal to the royalist government in
exile and voiced such opinions more freely as the anti-

240

communist purge started to spread. Omama, on the other hand, clearly was also not faring well: she had lost much of her memory and could not learn to orient herself in her new surroundings. She would go out on the street and not be able to find her way home. The police brought her back more than once.

—She is getting senile— my mother would say.

—She is just disoriented— my father would try to explain —she will learn, we must be patient.

—But can't you see that she doesn't remember what happened yesterday? She should go to a home. Life is impossible with her . . .

And so arguments over Omama continued. My father felt he would be betraying his mother by locking her up in an old-age home. It's a son's duty to take care of his mother in her old age. On the other hand, he could see how difficult life with Omama was for my mother. As usual, he was caught between his two women. I sided with my mother. More and more, we were able to talk to each other as friends. She had accepted much of her life with great courage. She learned to drive, she learned to deal with supermarkets and laundromats:

—In America you have to be able to read in order to buy food. That shows that it has a high literacy rate. You can't see the food, of course, all you see is boxes, but it is highly hygienic.

—The literacy rate is only high in some areas, in the South there is still a great deal of poverty and plenty of people who can't read— i would tell her.

I tried to share with her some of my newly acquired knowledge about the social injustices of our new land. But anything that sounded 'communist' made her very nervous. McCarthy's voice was being heard with greater and greater frequency. The Korean war raged on.

I was more and more in a hurry to graduate: i wanted to go back to Europe. I needed to get out of school to work and save money so that i could go back. In Europe i could clarify what i wanted to do with my life. I obtained a full year's credit by taking exams in various languages. It looked like i would be able to graduate by the end of the year. Clea, too, was making good progress at school. She spoke English fluently, with a 'cute' accent, as the girls at the dorms said. My accent was almost gone. They said it sounded like an affectation. That piqued me. There were certain sounds i could not pronounce correctly, no matter how much i tried, mostly 'o' sounds—words like 'sew,' 'precocious,' 'Lois' . . .

My last semester at Cal was arduous. I started the day by working the breakfast shift at the restaurant from seven to nine, then classes, then the lunch shift, afternoon classes, the dinner shift and then home or to the library to study. I liked the contrast between these activities: moving as fast as possible with greasy food lined up on plates along my arm, yelling out orders of 'eggs over easy,' in contrast to the lectures i would listen to in class on Paolo and Francesca, the adulterers condemned to burn in hell throughout eternity . . . At night i would lie in bed, my feet aching, talking with Clea about our friendship, about sex, about what life was going to mean for us. We agreed that we had to plan it carefully. We started by planning, in the immediate future, a trip through the South. Clea was going back to Italy and we decided to see something of the United States before she left.

—But i don't have the money— i said. —If i work all summer and live at home, at best i can save enough for a trip on the bus. You could travel in much greater luxury than that!

—But Micetta, i don't care about luxury, it will be interesting for me to go on the bus with you; that way we'll meet local people and see the country from close up. Let's do it!

And so it was agreed. The Korean war, in the meantime, was coming to an end. There was promise in the air.

I went to the graduation ceremonies, along with 11,000 other graduates, wearing a cap and gown. My parents were there and so was Braco. He had just arrived in California for the summer.

—This must not be such a good university if they let you out at eighteen . . .— he said.

—Ani is turning into an intellectual, just watch— my father conciliated.

Clea gave me a warm hug and whispered:

—I am proud of you, Micetta, life is going to be good, you'll see.

I was wearing the bracelet she had given me when i left Rome. It had brought me luck, i told her. My mother said:

—Let's go celebrate! Ani has a B.A. now and we are all reunited, the whole family, except for Baki, Dida and Vito, but that will come soon!

We sang Italian and Yugoslav songs all the way home.

That summer i worked in a glass company, saving my money for our trip across country. I was in charge of orders for new installations. It was rather interesting, better than my waitress or sales jobs. I was the only woman there and the men, coming in from their jobs to pick up new assignments, were jovial in a rough sort of way. They swore, exchanged crude jokes with each other and then turned to me and excused themselves; they treated me with care.

—Wow, did i have a good house-call today . . .— one of them said one day. —I ring the bell and this lady, see, opens the door, in her housecoat, unbuttoned halfway, ready for action . . . "I am the glass man, i am here to fix your window," i says to her, pretending not to notice her boobs. "C'mon in," she says; "would you like a cup of coffee before you start? I just made a fresh pot . . ." A cup of coffee her ass! So i go in and . . .

—Hey, watch your language, buddy, there are ladies present!— said the boss. They both laughed. I went on with my filing, pretending not to be listening.

—I am just joking, Anita— he pronounced my new name as if it were spelled with a 'd' —don't you go taking this talk seriously! I am a family man, you know that, you saw my missus with the new baby the other day . . .

When i went home at night i told Clea my work anecdotes. She, in the meantime, was spending her days reading, going to the beaches with Frederick, writing letters. Frederick was eager to show Clea around. We had discussed her seeing him without me and we decided that of course there could be no jealousy between us: our friendship came first, we could even share men if it came to that.

—But i wouldn't let him kiss me— she said.

—You can, it's all right with me, then we can discuss it . . . Did he try?— i asked.

—Of course not!— she exclaimed in mock outrage.

Clea helped my mother with the housework and sometimes even prepared some of the meals, which were always very 'balanced,' my mother would point out:

—The Swiss know a lot about nutrition— she said. Clea agreed.

They discussed the pros and cons of frozen vegetables.

—They lose some of their vitamins when they are frozen— Clea said—i learned that at school. (She had attended finishing school in Switzerland.)

—Yes, but look how much easier life is— my mother answered —i save an hour by not having to shell the peas . . . And they pick the best vegetables for the frozen industry, i understand.

Braco was there too, for the summer, reading the newspaper. He thought the cold war was progressing well, we were reaching an entente with the Soviets; of course McCarthy was somewhat excessive, but one had to be firm . . .

At night Frederick and i would go out with Braco and Clea; we double-dated. After the movies we often went to the beach. One night as we were sitting in the car, watching the waves in the moonlight, i realized that Clea and Braco were kissing in the back seat. Frederick and i got out and went for a walk to be discreet.

—It gives me a strange feeling— i said to Frederick.

—Why, what's wrong with it? Don't be a prude!

There was nothing wrong with it, he just didn't understand. It was one thing for my best friend to be friendly with my boy-friend, but with my brother, i just wasn't prepared. I decided to talk to Clea about it:

—How does he kiss?— i asked her. There was something very daring about this situation. I liked that.

—Pretty well, really quite well— she answered.

I was surprised. I felt a little closer to Clea.

# 8

On the day of our departure i had two hundred dollars in my pocket in traveler's checks, plus a Greyhound bus ticket to New York. We had planned our trip so we would travel at night to save money on hotel rooms, and sightsee during the day. Our first stop was Los Angeles, where Theodore was meeting us; he was spending the summer at home with his parents and he had offered to show us around Hollywood. He put us up at the "Garden of Allah" along with the other aspiring movie stars ... He drove us to Santa Monica, to Muscle Beach. We looked at the men exercising, lifting weights, bronzed, bulging Apollos ... We decided they weren't for us. Theodore's mother invited us to lunch and served a lavish platter of multicolored exotic fruit cut into bite-sized pieces. We toured a film studio and saw them make rain over a Mexican village. We also saw Deborah Kerr, filming a scene over and over again, a one-minute sequence, with great poise and patience. It seemed a humiliating experience: the director would interrupt right in the middle of a sentence and shout out: "Take it over!" without any explanation. He called her 'honey' ... Clea and i decided it was a profession we wouldn't be suited for anyway.

One night when we went to bed in our double bed at the "Garden of Allah," we talked about *us:*

—Have you ever thought of making love to a girl?

—I just thought of it since we have been staying here, never before.

We were lying in bed, our bodies touching slightly.

—I thought of it also, but i think it is best if we decide against it.

—Yes, you are right, but i am glad you brought it up— i said; —i felt strange thinking about it and not telling you.

—But, Micetta, we can tell each other everything, don't forget!

We kissed each other good night and turned over, back to back, and went to sleep.

The rest of the trip was very tiring: we'd had no sense of the vastness of the United States. We traveled for hours and hours on straight highways without seeing a single house. We were surprised by the uncultivated expanses, by the flatness, by the light. Our co-travelers were Mexicans, mostly men looking for jobs, some with families, beautiful women with small children on their laps; their skins were golden, their eyes deep and peaceful. They were friendly to us and shared their food, tortillas sprinkled with hot sauce. We wore pedal pushers. When we arrived in Dallas we suddenly became aware, while walking on the streets, that people were staring at us. We noticed that women didn't wear pants on the streets. It was a sinister city: a man told us with some pride that Dallas had the highest crime rate in the country. While waiting for a city bus, i looked at a beautiful baby in her mother's arms. I smiled and the baby smiled back. I went over to touch her hand. The mother moved away, without looking. They were Negroes . . . Racial tension was in the air, imperceptible, thick, unmistakable. We were shocked by the 'colored/white' signs over the bathroom doors.

As we traveled further south, the division between blacks and whites became more pronounced: in New Orleans we were told at the travelers' information booth not to go into the 'colored' section. We didn't pay much attention to such advice but we did go to our room before nine o'clock at night; the streets didn't feel safe. As we walked around the French Quarter, even in the daytime, deep, sad sounds of jazz filled the air. We agreed that we would come back one day, with a man . . .

We had our clothes laundered in "clean-while-you-wait" establishments, near the bus stations. We would go into a dressing room, hand over our pants and wait; then minutes later they would hand us our clothes, washed and starched. The pants legs were glued together by the steam and as we put them on we could hear them unsticking, like tearing paper. They were pressed through huge steamers which puffed big gusts of vapor into the shop. We peeked through the curtain in awe:

—You have to admit that America is really quite a country. Where else would you find such a place?— Clea remarked. She was getting sad at the thought of leaving.

—You only see the good side— i said.

—That's not true! The practical side of life is very well organized here. I always tell you that the affective life ['la vita affettiva,' she said in Italian with great emphasis] is greatly lacking: i don't think they hug and cuddle their children enough, as an example.

When we arrived in Jacksonville we were told that there were tornadoes in Miami. We decided to skip Florida; we were getting anxious to be in a city with familiar people. In New York we were going to meet Braco and Baki and Dida; i was looking forward to seeing them. They sounded lonely in New York and i thought our visit would cheer them up. Our suitcases had been sent to Miami before we changed our plans so that our first week in New York we had nothing to wear but our same old tired pedal pushers; but in New York it didn't matter, people seemed to dress any way they wanted; women walked around on the streets with their hair up in curlers and everyone wore pants, men, women and children. Generally people were dressed in a sloppy, casual manner as if they didn't notice what they put on as they got up in the morning.

The night of our arrival Braco greeted us and took us to see *From Here to Eternity* in Times Square. The line wound around the block when we arrived. We stood there, looking at the man smoking the Camel, blowing vapor rings into the night air, at the animated crowds, at the ornate plaster facade of the theater. Inside, the walls were red, imitation tapestry, with gold glittering from the ceiling. When Montgomery Clift appeared on the screen mumbling "If a man don't go his own way, he's nothin'," his face was larger than usual, more immediate: the screen was the largest i had ever seen. The film seemed simplistic in its attitude toward war, but the sex scenes were quite good, we thought.

Baki and Dida looked older, more frail than the last time i had seen them. They were living in a very small walk-up apartment on the upper West Side. The staircase was dirty and the apartment was furnished with recovered furniture. They greeted us cheerfully: Baki had made stuffed peppers and the table was laid out festively, with 'real' napkins. We placed the flowers Clea brought in a vase in the middle. This was a special occasion, we all felt it. Dida looked thinner, his eyes were sunken. He couldn't get a job and that made him feel useless, old. My grandmother was taking in some sewing, earning a few dollars here and there. She sat in her chair, giving orders to my grandfather:

—Just make sure the dishes aren't greasy before you put them on the table— and then, turning to me, she would add:

—He washes the dishes, yes, but they don't come out clean. What can i do? The streets are not paved with gold here, after all . . . But we can't complain, we have enough to eat, we are healthy, and now we are all together. Come, sit next to me, Ani, i want to hear everything. Tell me about your mother, how is she, about your father, how is his job, about Omama . . . Start by describing your house and then we will go from there.

After cooking the meal, Baki always liked to sit down and talk. She said her job was done now, the maid was off for the rest of the evening. The cleaning up was up to the men. Vito was there, a stranger to me, assisting his father. Braco was a 'guest,' not expected to participate. As i described our life in California her eyes filled with tears:

—Ah, who knows if i'll ever see it . . .

—Of course you will!— i protested, —you are going to come, both of you, and have a nice vacation!

—With God's help! Right now, my dear Ani, i can only think far enough to cover our next meal . . . But tell me more: how much do you pay rent, how much does a pound of potatoes cost in California?

Her questions were precise: she wanted to know about the climate, about my father's job, how mother managed without help in the house.

—Of course here everything is so much easier, they have such good machines to help the housewives!— She was happy to be in America, ready to see the good side.

—They have a club here, for us, the Jewish ladies come and make coffee and serve it to us with cakes. They treat us very nicely. They know what we have been through . . . They try to make it nice for us, to help us forget.

—Yes, but they don't invite you to their homes, do they?— i said.

—I didn't invite refugees to my house either when i was in Sarajevo! I should have, but i didn't. I didn't know how it felt to be homeless. They don't know either, they don't know who i am, that i won't steal from them . . .

As Clea's departure date approached, we spent more and more time making plans for our next reunion:

—Now it's your turn to come to Rome— she said.

—I will, i promise. This is my plan: i will go back to California, then i am going to get a job, a real job, and save money to come to Europe. I need to see Italy again!

—Yes, you haven't had a 'maritozzo alla panna' in a long time . . .— she answered, conjuring up memories for us both of cakes brimming with whipped cream eaten on the way back from the lycée.

Then Frederick arrived: he had decided to join us in New

York. He came by plane and suggested that he and i go back to California together in a car which he would pick up for his parents in Detroit. That way both his parents and we would save some money. It was comforting to see him; he started taking the initiative, organizing sightseeing trips for Clea to the Empire State Building, on the Staten Island Ferry, to Lindy's for cheesecake. Since this was her first visit to New York, she had to see everything. When it came to visiting the Statue of Liberty i told them to go without me.

That night when Frederick and Clea came back to the rooming house where we were staying, they came into the room Clea and i were sharing. I was half asleep. Lying on my bed, not wanting to wake up, i heard them whispering; they were sitting on Clea's bed, on the other side of the room. They didn't turn the lights on. For a while all was quiet. I opened my eyes and looked in their direction; i could distinguish their silhouettes lying next to each other. A ray of neon light was shining on them through the cracked dark-green shade. "They are kissing each other," i said to myself. I was quite awake by then. I wasn't sure what my reaction was, but i knew that it was going to be all right. It felt strange to be there, while they were kissing, unaware of my being awake. "Should i let them know?" i wondered. "No, of course not, i would just interrupt them, embarrassing us all," i answered to myself. "But i *am* feeling a little jealous . . ." "So what? a little jealousy never hurt anyone! They are both close to me, they both love me, so why can't they love each other a little?" The internal dialogue went on until i fell asleep. In the morning, Clea told me right away what had happened.

—Nothing can separate us . . .— i said.

I could see that she was relieved. Life was becoming complicated, adult, interesting.

When the day of her departure came, Frederick and i took Clea to the boat. She had a nice second-class cabin on the *Leonardo da Vinci,* a brand-new ocean liner. We visited the ship, looking at the mosaic murals. We all pretended to be cheerful. She, as usual, whispered some delicious words as we parted:

—Don't worry, Micetta, one way or another we'll get you to Europe soon!

We waved our handkerchiefs to her for a long time, until the boat disappeared through the grey New York harbor. I thought of our arrival to that same harbor four years earlier: it looked quite different to me, standing there next to Frederick, on the eve of our departure across the United States together.

We went to Baki's for dinner before our departure. She made 'pastel,' the meat pie she knew i liked, her specialty; she also made a Serbian salad—green peppers, onions, tomatoes and cucumbers, cut into small pieces. My grandfather made us sandwiches for our trip and they both gave me kisses for my mother. Dida looked grave.

—We'll be reunited soon, don't worry— i reassured him.

He nodded. As we got on the bus, on our way to Detroit, i sighed with relief at the prospect of days without schedules, open space.

# 9

When Maja was born we had a three-room apartment and i put her in a laundry basket, nicely outfitted with pillows, and since i didn't have any help to take the child out, i used to put her out in the courtyard and my mother-in-law would sit and watch this child . . . When Maja was born i was glad it was a girl; i preferred a girl to a boy. When Vito was born i was very dissatisfied; i wanted a female because a girl, when she gets married, stays with the mother and the male forgets.

I had a long and difficult labor with your mother: the midwife was there and Dida, but they didn't help me at all. The labor pains came on and they just kept getting stronger and stronger; the midwife just waited until the child started coming out, she didn't tell me how to breathe or anything; she didn't know about that. She told me to be patient: "It will come soon, it will come soon." But the child didn't come for a long time . . . the child didn't come until dawn. Then they bathed the child. It wasn't customary to call a doctor, so a doctor didn't come. But later a specialist in Zagreb to whom i complained that i have to go the bathroom all the time said: "When you gave birth to the child you tore a little and she didn't know how to sew you up." And that is why i have had that problem for years, not just now . . .

After the child was born she lay in the same bed as me and i nursed her. I had a cook and a maid and they helped me. We were very happy, but i didn't know how to nurse, how much and so on. When the child cried my mother said, "Give her to drink, give her to drink," and the child drank too much and then she would throw up. The child cried a lot. I worked with Dida in the store, so i said that we should come to an agreement: until twelve at night i would watch her, after twelve he would watch her. We made the agreement, but after twelve he didn't want to get up to hold the child so i had to. He said: "For my shift, let her cry." So i was often angry about that.

I nursed her some six or seven months and then i started her on a bottle. Cow's milk, boiled. The bottles needed to be washed in a special way and the nipples also; it was very complicated. When i was nursing they told me that i should drink a lot of beer, that from beer you get milk, but all that didn't help, i got fat and the child didn't have enough milk.

I told you that Dida had big ears and when Maja was a baby she started to get the same ears so i bought a special little hat at the apothecary's to hold the ears in all the time. Then, listen to our ignorance: we put the children on their feet too early and you can see on the picture, mother has slightly crooked legs, so the doctor told me we stood her up too early. There was this four-wheel cart and at nine months we put her in it and the poor thing couldn't stand up and she got bow-legged. The doctor prescribed salt baths and that helped so nicely that we started going to the seashore; every summer we went to the seashore. Your mother, as a baby, had been so sick that the doctor said that she wouldn't survive. I held the child like this and she would vomit from one end and make from the other end. I don't know what it was, maybe i nursed her when i was already pregnant; her stomach was always upset.

When Vito was born Maja was so jealous she wouldn't go out to the park; instead, she sat there. In those days we used to lie in bed for eight days, fourteen sometimes. And so i was lying in bed and mother would sit there, all dressed nicely, and wouldn't go to the park and when people came to visit it was like that, she sat over there and i lay over here. She was a year and some older than Vito.

In the meantime, Dida was going to the store so he wasn't with the children very much, but later when i also started going to the store the children would come to visit us at the store with the maid. Every day. That was the same for you and Braco when you were little. The first thing was to go to the store, then onward. The children went to the park every day with the maid. In those days they used to have their bath in the morning, not at night. At night they would sit with us at the table, eat and go to sleep. It was different when i was small, then the children ate separately; we sat on the floor around a low table and that's how we ate.

On Saturdays we all went to Nona's, my mother's, house, that was known, every Saturday and on holidays. There was always a big table at Nona's and all of us brothers and sisters with our families would go. We were all there together. Some of the men didn't get along with each other and this one and that one wouldn't talk to one another. They had differences over their work, one would be doing better than the other and so he was envious. The family grew so much that on holidays my mother had thirty-six people at the table: the sons, the daughters-in-law, the grandchildren, the brothers-in-law ... But the dinners were difficult because the sons-in-law didn't get along. My mother always said: "I don't feel well if they don't get along; if they are all satisfied then i am satisfied, but it pains me to see them not getting along."

She cooked Sephardic, she cooked very nicely. If it was Pessach she cooked matzoh balls, then she cooked chicken or lamb and we read the Seder. For New Year's everybody would go there to kiss her hand or to wish her a happy new year. For Yom Kippur it is customary to go, to ask forgiveness for the sins and so we all went to have our sins forgiven, all of us brothers and sisters, we ... we didn't quarrel, but the men did. The late Dida didn't quarrel with anybody because he didn't need anything from them.

I got along with all my sisters, we saw each other, we did. Other than sisters we didn't have time for friends. Every day i went to the store and then at night i went home, dead tired, to sleep and in the morning up early to work. But Dida had a friend, one friend, and we were always together; his wife and i were good acquaintances, but we didn't talk "my husband this, my mother this, or this ..." we talked about ... women's things, but we didn't talk if something was wrong. Every Sunday we would meet with my husband's friend and his wife, they were unusually good friends.

Dida didn't see much of his family, but his mother lived with us until she died. She minded the children. The old woman was a little senile so i left the children, locked the door of the apartment because she sometimes would go out and leave the door open, like your children, and i locked her up until noon. They had food, they had the bathroom, they had water, they had everything. She was old, she must have been seventy-five or eighty.

When i lived with my mother-in-law it was often hard for me, so i went to complain to my mother that it isn't easy for me, so my mother said to me: "My dear daughter, accept your mother-in-law. i had old Nona who was very sick and she was incontinent and i had to bathe her, wash her, everything ... She helps you, be patient because of the husband," and then i went back and i was much closer to my mother-in-law. My mother said that i should respect her and then i went back and respected her more.

Dida's father left her with the children and no one knows what happened to him. There was Dida's sister, Vito and Maja were very fond of her, but i, like all crazy women, didn't get along with the sister-in-law. What woman gets along with her sister-in-law? I used to see her, but i didn't like her. Dida was very fond of his sister, he loved her very much. She was bright, a hard worker, clean, neat. In her house it was as if they had a lot of servants, but all they had was someone to come in every day to wash the dishes. She was older than Dida; he had two other sisters, but one was in Vienna and one was in Caljina. We didn't see them, i didn't know them. He saw the one in Vienna, whenever he went to buy he would go to see her. When she got married she went to Vienna and she converted, she hid the fact that she was Jewish and there, as a Catholic, she survived through Hitler, nobody knew about her, she hid it a lot. She had daughters and she had a son, they are all alive. Dida had a brother who also converted and left them; he was in Sarajevo, but he never talked to him again nor to his mother ... Dida was very angry with his brother because he left the mother. The brother left the mother and converted and lived separately. The priest who converted the brother called on the mother to convert, but she didn't want to, she wasn't religious, but she didn't want to convert. The Jew was not the same as the Catholic. This probably didn't sit right with him, they were educated, modern ... Like now, for instance, the English and the Irish, they don't get along.

When we got married Dida accepted my family, he loved my mother very much. My mother was very intelligent and she adored Dida; he was very good, very generous. When he started going to Vienna, after my mother stopped wearing the 'feredza' [Turkish dress] and started wearing a silk kerchief fitted around the skull shaped like a cap with dukats hanging all around on the forehead, this silk kerchief Dida always brought from Vienna. He brought a meter of this silk—the women liked them with a design of large branches—and she would make three shawls out of that: she would keep one for the holidays and sell one so she earned some money and the third she gave to a good friend; i don't know who she gave it to, but it was a big gift.

Dida loved her very much. Dida was generous. When my parents came back to Sarajevo they were no longer well off, my father was already old, so each of us gave something every month for them to live on. My husband said to me when i told him that i wanted to give to my father: "You give, i don't want to know how much you give." And so i too gave. They had enough to live on, they had a good apartment, a maid; there was always a girl from the village or from the poorer families in the cities . . .

He was among the better off . . . and among the more generous. He had a very good nature, for the family and for others. He gave anybody what he could. He loved the family and he liked helping others. He put three or four people on their feet, people who wanted to start a store and didn't have the money, he lent it to them, to get started. One man divorced his wife and wanted to move from Sarajevo to Vienna and he came to tell Dida how in Vienna he could have a very good existence but that he didn't have the money to go to Vienna. "How much do you need?" He opened the drawer and gave him the money. The man left for Vienna the very same evening.

If my sisters needed some help they came to Dida, they didn't come to me, i had no rights . . . I liked helping poor people where it wasn't known that i was helping. There was a woman who came to knead dough for us for the winter, egg-barley, noodles and so on, and she asked me to lend her three hundred dinars. Naturally i gave it to her without any problems. Then i had a maid who didn't know how to read or write. There was a night school at six o'clock so i said to her to go and learn to read and write. Then there was another girl, a Sephardic girl, a relative of mine, who was working for me, so i hired a teacher for her to come to the house to learn to read and write . . . to at least know how to write her name. I couldn't watch people, women, who didn't know how to read and write. I liked to help like that, i wasn't gallant, but i liked to help in things like that.

Your mother was Dida's 'favorita.' I was sorry that Dida didn't love Vito as much as Maja, that bothered me, but we gave them both all the best. They didn't fight much, but once mother put Vito in a wicker basket, like the one you have in the children's room, and she sat on top of it. Poor Vito, he almost suffocated. Vito was always lower rank than Maja, she thought she was higher than Vito. Maja was first in the house and Vito second . . . Both children went to Serbo-Croatian schools and they did very well. When they were older, Dida bought a piano in Vienna and they started studying the piano, they played tennis and they studied languages, English and German. In those days, children were prepared for intelligence, it wasn't asked of children that they help in the house, or something, because all the better houses had a maid . . .

Dida thought that commercial school was better for Vito than the 'gymnasium' because then Vito would come into the store. He went to commercial school for two years and he was very unhappy because it was less interesting than 'gymnasium' and so he went back and did so well that he finished four years of 'gymnasium' in two. Then Vito wanted to study pharmacy but Dida said: "Here is a livelihood all set up and there is no point in his studying something else when here is a ready-made business. The store is here, it is going well and the son has to take over the store." And he came to take over the store, but he wasn't interested in it. Others thought that the child wasn't right, that he has to be introduced to the store so that he can take over.

I was in favor of his studying. The same with mother. When she graduated, i said: "Maja, you can go to Vienna and study what you like." But in the meantime she started talking to your father and she didn't feel like going to Vienna, rather she stayed in Sarajevo. Tata [daddy] thought she should study law but she didn't want to study law and she didn't study it.

# 10

Traveling with Frederick was quite different from traveling with Clea: he took the situation in hand, he read maps, decided on our itinerary, did most of the driving; he had crossed the country before, he was at home in America. With Clea, we mostly decided as we went along, changing our plans at the last minute, laughing together when we missed a bus. It was easier to travel through the North than the South, the customs were more familiar to us, and it was definitely easier to travel with a man; people seemed to approve, while with two young women alone on the road, the shopkeepers, the hotel keepers, the bus drivers all looked uneasy.

We picked up Frederick's parents' car in Detroit, a brand-new baby-blue Pontiac, and drove to Chicago. The city had an openness that surprised me pleasantly: large, well-kept parks, an enormous expanse of lake and a wonderful museum full of luscious Renoirs and rich Cézannes. I thought of Sandy briefly with nostalgia. Frederick and i spent nights in motels, sharing the same room to save money. We slept close together, chaste. We took long sensual showers, kissing and touching each other under the warm spray, until the bathroom floor was flooded. We piled towels into the puddles. I had decided to return home intact, possibly to prove to myself and to my parents that 'i was mistress of my emotions.' I wrote a postcard in Reno, addressed to my mother and father, in Serbo-Croatian: "Still a virgin. We'll be home on Tuesday. Kisses, Ani."

Frederick showed me the splendor of Colorado, the mining towns, the salt flats in Nevada. He was eager to show me his land, he was tired of all this talk about Europe, how everything was better there; with Clea and me together for a whole year he had had enough. The American in him really came out, inspired by the natural beauty of the landscape:

—We should camp out, sleep under the stars, breathe the pure air.— He was getting lyrical.

—No thank you— i answered —you can do that with your cowgirls . . .

I had a facility for making remarks that i immediately regretted. That was a stupid thing to say. I imagined that sleeping outside with the moon shining on my face would be wonderful, but i was scared and so i acted superior. The rest of the trip was uneventful.

When we returned to Monterey i decided it was time to 'go all the way.' Nineteen was definitely too old to still be a virgin . . . Now that i had proven to myself that i could travel across country with a man, even sleep with him, without succumbing, i was ready to go ahead. Frederick lived in a little cottage adjacent to his parents' house where we often spent time together, listening to music, reading to each other; he would declaim his poems, his plays to me, i would read him Baudelaire, Rimbaud in French . . .

One day, having returned to his quarters after a day at the beach, we showered and wrapped his large, brilliantly colored bath towels around our suntanned bodies.

—Let's put on Ravel's *Bolero!*— i said.

—Okay.— he answered with a mixture of embarrassment and excitement: he knew something was up.

—Let's dance— i suggested.

Frederick liked to dance to 'good' music. He felt that classical music needn't be considered sacred, that one can relate to it with one's body just as well as with one's mind. My strawberry-colored bath towel was precariously tucked in over my breasts. My feet were bare. As the music started to gather momentum so did we. He moved more emphatically than i, taking large leaps, swaying his arms, contorting his face. I was tempted to laugh but decided i should hold back that impulse if i wanted my plan to work. As the tempo of the music mounted, i felt my movements increasing in energy. My heart was pounding. "I wonder if this is what they call 'sexual arousal'?" i asked myself. Frederick's eyes, darker than usual, were staring at me. I closed mine. Then, suddenly, everything changed: colors appeared before me, light greens fusing with oranges and yellows, sinuously, like liquids, like electricity. The music became significant, intimate. It entered me. A strange sensation of flowing warmth permeated my body from the inside, centered around my bellybutton. My towel had fallen off. I was dancing naked with a naked man, feeling at ease, natural, "like an animal," i remember thinking. Then i touched his body with mine and we danced to each other's rhythm. The tempo was mounting still. Our bellies felt hot together, his slightly crouched, level with mine. We kissed. Our tongues touched. I put my arms around him and led him to the bed. He lay on top of me. He was trembling. I touched his penis. It was hard, springy. I guided it toward me. It met with some resistance.

—Am i hurting you?— he asked.

—A little, but it's all right.— I wished he would move in with decision.

He swayed in and out gently, in time to the music.

—Just push it in!— i commanded.

And so he did. The pain was sharp. I swallowed.

—Are you okay?

—Fine, fine . . .— I wished he wouldn't keep asking me.

Then he went in and out three times and came. I opened my eyes. His face was covered with sweat. He lay on his back, next to me. I ran my fingers through the hair on his chest and smiled.

Having accomplished phase one of my plan, i started

concentrating on phase two: finding a job to save enough money to go back to Europe. Standing in line at the employment office, filling out forms and sitting on benches waiting for interviews, i questioned myself: "Do i feel different? Am i a 'real' woman now?" I did feel different, lighter, but the sensations in my body hadn't changed. I knew that what i had done made me feel more adult, but there was another step yet to reach: passion.

Jobs were scarce. The people standing in line talked about recession, depression, war economy. There were those who believed that the country needed armed conflicts to stay economically healthy. Now that we were pulling out of Korea the jobless ranks were swelling. "How can war be healthy?" i wondered. I went to many interviews. How many words a minute could i type? How did i feel about filing? Was i planning to get married?

Finally i was sent to the telephone company. They had a training program for 'service representatives': the job involved talking to people on the telephone, taking orders for new installations and disconnections. They hired me because i said i liked people. "What a funny question," i thought to myself when the interviewer asked me that from her 'interview control' form. "Are there actually people who don't like people?"

I was enrolled in a six-week training program. After mastering the forms for ordering new telephones, moving a service to a new address or disconnecting, we started learning something called 'responsive listening.' This was a technique which consisted of listening to the customer and seizing the opportunity, when it arose in the course of their monologue, to suggest that they install an extra extension in their house. We would be rated on the number of extensions we sold each month, as well as on our manners. We were encouraged to assume a sugary tone of voice.

—If the customer says 'thank you,' immediately answer 'you're welcome'— they taught us —no matter how many times it comes up in the course of the conversation. A 'thank you' that goes without its 'you're welcome' is like a hat without a head. Besides, don't forget, you are being listened to and if you forget the whole office score goes down.

The other trainees and i were sitting in a room around a long table with dummy phones at our sides on which we practiced the situation the instructor set up for us. She explained that in each office there was a service observer spot-checking the calls for 'courtesy.'

—We are a public utility. Courtesy is of the utmost importance. Let's take this call over again and start cheerfully: "Miss Jones speaking, may i help you?" Let your voice rise at the end. We can help put our customer in a good mood. Okay, girls; ready?

—What's the matter, Anili?— my mother asked after my first day at work —don't you want to eat? I made roast chicken and mashed potatoes, your favorite dish!

—Oh, it's good, i am just not very hungry . . .

—You'll get used to it, the first day is always hard— she said, trying to comfort me.

After dinner, i went straight to bed and plunged into *Brave New World*. I had just discovered Huxley. He seemed to speak directly to me. His vision of modern society, while couched in futurism, seemed remarkably realistic. I missed the university context in which to discuss such issues.

My life had assumed a definite structure: i went to work every day from eight-thirty in the morning until five o'clock at night. Every other week i received a check for $87.55. At work i sat at a desk and filled out endless forms, answered innumerable telephone calls. I took coffee breaks at prescribed hours, ten and three. If i stayed more than ten minutes the supervisor pointed it out to me, very pleasantly. The lunch hour was eleven, twelve or one; we took turns. I wondered how people could stand to spend their whole lives in this manner. I watched the order-typist for clues: she had been performing her job for twenty years; she wore her service pin with pride. She was planning to retire soon. She seemed cheerful, healthy, involved in her typewriter; there were no signs of discontent in her demeanor. She fascinated me.

The office manager was a watery-eyed man who leered at the young girls, over his newspaper. One day i went to him to ask him whether i should adjust a customer's bill as she had requested. He looked up at me from his desk and said:

—Go ahead, don't be a Jew about it!

As i walked back to my chair i realized that he meant 'don't be stingy.' I regretted not having said something back to him. Repartee was not my forte, but i made a mental note to begin developing it.

In the company lounge, the conversation veered around marriage prospects, hair products, dress sales. I found it easy to participate in these discussions almost by rote, but they left me restless, dissatisfied. Everyone smoked. Filter cigarettes had just come out. They were more 'feminine' than the shorter, non-filter ones, everyone agreed. There was one woman, however, who was different from the others. Her name was Marion. She was slim and tall, with deep green eyes and light brown hair. She wore pleated skirts and sweaters with Peter Pan blouses underneath. She had a seriousness about her that the others lacked. She liked to talk about books. She too had gone to Cal and there, she told me, had developed a taste for literature and music. She seemed quite withdrawn, but at the same time she had a gift for directness which i liked:

—This isn't such a bad place to work. You complain too much— she said to me out of the blue, one day over coffee. —You can get promoted and even become a supervisor, like myself— she laughed. —There aren't many places where that is possible for a woman!

—Yes, but what about adventure, excitement, travel, exploration? I don't want to rot here all my life like . . .— and i pointed to the other women in the lounge.

—You are just impatient. It will change . . .

I estimated her to be about thirty, but she had a tendency

to act as though she were much older.

One night Marion invited me to dinner. She lived with her mother in a rustic house surrounded by trees. Her mother was a kindly white-haired woman who had prepared a dinner of creamed chicken and apple pie. She seemed pleased that her daughter had a new friend:

—This is a rare occasion, you know— she said to me —Marion is a hermit . . .

—I have you, Mom.

I looked at mother and daughter as they exchanged smiles; they both had the same gentle manner and a softness in their voices. Their movements were slow and deliberate, their skins slightly transparent.

—You seem to get along well with your mother— i said to Marion after dinner as we sat in her study. It was a wood-paneled room, lined with books.

—She is my best friend.

We listened to Mozart's *Piano Concerto no. 21* and we talked about Huxley. We agreed that he was a powerful writer, a philosopher, a prognosticator. She asked me if i had read Gertrude Stein.

—No. I have never heard of her.

—When you go home tonight i'll lend you one of her books. I don't know if you'll like her, but i think you will.

There was a tremor in her hands as she lighted her cigarettes, one after the other. I wondered if her fiancé had died in the war . . . I didn't feel free to ask. It was too early.

Frederick and i saw each other on weekends. We danced at Nepenthe, overlooking the Big Sur coastline. Legend had it that Orson Welles bought this enchanted spot overlooking the Pacific as a gift to Rita Hayworth but that she never saw it because they had a fight on the way up from Hollywood. Now it was a restaurant and night club where the waitresses wore flowing gowns and danced barefoot under the stars to the sound of Greek songs. Henry Miller would drop in and join the circle next to the roaring fire which was kept going to dispel the fog. After Nepenthe Frederick and i made love,

on the beach when it was warm, in his room when it was
cold. He was getting restless. I was getting edgy; he approached sex like a game of volleyball. I encouraged him to
branch out, to gain some experience from other women. He
said he had been thinking of going to France for a while.
When he left, several months later, i felt relieved.

Summer was approaching. One day during our coffee
break, Marion said:

—I am planning to take my vacation in June, what about
you?

—I haven't thought about it.

—You have to sign up early if you want to be sure to get it
in the summer. Why don't we go somewhere together?

—Yes, let's!

We decided to go to Santa Barbara for a week.

When the time came we drove off in Marion's open convertible all the way down the coast. The Pacific Ocean
stretched out in front of us, its waves splashing foam against
the cliffs. We exchanged confidences about our lives. We
talked about our mothers. I told her that i admired her for
having established an equal relationship with her mother.
With mine it was different, we loved each other, of course,
but there was greater definition between us, she was the
mother and i was the daughter, which meant that i should
listen to her.

—I guess that's because she is European— i said.

—I don't know, but you'll see, it will all change as you
grow older. You'll be friends, you'll calm down.

—Never! I don't want to calm down, that's like giving up!

We discussed our divergent approaches to life. She said
that i was a fighter, while she was a sculptor.

—What do you mean, 'sculptor'?

—It seems to me that one has to carefully carve out a place
for oneself, a beautiful, comfortable place. You have to know
your limits . . .

There was something in what she was saying, i agreed, but there was also a kind of defeat that i didn't like. We argued about that for years to come.

When we arrived in Santa Barbara we found a pretty inn near the beach. There were rose vines on the front of our cottage and we picked a few little red roses to put in a glass on the table in the kitchenette. We took some of the pictures off the walls and redecorated the room as best we could to make it ours. That night we went out to dinner and Marion ordered two rum cocktails. Much to my relief, the waiter didn't ask for my I. D. The drinks were served in tall frosted glasses with large slices of pineapple and twigs of mint. In the daytime we lay in the sun on the beach and talked. It was a real vacation, easy, pleasant, restful.

—I don't know why people consider Gertrude Stein so difficult— i said one night after dinner. I was reading *Three Lives*.

—It's probably because she affects them too deeply. If you let her draw you into her language, her sphere of consciousness, you have to give up some of your preconceptions about literature. She comes to you directly, as if she wasn't using words at all . . .

We were sitting on one of the twin beds. Marion looked at me with tenderness as she spoke, as if i were a child prodigy. That irritated me, but i could feel that the tenderness was real. On an impulse i bent over toward her. She was leaning against the pillow. I looked into her eyes, very close. Then i placed my lips on hers, lightly. They were shut. I opened mine slightly and hers followed my contours. There was moisture between us. Our tongues touched slowly, simultaneously. I felt her body heat. Her breasts were firm and small against mine. When we parted i knew that something momentous had occurred. I was surprised at myself, and yet not surprised, at the same time. Mostly, life had suddenly taken a much more interesting turn, once again. I thought of Frederick, his lips, his body. Hers seemed more familiar to me.

With him it was always a dialogue by trial and error. With her, i didn't wonder about her feelings, i knew what they were. I knew how to be with her. I also knew that neither she nor i would tell anyone about this.

**11**

—How was your vacation?— my mother asked after a nice, long hug. —You look very good; suntanned, rested.— She was clearly glad to see me.

—It was good, very good— i answered as we sat down together on the couch. My father brought coffee for all of us. At times like this, family reunions, he tended to look distracted, but he also didn't want to miss anything that was going on. He got up frequently, to go to the bathroom, to offer more coffee, to turn the heat up or down. He let my mother make the inquiries:

—How did you get along with Marion?

—Very well; she is a nice person after all, and very intelligent, you know— i said.

—Yes i know, but it's one thing to spend an evening with someone and another to be together twenty-four hours a day for a week!

—We got along very well, we have similar rhythms.

—Well, good, i am glad you found a friend, anyway. Maybe now you will miss Italy less. By the way, here is a letter from Clea for you!

After a full 'report'—my mother always insisted on a great many concrete details—how large was the room, where did we eat our meals, was the beach crowded—i went to my room and lay down on the bed to read Clea's letter. It was reassuring to me to see her generous handwriting with its regular,

**269**

well-formed letters. She said that she had come back re-
freshed from her year in America, that she had learned a lot
about living more simply, about treating people more like
equals. She was uncomfortable now having maids wait on
her, she thought people should do their own work. She was
happy. She had just met a man she liked, an architect, who
took her out dancing at night, in his sports car, and made her
laugh. He was very charming and professed to be in love with
her, which added to his charm, of course! The letter ended
with a reminder that it was my turn to come to Europe now.
As if i needed to be reminded . . .

I turned to my 'good citizenship' pamphlet distractedly.
We were all studying for our exam, which was going to take
place the following month on the fifth anniversary of our
arrival in the United States. My parents took this assignment
very seriously, going to evening courses, studying every night.
I started reading the introduction, but soon fell asleep. I went
to work the next day, ready to face the phones once again: the
prospect of seeing Marion made the office more palatable.
During breaks and lunch hours, at least, we could talk about
something besides telephones.

On the day of the American citizenship exam we all got up
early and dressed carefully. I paired off with Omama in an
attempt to avoid conflicts between her and my mother. She
put on her 'good' black wool coat and her pearl earrings. She
looked very pretty, her face glowing, her cheeks rosy. She
and i sat in the back seat of the car while my parents took
turns driving, a newly acquired skill for them, reading maps,
asking questions:

—Who is the president of the United States, mami?— my
father asked Omama.

—Truman.

—Ach, no! Eisenhower is president now!

—Oh, ya, i forgot— she said with embarrassment.

—Ani, every fifteen minutes or so, ask her again— my
father said.

So, periodically, i would pose the question, in German and

270

in English. Sometimes she said Eisenhower, but most of the time she said Truman, in whose era her memory had congealed. "Perhaps it's just as well for her," i thought to myself, but we were all worried that if she couldn't even answer that question correctly she would be denied citizenship papers.

When we arrived in San Francisco we found the Federal Building quite easily; it was near the Opera House where we had gone with Sandy, long before, to see *South Pacific*. We were told to sit down on benches in a room with about twenty other people, all speaking different languages, Spanish, Chinese, Japanese, Filipino . . . Omama was the first in our family to be called. I was allowed to go in with her, to help her with the language. I whispered "Eisenhower" in her ear as we went in and she smiled. We had been told that they didn't bother older people with too many questions, but that they always asked who the president was. The examiner was very polite to her, making sure that she had a comfortable chair. Then he said:

—State your full name and address.

I translated for her.

—Date of birth; these are routine questions we have to ask everyone— the examiner explained to me.

—August 24, 1874.

—Place of birth.

—Frankfurt-am-Main.

—Have you ever been a communist?— i translated.

—No!— she said emphatically.

—Have you ever been a prostitute?

I didn't know the word in German, but she seemed to understand the English. She looked surprised. I, too, thought this was an odd question to ask an old woman, insulting even.

—These are just routine— the examiner repeated, as if that were some kind of acceptable explanation!

—Okay, Petra— she looked startled again at being addressed by her first name, this time — can you tell me who the President of the United States is?— I translated the question.

—Truman— she said.

—You mean Eisenhower, right?— said the examiner.

—Oh, yes.

—Of course you did, Petra, it was just a slip of the tongue, right? That's all, thank you.

"That was easy," i said to myself.

My parents went in one at a time. They also passed. They were asked real questions—how many states in the union now, how many to start with—not very difficult ones, though. When i went in i knew right away that the examiner was planning to treat me differently; he asked me the questions about having been a communist or a prostitute, without looking up from his papers, dead serious. Then the interrogation began: the Constitution, the colonies, Washington, Lincoln, the Civil War; America's tricolored past was being explored through my accented answers. I felt i was doing all right. Then the examiner said:

—Name three ways of passing a law under the U.S. Constitution.

I could only think of two. He looked at me sternly and said:

—Sorry, miss. I can't pass you.

When i came out, my parents looked at me from the bench inquisitively. I didn't feel like talking, i didn't want to cry. I was humiliated. Irritated.

We went to the courtroom, all twenty or so of us, for the swearing-in ceremonies. The judge was sitting above us, behind a polished table, next to the American flag, under a large carved eagle.

—I want to congratulate you all for becoming citizens of the United States of America.

He read the names, stumbling frequently over the sounds. Our family was included, all except me. My mother, father and grandmother went up, raised their right hand and swore allegiance to the Constitution. I sat on my bench alone, thinking that things had been going too well for me lately, that something bad had to happen and this was it.

He called my name after all the others had sat down. I went up and stood in front of him, under him.

—It says here, on this form, that you are a graduate of the University of California. Is that correct?

—Yes.

He looked at me and paused. I knew he was waiting for the 'sir,' but i pretended not to understand.

—It also says here that you failed your citizenship test, is that correct?

—Yes— i whispered.

—What is happening to our educational institutions!— he exclaimed to the emptying hall. —In my day people had to know their American history before they were awarded a B.A. And now ... All right, i'll give you another chance: what was the basis of the conflict between the North and the South culminating in the Civil War?

Memories of *Gone with the Wind* conjured up all kinds of facts in my mind. He seemed satisfied with my answers.

—All right— he said —here are your citizenship papers. Raise your right hand and repeat after me ...

He congratulated us all and sanctimoniously walked out, his black robe disclosing a rather sad little grey suit underneath.

I reviewed my life as we drove back to Monterey. Becoming an American citizen seemed significant in one way—our stay here was more permanent now—just symbolic in another way: i was not going to change my allegiances; i still felt that Yugoslavia and Italy were at least as important to me as the United States. My longing for Rome had subsided somewhat, but i still missed the beauty, the warmth, the gentleness of Europe. At home, i often played Italian songs on the record player, in order to enjoy the pain of longing. But there were other aspects of Europe i didn't miss, the restrictions, the concern with appearances, with propriety. In the five years that i had spent in the U.S., i had gained a B.A., a full-time job, a sense of independence. Now i was going to acquire a passport.

That fall Omama was accepted into the Jewish Home for the Aged in San Francisco where she would be well taken care of, where she would be able to roam freely around the large park surrounding the buildings without getting lost. She was sad at leaving us, my father especially, but he promised to visit her often. He was feeling guilty about putting his mother in a home, but it was the only reasonable solution, he admitted. I was relieved and so was my mother.

Theodore drove up for a weekend in his new black Thunderbird. He was living in Pasadena, working on his Ph.D. at Cal Tech. He brought me a bouquet of wildflowers and told my parents and me about his laboratory experiments. We drove to Carmel Valley and took a long walk through the fields, holding hands. California poppies smiled their yellow glow at us.

—You know, Theo, our friendship proves that men and women *can* be friends. I like that.

—Yes, of course— he answered, but he didn't look pleased. —Friendship is part of love, after all.

—I am not so sure . . .

—Come, let's run!

I was glad he didn't pursue that discussion. I had been pondering that question for a while. Friendship seemed more solid than passion, but, of course, combining the two would be ideal.

That night we met a friend of his for dinner. His name was Doug. He was stationed at Fort Ord, having been drafted into the army where he was undergoing a series of interrogations concerning his past political affiliations.

—They are apparently upset by the fact that i belonged to the Progressive Party in college! They even questioned me about my mother's activities in New York: she is a member of the NAACP, as if that were some kind of proof of my communist leanings.— He spoke rapidly, in spurts.

—This country is going through a repressive stage. That always happens after a war— Theodore said, in an attempt to console him.

274

—It's McCarthy!— Doug said.

—McCarthy is a symptom, not the cause of the disease— said Theodore.

—It's all that propaganda about how wonderful America is— i said —you are all brainwashed from grammar school on, or even earlier, and you don't even realize it!

Neither of them seemed to like that comment.

—And you foreigners don't understand the complexities of this country— Theo said laughingly —but, of course, you add to them.

—All Americans are foreigners— i said —almost.

—Some more, some less.

I liked talking to them. Since i had been living on the Monterey peninsula i hadn't met any people who were very interested in politics; surrounded as they were by the mountains and the ocean, the local inhabitants seemed unaware that there was a real world out there, sitting behind steel desks, deciding their fate. At the end of the evening, Theo suggested that i give Doug my telephone number so that we could see each other again.

The following evening i went to see Marion. We sat in front of the fire, sipping sherry. I told her about my date with Theo and about having met his friend, Doug. She listened with interest, like an aunt or an older sister.

—Do you want to meet them sometime?

—Oh, no, i just like to hear you tell me about all that you are doing. You know that i have no desire to *participate*. I am an observer, you are a doer, and i like observing you doing things!

There was irony in her voice, mixed with tenderness. I was irritated by her aloofness from reality while i admired her for it. Our conversation drifted lazily from office gossip to books to music: we had been listening to the Beethoven string quartets, one by one, over the last few months. We agreed that the later ones were almost unbearable, their sounds hovering somewhere in that space where intellect and emotion meet. We lay on the rug next to each other, in silence.

Our embraces often seemed to include that space.

Doug and i started spending time together. His troubles with the army continued. After many weeks of interrogation, the army ruled he was to be denied promotion for the rest of his tour of duty and that he was not to be transferred out of Fort Ord. He would remain under constant surveillance.

—The irony of all this is that they are acting just like the Soviets in the name of anti-communism— he said one day after dinner.

—And to think that they would hold you responsible for the activities of your mother!

—Not only that, but my poor mother is just a nice Jewish lady from New York trying to be liberal, to show that she is free of prejudice, which she is, relatively speaking. The NAACP is not exactly a subversive organization, you know!

—They obviously think it is. The McCarthy hearings have had their impact, haven't they?

—Yes, more than we know— he said sadly.

My family had not yet bought a television set so that we were spared most of the spectacle, but the repercussions could not be ignored, even in the peaceful fishing town of Monterey.

Occasionally i went out with Michael, an arrogant, tormented young man who was studying Chinese at the Army Language School. He had joined the army as an act of desperation, having been expelled from Chicago Law School one semester before graduation for mysterious disciplinary reasons. He courted me with insistence, calling all the time, coming over unannounced. I sometimes mistook his persistence for passion, but mostly i drew away from it.

—So, Miss Unholy Vessel— he said to my great annoyance — tell me what a crass American like me is missing in the subtlety and finesse of the European cinema.

We had gone to see Cocteau's *Les Enfants Terribles* in which incest and homosexuality wove their inextricable web. Our discussions were always edgy, but in many ways i enjoyed the freedom that his nastiness offered me. I found it easier, sometimes, to be with him than with a more sensitive, easily hurt man like Doug. But i wouldn't let him touch me.

One morning, as i arrived in the office, the manager called me over to his desk:

—We're thinkin' of making some changes around here; we've got to shift our personnel around a bit and so i wanted to know what your plans are.

—My plans?

—Yes, in regards to marriage and so on.

—I have no such plans.

He was smirking at me.

—See, we've been talking about the possibility of promoting you to a supervisorial slot, but we wouldn't wanna invest all that capital in training you if you're just gonna pick up and marry some guy like you gals are apt to do . . .

—From what i hear, marriage isn't such a bed of roses . . .— i said, trying to lighten the tone of the dialogue. He nodded. A few days later i was promoted.

They sent me to San Francisco for a two-week training program. I stayed at the Hotel Plaza overlooking Union Square, along with all the other telephone company trainees from Northern California. We were taught how to fill out more forms and how to treat employees so that they perform their tasks with good humor:

—Absenteeism is one of the big problems with women, you know— said the instructor, reading from his manual. I didn't know.

—And most of our employees are women, as you have noticed.— I had noticed.

—Now, girls, there are a few simple techniques that i am going to teach you which will reduce this tendency. One of them consists of making the rounds first thing each morning, and asking each employee how she is. We want them to feel we care about them. The trick is not to take up too much time with that, just a simple question or two so they know that we care. But always bring them back to the work at hand; that will take their minds off their worries; you'll see, it works like magic.

He set up practice sessions during which we were to learn how to appear interested and remain detached at the same time.

At lunchtime i walked around the park in Union Square and watched the office workers and saleswomen sunbathing, surrounded by flowers and pigeons. San Francisco reminded me of Rome in its gaiety, its hedonism. In Chinatown the tourists mingled harmoniously with the inhabitants: the ones picking through the trinkets, the others through the fish and vegetables. Among the Chinese it was often the men who examined the food carefully, seeking the perfect asparagus, the liveliest crab, discussing them with the merchants with seriousness in melodious, incomprehensible languages.

One day i wandered into the basement of the City of Paris, one of the last 'belle époque' department stores, now defunct. I came upon a French bookstore displaying *Paris Match, L'Express, Elle.* The scent of fresh croissants from the adjacent bakery filled my nostrils. "The telephone company is not so bad after all," i thought to myself. I started going there every day. The salesman, a young Frenchman with soulful eyes, recognized me after the first few visits.

—The new issue of *Elle* has just arrived— he said one noon-hour, as i approached the newsstand.

—Oh, thank you— i said in French.

I glanced through the magazine; the horoscope predicted an unusual romantic encounter that week. I looked at him more closely.

—You are new in San Francisco. Like me— he said.

—Yes and no. I am here on business.

We smiled at each other.

—Can we see each other after work? We'll have a vermouth together. I know a quiet, pleasant bar not far from here.

His name was Pierre, of course. He had been in this country for a few months. There was something mysterious about him, but i didn't ask why he had left France. His

278

manner reminded me that in Europe it is not customary to ask personal questions, that it is best to wait for the time when confidences happen.

One night Pierre invited me to his apartment for dinner. He had put a red and white checkered tablecloth on the kitchen table, flowers in the middle and a bottle of good wine. Mouloudji was singing softly on the record player as Pierre cooked the 'steak et pommes frites.'

—Shall i make the salad?— i asked.

—Yes. As proof of my high regard for you i will let you make the 'vinaigrette' . . .

Afterward, as part of the conversation, we kissed tenderly. He told me i was beautiful and spoke of his mother. His best friend, Daniel, came to meet me. He had heard about me, he said, as we shook hands. He looked at Pierre with approval. They said they would come to visit me in Monterey.

—Do you play bridge?— Daniel asked.

—Yes, sometimes.

—Well, good, then we'll make it a foursome. And now i have to go see *'ma belle.' Au revoir, les amoureux!*

—Do you want us to come see you?— asked Pierre after Daniel left.

—Yes, of course!

And so they did, often, in the course of the following year.

# 12

Marion and i continued to explore our friendship, share books, listen to music, lunch together. When i told her that i was saving some money each month for my trip to Europe she smiled encouragingly but i sensed that she would prefer not to talk about it. We lay in the sun, next to each other, on her porch.

—My new friends, Pierre and Daniel, are coming next weekend from San Francisco. Would you like to meet them? We could play some bridge, go on a picnic— i said, changing the subject.

—No, that's not for me. When i can have you to myself i am happy, but when you are doing other things i prefer not to be around.

Her exclusiveness irritated me. I wanted her to participate in my life, in the mainstream of life, but she resisted.

—You will do what you have to do with your life— she said —but as for me let me live it at my own pace. I want to capture the moment, i want to stay still. You are all movement, it makes me dizzy!

I started to feel an urge to escape from the bubble we had created around us. I admired her courage in wanting to go deeper, but i was scared of my own feelings, frightened that i couldn't come back if i plunged too deep. I felt sad and confused. "Is it because i love a woman?" i asked myself repeatedly. "No, no, that's not it! Love is a positive force in all its forms and it is stronger than convention," i answered myself; "it's just that there is nobody to talk to about it!" I missed Clea.

One day, as if prompted by telepathy, Clea wrote that she was getting married, would i come to her wedding? I was nearing my twenty-first birthday, the deadline i had given myself for returning to Europe. I wrote back saying i wasn't sure that i could save enough money in time, but i would try. By return mail a letter arrived with a check in it: Clea's father was paying for my passage, as a wedding present to her. I waited several days before telling Marion that i was leaving. I was scared to tell her, scared of not being able to leave her, scared of hurting her, but most of all i was scared that i couldn't stand the pain that this separation would cause me. I also knew that i had to do it.

The next month was spent in making preparations for my departure. I wrote to Michael, who was stationed in Japan, to write to me in Rome. He was given to long, convoluted, passionate letters typed on the back of Abner Dean cartoons. Doug was finally being released from the army with a dishonorable discharge. Pierre went back to Paris, where he promised to find me a job so that i could come there after Rome.

My parents were resigned to my leaving. They couldn't understand my urge to return to Europe, with all its unpleasant memories for them.

—Don't you miss Yugoslavia, its air, its sea?

—I dream of Sarajevo every night— my father said —the way it was . . . If we went there now everything would be changed: none of our people are there any more; strangers are living in our house. It's better for me to visit it in my dreams, believe me!

—You can dream of Sarajevo all you want— my mother said —but i prefer California, wide awake! I have no desire to go back to Europe, i am an American now.

They advised me to get a leave of absence from the telephone company so that i would have a job when i came back. I didn't follow their advice. I wasn't planning to come back.

I spent the last evening with Marion. We had tickets to a concert, but we never went. We sat in her living room, quietly, with tension between us.

—You are behaving just like my mother— i said to her —holding on to me!

I knew this wasn't true. She had always been loving and generous with me. Why was i being so nasty to her, all of a sudden? Was it guilt? Why couldn't i just love her back without this cruelty? She didn't answer. She got up and put another log on the fire. She gave me a copy of André Gide's *Corydon* to read on the boat.

I took an unscheduled flight to New York which took sixteen hours, with all the stops. When i arrived at Baki's and Dida's apartment in New York i was exhausted, but very happy to see them. They had settled into a more comfortable life. My uncle was working and Braco came to see them regularly. They didn't feel as isolated as before. They had gained weight, they looked healthy.

—How do you get along in the neighborhood with your English? How do you manage with the shopping, the laundry?

—I don't speak English— Baki answered with a glitter in her eye —i speak Spanish! They all think that i am Puerto Rican! We are doing all right. I take in sewing and Dida, you know, has a job!

—Yes, i do!— he said.

I looked at my grandfather, at his light, generous eyes, at the silver hair on his temples. He was a messenger on Wall Street, he who had once been the boss, with employees to run errands for him. I flashed on *his* messenger, wearing a fez, bringing him Turkish coffee on a copper platter, while he sat in the sun in front of his store greeting passers-by. Now he was an old man, an immigrant in New York, carrying manila envelopes up and down elevators and nobody knew who he had been in Sarajevo. But this didn't seem to bother him: he was a proud man, not readily humiliated.

—It's just for something to do, isn't it?— i tried to cheer him up.

—Oh, it's much better than sitting at home, being useless. I have worked all my life, i don't want to 'retire!' But tell me about Mama and Tata. How does Omama like her 'home'?

—She complains, but she seems happier there. She has a friend now, another German-Jewish lady, so she has somebody to talk to.

—That's good news. The worst is if you are all alone . . .— said Dida.

—What can you do? She's lost her memory— Baki said. —My late mother used to say: "Take care of your head and of your legs!" Let's hope it won't happen to us, but you never know . . .

They turned to more cheerful topics: they were making plans to visit my parents while i was in Europe. The family would be reunited again, at least some of it.

Stepping on the Italian ocean liner to Naples, i immediately felt a change of atmosphere: i was in Italy once again! The cabin attendants treated me with that special mixture of courtesy and flirting for which their countrymen are famous.

—*Ma certo, bella signorina*— they would say in answer to a request.

I was traveling third class and i spoke Italian: they could allow themselves to be somewhat familiar with me, i was one of them, after all.

—Italo-American girls are the best in the world!— they said, assuming i was one —beautiful like Italian girls, free like Americans!

With each meal, each taste of prosciutto and melon, i recaptured Italy. I lay lazily in the sun and imagined my reunion with Clea and with Rome. At night i danced to the sounds of "Guaglione," "Anima e core" and let the words shape my mood.

As soon as i disembarked in Naples i realized that Italy had undergone a transformation in the seven years i had spent in the United States. The port was teeming with activity. Little boys straight out of *Shoeshine* were busy running errands, offering to carry luggage, extending their hands. The customs official pompously asked about my phonograph. What was i planning to do with it, sell it on the black market?

—Oh, no!— i answered indignantly —it's for private use!

It was Clea's wedding present, in reality, but somewhere from deep in my memory came the appropriate words.

—What are you, a musician?

—Yes, yes, i am a musician.

—Why does it say student on your passport, then?

—Student of music— i clarified.

We were going through the motions, but neither of us was duped by any of this.

—And you plan to take it out of the country when you leave?— he persisted.

—Yes.

—Va bene. Sign here.

The train ride from Naples to Rome was short. I looked at the countryside, and a sense of well-being enveloped me. There were still reminders of the devastation, buildings not repaired, scattered bomb holes but by and large the people in the fields looked peaceful once again, as they waved to the passing train. Everything in the Italian landscape was on a smaller scale than in California; even the cows were less ominous.

Clea met me at the train station with her fiancé, Mario. I liked him right away; he was a handsome man of medium height. He took Clea and me by the arm on the way to the car and announced:

—I am going to have a wonderful time with my two women!

He accepted me as Clea's best friend, a role he obviously respected. He asked me about my parents, my brother, my grandparents. Clea had told him about me; there were no secrets between us. Driving through Rome, i noticed that it too had been transformed in my absence: the city looked prosperous, with people milling in the streets, beautifully dressed, hundreds of cars zigzagging their way around the narrow streets, honking, the drivers cursing at each other.

—We hide our poor— said Mario in response to my observation on the apparent prosperity. —The economy is not healthy, it will all crack one day.

The atmosphere in Clea's house was one of preparation; the wedding was two weeks away and it was going to be very elegant. Clea's mother kissed me and greeted me with much warmth, her brothers looking on, smiling, all grown up, handsome. Her room had changed: it now looked like a sitting room, with the two beds serving as couches in the daytime. We retired under the pretext of unpacking. We were eager to be alone.

—You haven't changed at all, Micetta, and yet you have, at the same time— she said.

—You look more beautiful than ever. Like Elizabeth Taylor. And i like Mario very much, i was worried what would happen if i didn't but i do!

—I knew you would, but i am glad to hear it. It's a big step, you know, and it reassures me to know you approve.

—It will all go well— i said. I knew she was nervous about getting married. I was nervous for her! Marriage seemed more and more problematic to me in general, but hers seemed promising: they were in love, after all.

One afternoon, while Clea and her mother were at the florist selecting the flowers for the wedding, i went to see Cara. She was a doctor now. She was still living at home, as everyone does in Italy until they get married, and *that* she wasn't planning to do.

—What about your engagement?— i asked —you wrote me you . . .

—Have you forgotten?— she interrupted. —In Italy everyone has a 'fidanzato!' That way we can go out at night, as we please, within the limits of propriety, but these engagements can last for years sometimes and then break up without the marriage plans ever even being discussed.

—That seems like a reasonable arrangement— i said. —But still, doesn't it bother you to continue living at home?

—Yes, it does, but i don't earn enough money to have an apartment of my own.

—Even as a doctor?— i inquired in disbelief.

—You don't know about Italy any more! We are all doctors here— she laughed at her reminder to me that 'dottore' was a loosely used title in her adopted land.

We were talking to each other with ease as if we had seen each other all along. We had not lost contact. She wanted to know a great deal about America. She wanted to go there for a visit.

—Perhaps you can come for a year, to do your specialization work— i said.

—It is not so easy; the Americans do not accept the Italian degree, i would have to take all kinds of exams over again.

She moved around with grace, her hair up in a French twist, her freckled face lightened by her green eyes. I liked her very much, i confirmed to myself: she was intelligent and quick and still didn't take herself too seriously. She laughed easily.

—Our friendship is as strong as ever, isn't it?— she said, taking my hand.

—Yes, as though no time at all had gone by.

On other afternoons Clea and i ran endless errands in the crowded Roman 'centro,' downtown. Specialty shops displayed the finest goods—leather garments, shoes, handbags, knits. Some said Italy was becoming a focal point for European fashion, replacing Paris even. We went to pick out the suit i would wear to Clea's wedding. We decided on a grey brocade to be made to measure, tight in the waist, with large lapels around the face and neck and a fitted skirt, midcalf in length. We also picked out a dark violet straw hat and matching, long leather gloves. As i was being fitted into these garments i felt that i was shedding a part of me, the casual California part. It was exciting to be 'elegant' once again, but i was no longer used to being restricted in my movements, pinched.

We went to see Clea and Mario's future apartment. He was overseeing the renovations: the kitchen was going to be modern with florentine tile; the bedroom was outfitted with wall mirrors on three sides and large doors opening onto a sunny balcony. They had selected a mixture of well-designed modern furniture, mostly by Italian designers, and antique pieces with Persian carpets from their parents' collection. The parquet floors were stained dark; it was going to be beautiful! Mario's architecture students were working on it, whistling popular songs. Mario and Clea smiled at each other, embraced, held on to one another. They exuded their passion for each other, their sense of anticipation. It was pleasant to be with them; they encircled me with their warmth. At night we went to restaurants, dancing, on long rides into the Roman countryside: the Appia Antica had become a popular night-club area. Prosperity was in the air.

—Italy has really recovered from its wounds— i said one night as we sat drinking 'spumante.'

—We recover fast— said Mario —with the help of our former enemies, that is. Look at England, their ally, they are doing much worse than we are! But don't let all this glitter give you the wrong impression. The Italian economy is not healthy, the workers are organizing, they are not satisfied, there will be much unrest in the months to come. Let's enjoy it while it lasts, the proletariat is rising, they will win. Drink up your champagne . . .

The wedding was somber, subdued, elegant. The reception was in an old Roman hotel on top of the Piazza di Spagna steps, a select group of elderly, refined people in attendance and some of Clea's and Mario's younger friends. Clea looked beautiful in her long embroidered gown, but her face was quite pale. As she stepped into the black limousine, holding onto the train, and drove off with Mario, she wore a slightly forced smile.

I stayed on in Clea's room, as she had asked me, to keep her mother company, in an attempt to alleviate the sense of loss caused by her daughter's departure. I tried to emulate Clea's ways. I sat with her mother in the 'salotto' sipping tea, discussing Clea's apartment, her wedding, her honeymoon plans. She was making the best of it, being cheerful, but i could see that her bond to her daughter was strong and that the marriage represented a change in that bond.

—You'll see each other all the time; she will be living near you, after all.

—What do you think, that i have nothing better to do than sit around gossiping with Clea?

A few days later came a phone call from Mario: Clea was very sick, they were coming home. When she arrived she was hot with fever, her eyes glazed, we weren't sure she recognized us. She lay down in her bed, in 'our' room, while Mario went back to his house to live with his parents. Clea's mother and i took turns caring for her; doctors streamed through the apartment, spreading the smell of medicine wherever they went. At night Clea often talked incoherently, calling for Mario, her mother, even in their presence. Mario sat by her bed hour after hour, holding her hand, comforting her. She couldn't tolerate any strong smells so the room was filled with odorless flowers.

I walked around Rome while Clea was sleeping, alone or with Cara. It was a pilgrimage. I visited the lycée and made a point of speaking English to my former English professor. He did have a thick French accent, just as i had suspected. I didn't know if he remembered the slap but i felt vindicated. Rome was still familiar to me, i remembered every alley, every streetcar. I circulated through its intricate streets as if by instinct. But there were many aspects of Roman life that shocked me now: the way the beggars were treated, the poverty, the corruption. I wrote to Marion:

Dear Marion, i miss you very much, but i am glad that i came; it was the right thing for me to do. I had to do it. When i stepped on European soil i felt whole again. The rhythms and the smells suit me; i will undoubtedly always have to come back to regenerate myself. I am no longer in love with Rome. It is more beautiful than ever but it seems small all of a sudden, even stifling. I can't tolerate the conventions any more, all those things 'proper' young ladies do or don't do. America has emancipated me. Surprised?

It helped me to write these thoughts, sitting next to Clea, waiting for her to recover. When she did i told her i would be leaving soon:
—We have taken different directions in life, but in our souls we will stay together, of course— she said. —You are ready to move on now, i can see that.
Pierre had written me from Paris saying that he had found me a job with a family, as an 'au pair'; i would have room and board and thus stretch my stay in Europe. I wrote him that i would accept.
—Perhaps in Paris i can decide what to do with my life— i said to Clea.
—Whatever you do will be good, even if you change your mind once you decide . . .— Clea said with her wonderful smile.
—Yes, i am going to go to the Left Bank, write my thoughts on paper napkins and send them all to you!
We shook hands.
—We are blood sisters, after all— we both said at the same time.
When i boarded the second-class compartment on the train to Paris, i looked at Clea through the window. We both had tears in our eyes. I waved to her. As the train pulled out of the station she made a 'V' for victory sign with two fingers.

# Epilogue

You know that in my youth women didn't have the right to vote. I was often angered about this injustice. We used to go to Oplenac to visit King Alexander's grave and our leader was a woman, a cousin of the man who killed Ferdinand and her cousin was then an important man because he had killed the Archduke of Austria. She started to organize women and to open up their heads. She told them that they had to have the right to vote. And i started going to her meetings, unbeknownst to my husband, to hear what she had to say. She interested me. Very few women went to hear her . . . She said: "I, as a woman, i am intelligent, i know how to read and write, i have a job and i don't have the right to vote, while my servant who doesn't know how to read or write, *he* has a right to vote!" And i always fought against that, it was always upsetting to me that we women didn't have the right to vote.

I knew one case where the husband had a big house and it was in his name and the wife was so dissatisfied that she went to the lawyer to contest the fact that she didn't have any rights to the house. She was very smart, very agile and this bothered her a great deal, so she went to the lawyer to find out what to do and how to do it . . . But the lawyer said there was nothing to be done. Women had the right to get a divorce, but they didn't ask for one. The mother would say: "This is your luck, don't leave the children," and so they didn't get a divorce. There were women who were unhappy, many women knew that the male cheated on them and so on, but they didn't get a divorce. Instead, they suffered.

People didn't think about dissolving their marriages in my time. Mostly they were patient and they thought to themselves, "This is your fate." For women there were problems of need, they didn't have what to live on, so they stayed even if they were unhappy, dissatisfied. They didn't earn money, they were second-rate citizens ... The woman didn't have the right to say much, she ran the household all day, everything nice and neat while the man ... Many men were incompetent, not qualified for work. He came home drunk, picked a fight with the wife and the woman put up with it all. They didn't think about separating, they didn't have any options.

Complain? To whom should they complain? *He* was the boss in the house, not she! The way i lived, things weren't so bad with us that i had to complain. If something bothered me i told him directly. For me and my sisters and my friends it wasn't so bad that we had to complain. I was better off than other women; just like today, there are women who live better, under better conditions than others. If they asked *me*, i would say that to get married is no great happiness because men and women have two different ideas: *he* can be very good, *she* can be very good, but they are of two different opinions ... I think that the way people are talking nowadays, about abolishing marriage altogether, is right. I think that no marriage, or better said, very few marriages, can work. It's all right if one doesn't get married and just lives with a man, but what about the children, whose children will they be?

I would say to the young women: first of all find a place for the children, a good place where they are well taken care of, something like a kibbutz—i visited kibbutzim in Israel—something like that, where there are schools, where there is wonderful food, where they go to bed on time. You should see how clean and beautiful it is there, you would be amazed! They have men and women teachers for those children. Then the women can be free to earn money ... And if she wants a ... relationship, let her have a relationship! Does she get along with this one? If she doesn't get along with this one, let her get along with a different one ... They should be independent, they should not be tied down. But in the first place they must think of settling the children somewhere, that has top priority, before she goes out to have fun. They must establish good schools for the children and then, let them live as they wish, let her work, let her make money and at night if she wants to go dancing, if she wants to go to the movies, if she wants to be with a man, let her do what she wants!

I was a member of a women's organization, the 'Frauenfahreind'—Omama was the president—and some other charity groups. I was just a member, i didn't have time to work for the groups, so i didn't do anything about these injustices, i was just angry with Dida. When i was angry about my lack of rights, i took it out on my husband. I held him responsible. The poor man wasn't really responsible . . . I blamed *him* and he wasn't to blame, but such was the custom. I was never interested in politics, knowing that i didn't have the right to vote, so i didn't discuss politics with him or anyone else. He never asked me for my opinion about that. We worked together and we always decided together what to pick out from the fashion shows for the store, but it bothered me very much that i didn't have the same rights as the men. The store was just in the man's name, the house was in *his* name, all we had was under him and i was also working and i thought to myself: "What am i? I gave the money for this store, i work in this store and how come i don't have the same rights?" I didn't have the right to do something without my husband's agreement.

When i was in Sarajevo, working in the store, it bothered me a great deal that, even though i knew everything a man knew, that was not acknowledged. That was my problem. It bothered me that women didn't have the right to vote. It bothered me that if a decision had to be made, they only asked him and not me also. It bothered me that if something needed to be bought, a house, a store, they didn't ask for my signature, just his, that he could decide without me while i couldn't decide without him.

This happened to me once: i was sick and i went to the baths and when i came back i had to go to the sanatorium for three days because i wasn't cured at those baths so i stayed in Zagreb for a general checkup. It was Friday night and when i got to the sanatorium they wouldn't take me without money. I didn't have any money. I went to see an acquaintance with whom we traded, we bought goods from him, and asked him to give me three thousand dinars so i could go to the sanatorium. He asked me if i had Dida's authorization! I felt *very* bad and *very* angry about that, that i, as a woman, who is in the store, who

works, who gave the money to start it, that i don't have the right to
three thousand dinars! I reproached Dida greatly for that. And he said:
"That is the custom, it is the same for this woman and that woman."
So i saw that i am nothing.

Another woman, she worked in the store next door to ours, they
sold watches, she too protested. Other women were more clear than i:
they knew how to be the big wheel and make the husband less
important. They kept track of everything. They bought their houses
right away half and half, they were smarter than i. Some were and some
weren't. But in my family they considered me like the most adamant
about my rights. For me it was already better than it had been for my
mother.

In her time, the parents chose the bridegroom. The young couple
didn't even know each other. The parents got them together and
looked: this is a good young man, hard-working, or from a good family,
so they called a middleman to go and offer their daughter. This man
would get paid for this service. Many times they offered more than they
could give and when it came to the marriage, the middleman would
disappear . . . He would take the smaller dowry to the groom and then
disappear. In the meantime everything had been readied for the wedding, so they would get married anyway. In my time this was still
practiced, but not always. Sometimes the young man would go and ask
for the girl's hand, but for the most part they watched out for their
interest. Whatever girl was rich, she was good. And the smart girls from
poor families couldn't even think of marrying someone from a good
family; that young man didn't even notice her.

Money was more important than beauty, more important than
anything. In my time, after people were married they would go off on
their own. In my mother's time they went to live with the husband's
family: there were three or four sisters-in-law all living together and
they took turns cooking, each week a different one, while the others
did the housework, like maids. And the old woman ran the household.
They had to listen to her. For instance, my late father worked in the
store with his brothers and his father and the women ran the house
with his mother in charge. In my time we all lived separately, except
when the mother-in-law was left alone, then she would come and live
with the son, or the daughter sometimes . . .

With us it was customary for young girls to marry older men. Since the doctors weren't one hundred percent adept, many times at childbirth young women died so the widower would look for another wife, for a girl who was a little older, twenty-one, twenty-two . . . If you weren't married at eighteen, nineteen, you were considered an old maid. The widowers would look over the old maids, or the widows . . . The woman died in childbirth because they didn't know how to cut the cord properly and she would get an infection. And then those poor children would get a stepmother. My own mother had a stepmother, but she was very good to my mother.

I believe that there isn't much difference between men and women. Often women are more intelligent than men. Man's nature isn't so . . . so smart. I don't think only men count. Women do too. I am in favor of women also being in high positions, that they have the same rights. Today very few women are in high positions. There should be more. But i also believe that if a woman works outside she should have help at home so that when she comes home she has time for the children, for friends, for reading. Because that leads to a lot of tension when a woman comes home tired and has to do all the housework.

* * *

When i went back to Sarajevo in 1965 i didn't see those people that i left, but i saw a great change. Women are much more appreciated now in Yugoslavia than before. They got jobs, things changed a great deal. I noticed that the people don't work as hard in the stores because they are just employees; they have salaries no matter what they do, so they don't care whether they sell anything or not. I went to buy some presents, they didn't go to too much trouble to find what i wanted . . . But i liked very much how these communists made it possible for poor people to send their children to the university, that the poor who in the past could never go on vacation now could go to these nice villas which before were only for the rich. Now the workers can go and sun themselves, swim . . . They have food, not too much meat, but it is better for the people, better than before both Austria and Serbia. Under them the poor could not become lawyers and doctors, now they can. I like that. And doctors have ambulances for the poor also. I liked a lot of things and i didn't like a lot of things.

294

For the rich it wasn't easy to change. We, who used to have riches, had a hard time getting used to not having any more. I would have gotten used to the Partisans but what should i live on? Young people got jobs, but it wasn't easy for the older people . . . Conditions are much better for most people now. But i don't like the fact that the pay is the same: the doctor who studies a lot and who is intelligent gets as much as the one who doesn't know how to work much. Because he fought he sits in a good seat now but he doesn't know how to steer . . .

But i liked what i saw in Israel also very much; i liked Israel first of all when i saw the Israeli flag, that it can fly, that it is not afraid that it is Jewish, to show our flag . . . I liked Israel, i liked seeing how people adjusted, how they rolled up their sleeves, these people, how they started working, each in their way, to earn the most modest progress, how they made sure that the children were well taken care of. I like the fact that they didn't only look for wealth, that the rich man is not the only one that counts, that the one who doesn't have lives well also, as well as possible: he has an apartment, he has food, nothing extravagant, but he has that . . .

When communism first came we were horrified at what was happening, that the communists had come, this so-called terror, that everyone was going to be the same, that they took everything away, that the one who knows more and does more gets the same . . . Then why bother studying? You can be a coachman right away!

When i lived in Sarajevo i didn't bother much with politics, politics didn't interest me much. I know more about politics today than then. Today i have more time to read, i have more newspapers from all sides, and because we went through so much, i am interested in other people. I feel sorry for some nations and about others i think: "Do you need to get more?" For the Germans i think it is going too well again. I worry that they should become too strong again, because such evil . . . such evil very few nations have committed. Spain kicked the Jews out but they let them live, in Russia Jews suffer today, but still . . . they have a bed. What the Germans did, in such a way, this so-called cultured people, that doesn't exist! And it isn't taught in the schools, it isn't spoken about much, it is hidden today . . . Good old politics, all that is forgotten!

The Germans are educated, very well educated, very clever, in every line of work. A German, he is capable, each knows his trade, each knows how to work, each one knows how to earn money. But . . . they are still great criminals; there are great criminals among them because they didn't all flee from Germany, most of them still live in Germany. When Hitler first started to make Germany 'rheinedeutsch' [pure German], he started to organize in order to free it from the Jews. And they all liked it because they had the possibility to take the Jews' wealth away from them. Whoever was a leader could take a house, a store, could take whatever they liked; whoever was a Hitlerite had a good job, well paid. They did it out of greed. That janitor immediately got a big apartment, a big salary, in order to become a criminal. I read about a German woman who said that she was young when she became a Hitlerite, that they gave her a well-paying job, that today she is ashamed of all she had done, that she wants to go to Israel, to see this Israel and to help this Israel as much as she could. But there are very few people like that, there are many people who say: "More Jews should be killed, more Jews should be burnt . . ." There is still great evil.

* * *

Now people live much better, much more modern, much nicer, more comfortably. Before everything was so complicated but people were more peaceful, people weren't as nervous, they didn't have more worries than time. If you didn't finish at seven you worked until nine, everything was slower. But now it's better. If a person has a good schedule, it is better now. There are all the comforts. Even if you don't have a very big job, you can live very nicely with a medium job, if you know how to live, if you know how to manage your pay . . .

I don't miss anything in my past, on the contrary, it is nicer and nicer for me when i see how many better things there are. At home the laundry was washed by hand, we had to rub it by hand. I didn't do it because i didn't have to. I had maids, i hired a laundress when there was too much. We didn't have all the conveniences that you have. We washed the children's laundry every day. All that mud, all that we had to wash. Then, we had to boil the white laundry to get rid of the spots. After that we had to iron . . . Now it's much easier, much nicer. A washing machine, a drier, the materials are mostly such that they needn't be ironed. All that is a help. In our time it was much harder for the children, we watched a great deal over them so they wouldn't get dirty! We didn't let them go to the park and jump around as they liked. We told the maids to watch so they wouldn't get dirty. And so the children couldn't jump around much, they couldn't play much.

Of all the places we could have gone, it is still best in America. In America there is great wealth. When i came to America i saw that the garbage man wears gloves, that the garbage man has a car, that the garbage man owns a house, with hot running water and a refrigerator! I hadn't seen that in Yugoslavia! Even when we were well to do we didn't have a car; i had an ice-box but i didn't have a hundred and one things. In Yugoslavia a maid was a real maid. Here in America i saw they worked eight hours, because if you work ten you get paid more, i had never heard of such a thing. I liked that. In Yugoslavia people would let the maid go and the maid was poor and often she couldn't find another job. Here today if she is fired there is a union that defends them, which protects them, i like that. But i didn't like that they didn't give blacks equal rights. I was very surprised when i heard, after i came to America, that a black student couldn't sit on the same bench or go to the same school as whites and even if he did go to the same school he would have to sit separately. That bothered me a great deal because i know how much we Jews suffered because we were Jews. And that bothers me even today, that they are not equal. But it is all changing and that doesn't happen all at once. This will get better. Tomorrow a black will be president. In my opinion they should get together, cooperate, organize, and then they will be first!